THE ANSCHLUSS QUESTION IN THE WEIMAR ERA

A STUDY OF NATIONALISM IN GERMANY AND AUSTRIA, 1918–1932

By STANLEY SUVAL

THE JOHNS HOPKINS UNIVERSITY PRESS

BALTIMORE AND LONDON

Manufactured in the United States of America

The Johns Hopkins University Press, Baltimore, Maryland 21218
The Johns Hopkins University Press Ltd., London

Library of Congress Catalog Card Number 73–17174
ISBN 0–8018–1502–9

Library of Congress Cataloging in Publication data
will be found on the last printed page of this book.

TO MY FATHER AND MOTHER

CONTENTS

ACKNOWLEDGMENTS

SINCE IT IS impossible to acknowledge all the people who aided me in this research, I would like to thank collectively the staffs of the libraries of the universities of North Carolina State, North Carolina, Duke, Munich, and Vienna; the Bavarian State Library, the National Archives, the Bundesarchiv at Koblenz, the Haus-, Hof- und Staatsarchiv, Vienna. I am particularly grateful for the assistance of Anton Nemeth, who made possible the perusal of a large number of documents in Vienna in a limited time. I would also like to acknowledge the financial assistance received from the Professional Development Fund, North Carolina State University. I am grateful to Professors Marvin Brown, Boyd Hill, Joseph Hobbs, John Riddle, and A. J. Slavin who read all or part of the manuscript. I am, of course, indebted to other scholars for their published work. Unfortunately Klemmens von Klemperer's biography, *Ignaz Seipel* (Princeton, 1972), and Nikolaus von Preradovich's *Die Wilhelmstrasse und der Anschluss Osterreich* (Bern, 1971) were only available after this manuscript had been sent to the press. I wish to thank Kenneth Arnold of the Johns Hopkins University Press for his suggestions concerning the expansion of the study, and Nancy Middleton Gallienne for her careful editing. The same thanks go to John Rath, editor of the *Austrian Yearbook,* and Douglas Unfug, editor of *Central European History,* who accepted a part of this work for their journals.

A great deal of my enthusiasm for history is drawn from three historians who have since died, the first two in the prime of their careers: James Edward King of the University of North Carolina, Walter Simon of Cornell University and the University of Keele, and Franz Schnabel of the University of Munich. This manuscript would never have come to fruition without the active encouragement from its initial stages by Carl H. Pegg of the University of North Carolina. I would like to thank all those who have consistently thought more of the author's work than the author himself, and among them my wife Elizabeth in particular, who took time from her own professional career to help prepare the final manuscript.

ABBREVIATIONS FOR UNPUBLISHED DOCUMENTS

AA   Auswärtiges Amt (Microcopy in National Archives, Washington)

ARk   Alte Reichskanzlei (Bundesarchiv Koblenz)

NPA   Neues Politisches Archiv (Haus-, Hof- und Staatsarchiv, Vienna)

FM   Finanzministerium (Bundesarchiv Koblenz)

USDS   United States, Department of State (National Archives, Washington)

VA   Ministerratsprotokolle (Verwaltungsarchiv, Vienna)

The Austrian documents are cited as follows: NPA Faszikel number, document number.

The German microfilmed documents are cited as follows: AA roll number/serial number/document number.

INTRODUCTION

NATIONAL UNIFICATION was the primary goal of nineteenth-century politics in Central Europe. Yet after over one hundred years of struggle the German nation remained fragmented both politically and territorially. The unification of Austria and Germany in many ways would complete the unfinished business of the nineteenth century. The failure of Anschluss in the Weimar era illustrates the specific problems in this period as well as the dilemmas involved in the process of national unification in general.

Essentially this is a study of nationalism and its effect upon foreign policy in both Germany and Austria. It approaches the Anschluss problem in the 1920s from the following four perspectives:

1. The Anschluss was an important component of German revisionist foreign policy. A study of the Anschluss movement not only shows the depth of revisionist sentiment in Germany and Austria but also the difficulties of transforming this sentiment into action. The movement can also be viewed as a case study of the effect of political pressure groups upon Weimar foreign policy.

2. It involved domestic as well as foreign policy considerations. In the Reich, Austro-German union was most strongly advocated by democratic forces and the fate of this union had become bound up with the fate of German democracy. In both Germany and Austria, class and political conflicts often took precedence over concerted action on foreign policy.

3. The Anschluss question was handled more intensively in Austria than in the Reich. In Germany the Anschluss was only one of many revisionist goals, but Austro-German union involved the whole political future of the small Alpine land to the south. For many Austrians, Anschluss appeared as the only salvation from their economic and political difficulties. For others, it meant abandoning their traditional patterns of living for the uncongenial politics and business

practices of the north, and many Austrians were unwilling to accept this drastic change. These opponents of Anschluss dominated Austrian foreign policy from 1922 to 1928 and sought to find alternative solutions to union with Germany.

4. The Anschluss movement in the Weimar era presents an interesting model for the study of German nationalism at a time in the interwar period free from much of the hysteria associated with the active expansionist policy of the Hitler period.

THE ANSCHLUSS MOVEMENT AS A MODEL
FOR THE STUDY OF NATIONALISM

Aside from periods of hysteria, nationalism is actually much more fragmented than most definitions will admit. Scholars have consistently underestimated the pluralistic components of nationalism and most often treated it as a single monolithic phenomenon. They have too often confused agreement upon a specific objective with agreement upon the political goals of society. Yet a study of the Anschluss movement in the 1920s suggests just the opposite: that national aims are only a catch-all to describe a number of diverse interests cooperating for some tangible short-term objective.

There are a number of reasons for this underestimation of pluralistic interpretations. Scholars have had exaggerated expectations that the nation-state would provide the cement to hold the political framework together by overcoming the centrifugal tendencies of tribalism, regionalism, and differences in caste and color. As Reinhard Wittram maintains: "The nation undertook a function it could not fulfill. . . . Composed of obviously unrelated branches of society, of men of different regions and social classes, the nation was more promise, dream and ideal than communal reality."[1]

---

[1] Reinhard Wittram, *Das Nationale als europäische Problem* (Göttingen, 1954), p. 78. See Louis Snyder, *The Meaning of Nationalism* (New York, 1954), pp. 4–5; Wittram, *Das Nationale*, pp. 35–36. This study cannot discuss all the literature; for bibliography see Boyd Shafer, *Nationalism: Myth and Reality* (New York, 1955), pp. 295–314; idem, *Nationalism: Interpretations and Interpreters* (Washington, 1963); Karl Deutsch and Richard Merritt, *Nationalism: An Interdisciplinary Bibliography* (Cambridge, 1966). As the title of Deutsch's bibliography suggests, nationalism can be approached from many directions, if almost all authors consider it as a holistic form. The standard Anglo-American works on nationalism generally accept this monolithic interpretation; see especially Carlton Hayes, *The Historical Evolution of Modern Nationalism* (New York, 1931); Royal Institute for International Affairs, *Nationalism* (London, 1939). Two of the most important searches for its historical roots are René Johannet,

Even the definition of nationalism mitigates against a pluralistic interpretation. To expect more than a monolithic interpretation of nationalism would mean to question the *sine qua non* of the definition. Yet this has to be done. Modern societies, even the totalitarian, are more pluralistic than homogeneous. And pluralistic cultures engender a pluralistic symbolism. National goals vary with the specific interest groups from which they emanate and with the geographic, class, and political background of those who hold them. There are as many different kinds of nationalism as there are differing visions of the good society. Instead of one set of patriotic symbols there are many. Instead of one homogeneous nationalism there are often several sets of national loyalties within the same community. Some historians have already recognized this fact. Hans Kohn has shown how there were two distinct forms of French nationalism in the period 1789–1915. Otto Pflanze has demonstrated that there was more than one nationalism operating functionally in the German political culture of the 1860s. As early as 1912, Max Weber reminded his fellow colleagues in the German Sociological Society: "All in all, if we find it generally of use to differentiate national feeling as an undivided, specific, monolithic phenomenon, we can only grasp it as a condition of a tendency to form its own state, and we must be

---

La Principe des nationalités (Paris, 1923), pp. 34 ff.; and Hans Kohn, *The Idea of Nationalism* (New York, 1943). Some studies emphasizing sociopsychological phenomena are Leonard Doob, *Patriotism and Nationalism: Their Psychological Foundations* (New Haven, 1964); Friedrich Hertz, *Nationality in History and Politics* (London, 1944), pp. 26 ff.; Eugen Lemberg, *Nationalismus* (Hamburg, 1964), II: 100 ff.; Robert Michels, *Der Patriotismus* (Munich, 1929); Louis Snyder, *The Meaning of Nationalism*. See also the sociological studies of Karl Deutsch in *Nationalism and Social Communication* (New York, 1953) and *Political Community at the International Level* (New York, 1954). For similar studies on the growth of nationalism, see Seymour Lipset, *The First New Nation* (New York, 1963); Richard Merritt, *Symbols of the American Community* (New Haven, 1966). Two studies which approach nationalism from the standpoint of cultural and intellectual history are Elie Kedourie, *Nationalism* (London, 1960), and Friedrich Meinecke, *Weltbürgertum und Nationalstaat*, in *Werke*, II (Stuttgart, 1957–1962). Exaggerated expectations of historians are evident in G. P. Gooch, *History and Historians in the Nineteenth Century* (London, 1913). For American historiography, see David Noble, *Historians against History* (Minneapolis, 1965). See especially the discussions on Friedrich Meinecke and Max Weber in Georg Iggers, *The German Conception of History* (Middletown, Conn., 1968), pp. 169 ff.; J. P. Mayer, *Max Weber and German Politics* (London, 1955), pp. 41–78; Richard Sterling, *Ethics in a World of Power: The Political Ideas of Friedrich Meinecke* (Princeton, 1958), pp. 54–163. For the commitment of Wilhelmine historians to German nationalism, see Ludwig Dehio, *Germany and World Politics in the Twentieth Century* (New York, 1959), p. 66; Walther Hofer, *Geschichte zwischen Philosophie und Politik* (Stuttgart, 1956), pp. 42–43; Hans Kohn, *The Mind of Germany* (New York, 1960), pp. 309–11.

clear that thereunder are brought together feelings of community very heterogeneously formed and caused by a multiplicity of factors."[2]

Certainly German history has enough examples to support Weber's contention. Pflanze has shown how the tension of the 1860s was partially caused by the conflict between Bismarck's Prussian nationalism and the German patriotism of his liberal opponents. True, the new Reich generated its own symbols of national unity, but these were late in coming and never robbed German history of its conflicts. Theodor Schieder has indicated that as late as 1914 there were at least two contradictory symbols used to describe the goals of German nationalism. He claims that Germans had never decided between the aspirations of *Rechtsstaat* and *Weltpolitik*.[3]

The postwar world had done nothing to change the situation. Evidence drawn from the Anschluss movement demonstrates that general agreement upon the ultimate political aim could not insure against disagreement as to its meaning. The German people were fundamentally divided about the nature of their political society's final goal. These differing visions of the good society led to jealousies, conflict, and disorganization within the Anschluss movement. This movement became more of an example of the divisions within German society than a means of providing a common political framework. It did not heal the old wounds; it was hardly a showpiece for a unified conception of national aims.

German federalists and Bavarian separatists hoped to use the Anschluss question as a lever by which to overturn the central government's prerogatives. German democrats attacked such a position as parochial. For some, Austro-German union was to be part of a general democratic reform of German institutions. For others, it simply meant the addition of an appendage to the national community without changing its internal structure. Democrats and socialists sought to use their support of Anschluss to legitimize their reputation as German nationalists. More conservative politicians were concerned that the addition of Austrian voters to Reich elections would irremediably turn the balance of power in the direction of the democrats. Middle-class Germans feared to join an Anschluss organization dominated by the socialists and thus split the German Anschluss movement into two separate groups, differing in methods as well as

    [2] *Verhandlungen des Zweiten Deutschen Soziologentages* (Tübingen, 1913), p. 52. See Kohn, *Prelude to the Nation-States* (New York, 1967), pp. 41–47; Otto Pflanze, *Bismarck and the Development of Germany* (Princeton, 1963), pp. 71 ff. The author is indebted to Lee Benson's advocacy of pluralistic interpretations in *Turner and Beard* (New York, 1960), pp. 222–26.
    [3] Pflanze, *Bismarck;* Theodor Schieder, *Das Deutsche Kaiserreich von 1871 als Nationalstaat* (Cologne, 1961), p. 86.

membership.[4] In Austria the same phenomenon was apparent. The Austrian Anschluss movement was just as split by fear of socialism as the German. These fears also turned the Viennese middle-class nationalists away from an alliance with the Social Democrats, the other major pro-Anschluss party, and into a political coalition with the Catholic enemies of Anschluss.[5]

Sometimes these conflicts were present in the mind of the same individual. German businessmen gloried in their role of patriots who favored the Austro-German union as well as in their dreams of using Vienna as an *entrepôt* into Southeastern Europe. Yet the same businessmen in their role as company directors complained about the most minute trade concessions to the Austrians. Similar conflicts were present in the mind of Gustav Stresemann. There is a good deal of evidence to show that he had a strong emotional attachment to the Anschluss. Against the advice of his subordinates, Stresemann intervened on the Austrian side in the question of South Tyrolean minority rights. More important, he confided to the Italian Ambassador in Berlin that he thought Anschluss was both necessary and inevitable. He also made pro-Anschluss statements that disturbed his relations with Aristide Briand and especially the old German-baiter Poincaré. Yet Stresemann had reservations about adding so many Catholics to his Protestant Reich and doubted that the Austrians would contribute to the political stability of Germany. Almost certainly, Stresemann gave the Anschluss a lower priority than the task of regaining the lost Polish land that, unlike the Austrian, had once been part of the empire of William II.[6]

Monolithic nationalism is not the element that precludes conflict within the political framework. Still those who have differing views of the good society and the meaning of the nation can unite for specific reasons. Various groups representing conflicting ideologies can cooperate with each other in a national community for the achievement of certain fixed and popular goals. This hypothesis is hardly new. Historians and political scientists have always known that the most diverse groups are capable of acting in concert with one another. After all, Bismarck and many German liberals worked reasonably well together after 1866. Socialists and middle-class conservatives might not be able to live within the framework of a single pro-Anschluss organization, yet they could pursue the same aim along independent lines.

This holds true for other aspects of the Anschluss movement.

[4] See chapter II.
[5] See chapter III.
[6] See chapters VII and VIII.

Many German conservatives even adopted the democratic rhetoric. They advocated the Wilsonian principles of self-determination that were certainly heretical by Wilhelmine standards. But these conservatives now realized that self-determination was the best argument to use in convincing the recalcitrant allies that Germany had a just case. This common rhetoric was reinforced by an apparent unanimity of support for the Anschluss question in Germany. Yet again this support represented a coalition of competing interests rather than a perpetual unity under the national banners. The large Anschluss demonstrations held in almost every major German city were primarily the work of socialists and middle-class democrats. The plethora of pamphlet literature published on various aspects of the union was primarily the work of middle-class conservatives. The attempts to create a common legal system and an economic union were also generally confined to the middle class, democratic or not. Yet all this division was forgotten, and these acts were simply filed away under the heading: evidence of support for the Anschluss. It gave a sham appearance of a harmony of interests, and the Anschluss movement did nothing itself to challenge this belief. Its leaders maintained that their organizations were of a supra-party nature. They believed that the allegiance of their membership to patriotic goals far outweighed any parochial considerations. As Friedrich Meinecke wrote in 1922, "The unification of German-Austria with Germany belongs to those extraordinary and great political questions in which the irrational strength of events comes together harmoniously and absolutely."[7]

There was one serious attempt to create a unified German symbolism. The Weimar republicans had to junk some of their inherited symbols that had long been intertwined with those of the Hohenzollern dynasty. Thus events such as the victories of Frederick the Great over Maria Theresa were celebrated in the schools as German national victories. These loyalties to the Hohenzollern past would have to be overcome if the Austrians were to be integrated eventually into the national community. New symbols would have to be created in conformity with the new reality of the postwar Austria. Austria was no longer the name of a state with a Slavic majority; it no longer slipped off the tongue in conjunction with Habsburg interests. The new Austria was a German republic, most of whose citizens wanted to join the Reich. And, if the Germans wished to append this land, they would have to treat the Austrians as fellow nationals.

German and Austrian historians alike went about transforming

---

[7] Meinecke, *Werke*, II: 336. See also chapters V and VI.

their interpretations to take these new facts into account. By rewriting Austria's role in the German past, they attempted to show that Austrians had always had a common identity with other Germans. Most of these historians were not committed to overturning their old ideas completely. They still sought to justify Bismarck's work as a necessary step in the movement toward complete national unification. They were often still unsympathetic to the Habsburgs as well. Most historians rejected the two simple solutions to the problems accompanying revision. Attached to Prussia as an historical entity, they refused to accept a federalist-oriented historiography that offered an anti-Prussian view of German history calculated to please many Austrians. Attached to the Hohenzollern dynasty as a historical necessity, they were also unwilling to accept a socialist and democratic historiography that sought to achieve a common sense of identity by relating the present German desires to those of the 1848 republicans.

Yet again diverse groups cooperated and gave the impression of a harmony of interests pursuing a unified national policy. Most conservative historians agreed with democrats and socialists in seeing some new role for Austria in classroom lectures, primary and secondary school texts, even in curricular changes. Although this attempt was only partially successful before 1933, these new symbols of Austria were well on their way to becoming an integral part of the baggage carried by German nationalism.[8]

This temporary union of interests also took place in the country that was the object of the German nationalist sentiment. Austria itself presents an interesting, if extraordinarily exotic, example of diverse interests working toward the same end, in this case the destruction of their state. In their different ways, both proponents and opponents of Anschluss hoped to dissolve the apparatus of central government and merge into some larger political unit. The major difference was the nature of this political unit and the means chosen to effect it. Committed to an immediate union with Germany, the Anschluss supporters rejoiced at all signs of Austrian economic instability, considering such the surest means for convincing the allies of the need of an immediate union with Germany. They had a stake in keeping their fellow citizens permanently in misery. On the other hand, the opponents of union did work for the maintenance of the Austrian economy, but their efforts were undermined by a disbelief in the efficacy of their labors. The opponents were just as unwilling as the Anschluss supporters to accept the Swiss model for Austria. They ultimately

[8] See chapter IV.

hoped that Vienna would become part of some Danubian or Pan-European federation.[9]

THE ANSCHLUSS PROBLEM AND THE SHAPING OF AUSTRIAN AND GERMAN FOREIGN POLICY

Although the majority of Austrians and Germans favored Anschluss, the governments were never able to take advantage of this fact. The consistent opposition of France, Czechoslovakia, and Italy made any such move impossible. This fact forced the Germans to practice the *Realpolitik* of the losers; even Stresemann had to discourage Anschluss demonstrations that disturbed the allies while bringing no tangible benefits in return. The German Foreign Minister could not pursue an active policy vis-à-vis Austria until the Rhineland occupation had ended and a new reparations settlement had been reached. But this policy did not mean that Stresemann was opposed to Austro-German union. Hans Gatzke and Anneliese Thimme have already shown that Stresemann was committed to the union, at the very least as a means for overturning the entire Versailles system. If the German Foreign Office did not wish to disturb the entrenched foreign opponents of Anschluss by open demonstrations, this did not mean that it was not involved with the Austrian question. German diplomats were, however, mainly concerned with future possibilities not present actions. They particularly worked to forestall any additional treaty obligations that would make the accomplishment of Anschluss even more difficult. This stand was taken even at the cost of endangering further rapprochement with the Western allies, particularly Italy.[10]

Yet Stresemann's own successes contributed to the revival of the agitation for Anschluss after 1925. The Locarno Agreements and Germany's entrance into the League of Nations raised expectations for a peaceful revision of the Austrian question. There were not only those massive demonstrations which were discouraged by the Foreign Office but other substantial efforts that did not openly conflict with the short-term goals of German foreign policy. German jurists and politicians worked to solve the legal and economic problems in-

---

[9] See chapters X-XIII.

[10] See chapters I, VI, and VIII; Anneliese Thimme, " Gustav Stresemann: Legende und Wirklichkeit," *Historische Zeitschrift* 181 (1956); 292–338; idem, *Gustav Stresemann* (Hanover, 1957), pp. 20 ff.; Hans Gatzke, *Stresemann and the Rearmament of Germany* (Baltimore, 1954).

volved in the eventual union so that political amalgamation could be achieved with the least possible conflict. In addition, both the German and Austrian governments initiated discussions on the possibility of cooperation even before the Anschluss was achieved. Many German and Austrian leaders sought to create such far-reaching legal, educational, and economic unification that would complete the Anschluss in all but name.[11]

Although the Austrian government accepted some limited cooperation in legal and economic matters, the German nationalist ideology was not often present in those who directed Austrian foreign policy, particularly between 1922 and 1928. Ignaz Seipel and Heinrich Mataja, who shaped Austrian foreign policy for most of this period, were suspicious of the Protestant, Bismarck-unified Reich. They sought to create some surrogate for the old empire. Yet, like Stresemann, these statesmen were trapped by the postwar situation of their country. Their state was in a perpetual economic crisis and lacked the muscle necessary to carry out a strong foreign policy. Seipel, especially, had to seek coalition with the German nationalists and thus permanently weakened his ability to oppose the Anschluss. The French, Czechs, and Italians were sympathetic, but they could offer no more than temporary palliatives for the Austrian problem. Czech Foreign Minister Eduard Beneš could hardly convince all his own people, not to speak of the successor states, on the feasibility of reconstructing this surrogate empire in the form of an economic Danubian union. Mussolini was ready to propose a simple Austro-Italian customs union as an instrument for his expansion into the Balkans. But this scheme raised opposition from the Czechs and was considered as only a last resort by Austrian diplomats. Mataja's policies ended in failure. Forced to reject Danubian union, Seipel still hoped that an Anschluss could be avoided by the fruition of some other plans that would make Austria a center in a larger economic and political area— a Central European union that included Germany or a united Europe.[12]

Seipel and Stresemann were certainly extraordinary men who in more propitious times would have been able to mold the course of events in their states for generations. But their styles were different, and these styles raised a barrier against Austro-German cooperation almost as great as that of ideology. Stresemann was the sophisticate, the cynic. He could joke. On New Year's Day 1929, feeling the effects of champagne and conviviality, he took the Austrian Minister to Berlin

[11] See chapters VI and VII.
[12] See chapters X and XIII.

aside and suggested that "we call the papers and tell them that Bavaria has just completed an Anschluss with Austria."[13] The only priest in the twentieth century to be a prime minister, Seipel waged an intense and humorless war to save his church and his society— "my task in my first ten years of political life was to maintain a counterreformation against all those tendencies and experiences that lead people away from religion and the Church."[14] Yet he often anguished in the accomplishment of this task, since his daily round of duties impeded the complete fulfillment of his priestly function and jeopardized, he thought, the state of his soul.

It was difficult for two such men to communicate with each other. Their common meetings often appeared more like sparring sessions. In the end, these political enemies were brought together by the logic of events, by the fact that neither Austria nor Germany could pursue an independent foreign policy. Seipel's schemes for a Pan or Central European union were too visionary to be achieved in the 1920s. Stresemann, however, was hardly more realistic. The Reichsminister was not convinced by the arguments of German democrats that the Czech and French opposition might be removed by the justice of Germany's moral stand. Yet his own alternative was scarcely less utopian, since he believed himself able to overcome allied opposition through diplomatic means. Thus it was the frustrations of these statesmen that induced their cooperation, not their desires. Stresemann was forced to accept Seipel's struggle to maintain Austrian independence because he could not immediately achieve the Anschluss. Seipel would become increasingly interested in economic cooperation with the Reich because of the failure of all alternative policy.

Frustration summarizes the Anschluss movement as no other word can. A large propaganda effort brought no visible results. Chained by the clauses of the peace treaties, the Reich could not give the necessary support to the demands for economic and legal union. Without the full cooperation of the state these aims were unattainable. Thus statesmen were not the only Germans and Austrians with unfulfilled desires. The restrictions upon an active foreign policy brought forth hyperbolic reactions, particularly within the Anschluss movement. There were extreme assertions of moral superiority over the allies who refused to carry out Wilsonian self-determination to its logical conclusion, or of the reverse, unleavened despair. In either case, the Anschluss question was a constant reminder of a failure

[13] Frank (Berlin) to Vienna, January 2, 1929, NPA Fasz. 11, Zl. 1 Pol. See bibliography for discussion of the footnoting methods used for documents.

[14] *Ignaz Seipel: Mensch, Christ, Priester* (ed.) Rudolf Blüml (Vienna, 1933), p. 162.

that concerned more than foreign policy. The whole political process was involved. Both the Austrian and the German republics desperately needed results that would buttress the belief of their citizens in the ability of their governments to rule effectively. The continually unresolved Austrian problem was scarcely calculated to restore this faith in a purposive national community. There was one great period of activity in the era. The Austro-German customs union project of 1931 was calculated to provide some success. The Austrian government at this time was controlled by Johannes Schober, hardly a follower of Seipel. Julius Curtius, the German foreign minister, was inclined to take more chances than Stresemann. However, the allied opposition was just as strong in 1931 as it had been in 1919. The defeat of the customs union project was a serious blow to political stability in both countries and marked an end to the attempts at peaceful revisionism.[15] Anschluss was to be achieved by other means in another era.

[15] See chapter IX.

THE EMPIRES' COLLAPSE

CHAPTER I THE SPARK AND THE FLAME: THE ANSCHLUSS QUESTION FROM NOVEMBER 1918 TO SEPTEMBER 1919

THE ANSCHLUSS MOVEMENT in 1918–19 was a direct response to the new political environment. Some historians would later contend that it was the logical culmination of German history, but such judgments were manufactured more out of present hopes than out of the reality of the historical experience. The spark that ignited the movement was the fall of the Habsburg and Hohenzollern dynasties and the destruction of Austria-Hungary. The Anschluss appeared as the only solution for the rump Austria and as something to salvage from the wreckage of defeat for Germany. Public opinion in both countries was united on the issue. After some initial hesitation in Berlin, the two governments would jointly conclude an agreement to accomplish this goal. But the flame ignited by the events of November 1918 would be extinguished rapidly by the allies. The peace treaties prohibited Anschluss and the movement died what appeared to be a natural death by September 1919.

As late as the summer of 1918 the political separation of Austrian Germans from their co-nationals in the Reich was an unquestioned fact. Bismarck's solution of 1866 appeared both adequate and irrevocable. However, by the 1870s a small group of radicals within the Austro-Hungarian empire desired an amalgamation of the German-speaking peoples of Austria with the Hohenzollern state. Georg von Schönerer was the spiritual leader of these radicals. Although a whole generation of Austrian youth had found these views appealing, Schönerer had never been able to develop a mass following among the Austrian Germans. The majority of the German liberals were more concerned with protecting their special position within the Habsburg empire than advocating its destruction. German-Austrian Catholics distrusted the Protestant Prussians who had been bitterly anti-Roman as late as the 1870s. The socialists were almost exclusively concerned with reconciling the differences between the nationalities within the empire. Thus Schönerer often found himself isolated and condemned as a disturber of the peace. A typical confrontation between Schönerer

3

and the majority of Austrian Germans occurred during his speech to the House of Delegates on December 18, 1878.

More and more one hears in these lands the call: if we only already belonged to the German Reich. (*Cries of Oho! Oho! Oho! That is not true. Lively contradiction.*) I maintain this is so. (*Renewed lively contradiction.*) As someone said at another time that something was rotten in the state of Denmark, so I will slightly paraphrase this statement and say: Today in the state of Austria almost everything is rotten. (*Cries of Oho!*)[1]

German policy and public opinion were equally opposed to the union. Such a continental expansion clashed with the aims of *Weltpolitik* which focused on overseas adventures. Thus even an expansionist such as Heinrich Class, head of the Pan-German League, rejected a political union with Austria-Hungary. The struggles over linguistic policies within the Habsburg state did evoke some sympathy, especially in the late 1890s. Yet support for the Germans in the Austro-Hungarian monarchy was more often simply an expression of the *Realpolitik* in Berlin's foreign policy than of nationalist feeling. Many Germans were convinced that a Slav-dominated Austria would be an unreliable ally. An isolated voice might proclaim in the Reichstag that "Blood is warmer than the cold ink of diplomats. . . . The whole Germany it shall be from the Belt to the Adriatic,"[2] but official German opinion was more correctly stated in a memorandum written by Bernhard von Bülow when he was German foreign minister:

Our political interests, to which all platonic sympathies must be subordinated . . . demand the recognition of the maintenance of Austria-Hungary as an independent power. This interest demands from us that we abstain from encouraging any divisive attitudes in Austria, whether they be Polish, Czech or German. The Austrian Germans must not doubt that so long as they fight to preserve Germandom as the cement for the internal cohesive force and to preserve the Austrian state in its present form, we will follow their struggle with the fullest sympathy, but that as soon as this struggle seeks as its final goal to separate the German lands from Austria and with it return to the *status quo ante* of 1866, the German nationalists are to expect no support for their plans from here.[3]

The war naturally brought the Germanic peoples closer together. But a political union cannot be created upon the basis of common

[1] *Stenographische Protokolle über die Sitzungen des Hauses der Abgeordneten*, VIII Session, Bd. XII, 13112. See also Heinrich Schnee, *Georg Ritter von Schönerer: ein Kämpfer für Alldeutschland* (Reichenberg, 1941).

[2] *Verhandlungen des Reichstags*, X Legislaturperiode, I Session, Bd. I, 118.

[3] *Die Grosse Politik der europäischen Kabinette, 1871–1914*, XII: 120–21. For a description of similar views by Bismarck, see Henry Cord Meyer, *Mitteleuropa in German Thought and Action* (The Hague, 1955), p. 47.

enemies. There were still two competing sovereigns in Berlin and Vienna. The two empires often pursued different goals. The general staffs often disagreed on the conduct of the war. Austrian generals and diplomats were bitter about the German-dictated solution to the Polish problem. The main effect of wartime cooperation was to initiate planning by public officials and opinion leaders on the postwar reconstruction of Central and Southeastern Europe. Friedrich Naumann's book *Mitteleuropa* called forth a flood of imitative pamphlets advocating a joint German-Austrian enterprise in Southeastern Europe. However, this cooperation was to be basically economic and was not necessarily conceived as a prelude to a political amalgamation. It was to be an enterprise to be administered jointly by independent partners for the mutual benefit of both. The first step in Naumann's scheme was achieved by the Treaty of Salzburg on October 11, 1918, that provided for a customs union between the two states. Except for some discussion concerned with uniting Austrian and German legal codes, this was as far as the cooperation got.[4]

By the time the Treaty of Salzburg had been signed, the question of postwar entente between the two empires had become academic. The recognition by the allies of an independent Poland and Czechoslovakia in August 1918 meant the virtual end of the Habsburg empire. The collapse of the Balkan front in September accelerated the creation of governments in exile by the Slavic peoples of Austria. The Emperor Karl sought for some last-minute reform that could still hold the Slavic people within the monarchy. On October 16 Karl published a manifesto calling for the creation of a new Austria "in which every people would build its own political community in its own area of settlement."[5]

The Emperor's manifesto precipitated the Anschluss movement in Austria. Any attempt to undermine the privileged position of the Germans would necessarily weaken their support of the monarchy. The fifteen radical nationalist deputies in the Reichsrath suddenly found popular support for their view that the Austrian Germans had to dissolve their ties with the other peoples of the monarchy. Mass meetings were held under nationalist aegis in Upper and Lower

---

[4] The Treaty can be found in AA 3270/7478/H187393–H187402. See also Gustav Gratz and Richard Schuller, *The Economic Policy of Austria-Hungary during the War in Its External Relations* (New Haven, 1929), pp. 114 ff.; Cord Meyer, *Mitteleuropa in German Thought*, pp. 194 ff.; Friedrich Naumann, *Mitteleuropa* (Berlin, 1915); Gerald Silberstein, *The Troubled Alliance* (Lexington, 1970).

[5] Hans Leo Mikoletzky, *Österreichische Zeitgeschichte* (Vienna, 1962), p. 41. See also Helmut Rumpler, *Das Völkermanifest Kaiser Karls* (Munich, 1966).

Austria, Bohemia, Styria, and Tyrol to demand an immediate union with Germany. The antisemitic radical nationalists found allies in unexpected quarters. On October 12 the Jewish socialist leader, Otto Bauer, stated that union with Germany was the only salvation for the Germanic lands of the Habsburg empire. By the end of October the German-speaking socialists were calling for the creation of a democratic republic that could unite with the Reich.[6]

The manifesto of October 16 was more than a stimulus for the creation of pro-union propaganda. It created the vehicle by which the Anschluss might be achieved. The manifesto did no more than validate the councils already set up by the Czechs and Poles, but the Germans had no council, nor had there been great agitation to set up one. In imitation of the Slavs, and now with the consent of the Emperor, the German-speaking deputies in the Reichsrath established the Provisional National Assembly on October 21. This was the first recognized political expression of a distinct German political entity in the history of the empire. Thus the German political leadership could, for the first time, think of its future unencumbered by the problems of the other nationalities. For many this future meant a union with the Reich.

There could be no union as long as the imperial institutions and monarchist sentiment remained. The Habsburgs would never submerge themselves under another German sovereignty, and they lingered on long after their demise appeared imminent. The German liberals were too timid to make the break; the Catholic Christian Socialist Party was still loyal to the empire. Through the end of October many lived in the hope that the reality could suddenly change. Chancellor Hussarek even claimed that the Slavic peoples would return to the Habsburgs once the first ecstasy of national liberation had passed. The provisional government instituted on October 31 might have a prominent socialist minister, Viktor Adler, and a chancellor who believed in the inevitability of Austro-German union, but it was far from ready to proclaim the Anschluss. The Austrian government gave no positive response to Prince Max von Baden's announcement of forthcoming elections to a German constituent assembly that would have the task of determining the future of the entire nation. The German diplomats became convinced that Emperor Karl was attempting to save his crown by promising the allies that he would forestall a union with Germany. Count Botho Wedel, the German ambassador to Vienna, was extraordinarily disturbed by the continuing monarchical loyalties. He stated that the Viennese were beginning to realize what would

[6] Duane Paul Meyers, "Germany and the Question of Austrian *Anschluss*, 1918–1922" (dissertation, Yale University, 1968), pp. 38–74.

happen to their city robbed of its imperial residence "and, when the entente will have supplied the country with food, interest in the republic and the German idea will slacken in the face of *café au lait* and rolls, owing to the superficiality of the Austrians."[7]

It took the collapse of the Italian front and the German Revolution to seal the fate of the Habsburg. On November 2, 350,000 Austrian troops became prisoners of the Italians. The Italians were marching into Tyrol not only as conquerors but as permanent occupiers. The final collapse of the armies persuaded the Hungarians to seal off their borders, the last major source of food for a Vienna which had been undergoing serious shortages since April. The imperial government in Vienna had all but ceased to exist after October 30.[8] Finally the German liberals lost their timidity and began advocating a union with the Reich. The Christian Socialists' loyalties were wilting under the pressure of events. The provincial parties in Tyrol and Styria began to demand Anschluss as their only protection against Italian or Serbian rule. The leader of the Upper Austrian Christian Socialists also admitted that the majority of his constituents favored the union. The proclamation of the German republic on November 9 removed the last possible obstacle to the union. Workers marched through the streets of Vienna demanding a republic and union with their comrades in Berlin. No one could now resist the tide. The Christian Socialists capitulated; there was nothing else to do. On November 11 the Emperor issued his last manifesto. He renounced "any participation in the business of state."[9] On the next day the Provisional Assembly proclaimed Austria a republic that wished to unite with the Reich.

The republic and Anschluss had by then become almost interchangeable terms. On November 12 the Provisional Assembly proclaimed the new democratic republic of German Austria in one breath and its suicide in the next by declaring that this new state was "a constituent part of the German Republic."[10] The first chancellor of Austria, Karl Renner, reiterated these demands in his inaugural address to the Assembly. "In this hour our German *Volk* in all areas

---

[7] Wedel (Vienna) to Berlin, November 26, 1918, Microfilms of the German Foreign Office 1870–1920, Saint Anthony's reel 25 (hereinafter cited as SA 25). See also Wedel to Berlin, September 26, 1918, AA 3270/7479/H187435; and Arthur G. Kogan, "Genesis of the Anschluss Problem," *Journal of Central European Affairs* 20 (1960): 46–49; Meyers, "Germany and *Anschluss*," pp. 90–128.

[8] Ernst Hoor, *Österreich 1918–1938* (Vienna, 1966), p. 82.

[9] Mikoletzky, *Österreichische Zeitgeschichte*, p. 52. See also Friedrich Funder, *Vom Gestern ins Heute* (Vienna, 1952), pp. 588–97; Walter Goldinger, "Der Geschichtliche Ablauf der Ereignisse in Österreich von 1918 bis 1945," Heinrich Benedikt ed., *Geschichte der Republik Österreich* (Vienna, 1954), pp. 37–41.

[10] Ibid., p. 53.

shall know that we are one people and one community of fate. (*The Assembly rises. Stormy, long-lasting cheers and handclapping on the floor and in the galleries.*)"[11] But until the time of union, the German Austrians were in a limbo. All political arrangements had to be considered impermanent. Until the Anschluss was achieved, the Austrians were, in Renner's words, "a people without a state."[12]

All now depended upon the Germans. As early as November 16, Otto Bauer, then under-secretary of state in the provisional Foreign Ministry, entered into negotiations with the German People's Commissar Hugo Haase. Bauer desired that the two new states should immediately demand recognition of the union by the entente. He claimed that Germany and Austria were simply exercising what Woodrow Wilson declared as "the right of self-determination . . . . They intend to re-constitute the close constitutional tie with Germany which was cut by the sword 52 years ago."[13] Ludo Hartmann, the republic's Austrian ambassador in Berlin, argued that the two powers should immediately unite. Once the union was achieved, the entente powers could never forbid it. Hartmann stated that "the more *fait accomplis* that are created before the peace conference, the easier the situation will be for Germany and for us."[14]

The Germans were slow to respond to the Austrian initiative. The imperial government had flirted with the idea of Anschluss during its last days. William II thought that the demise of the Habsburg rule might pave the way for the entrance of the Austrian Germans into the Hohenzollern-led Reich.[15] In late October Ludendorff suggested that the collapse of the Habsburg armies required a change in the position of the German government. He believed that: "In the not too distant future, we will perhaps be faced with a situation in which we have to extend our military protection to the Germans in Austria."[16] However, such a situation did not come about. German troops did advance in Tyrol after the collapse of the Italian front, but this move was only undertaken to create a buffer zone between the advancing Italian armies and the Bavarian border. Both civilian and military authorities were reluctant to move German troops into Bohemia after the Czech revolution of October 28. There had been some contingency

[11] *Stenographisches Protokolle der provisorischen Nationalversammlung für Deutschösterreich,* p. 66.
[12] Goldinger, "Geschichtliche Ablauf," p. 42. For the attempt to assimilate the new Austrian basic law with the political movements in the Reich, see Friedrich Kleinwaechter, *Von Schönbrunn bis St. Germain* (Graz, 1964), pp. 98–100.
[13] Meyers, "Germany and *Anschluss*," p. 168.
[14] Hartmann to Bauer, December 31, 1918 quoted in ibid., p. 169.
[15] Kogan, "Genesis," p. 30.
[16] Ibid., p. 28.

plans made for such an event but neither the Foreign Office nor the army high command was willing to take responsibility for such an action. It was left to the Austrians to request military intervention. After some hesitation in Vienna, the new Austrian government reported on November 3 that the movement of troops was unnecessary.[17]

While accepting the Anschluss in principle, the Foreign Office Under-Secretary of State Wilhelm Solf had always been reluctant to intervene in Austria and to initiate a thoroughgoing pro-Anschluss policy. Solf argued as early as October 19 that German demands for the inclusion of Austria might strengthen the French in their intention to annex Alsace-Lorraine and the Rhineland. He stated that France could contend that Austria would be an adequate compensation for such losses. After November 11 this position was still maintained. Solf, still in charge of foreign affairs under the revolutionary government, stated: "We had to curb our expressions of joy . . . for tactical reasons since it appears that our opponents, especially France, do not wish the union."[18]

With the experts opposed, there was little action from Berlin. The situation in Germany was too desperate for the political leadership to concentrate on the Austrian situation in November. The new Council of People's Commissars in Berlin faced a much more dangerous internal political situation than the provisional government in Vienna. The leading parties in Austria had easily agreed upon the composition of a coalition government. In Germany the loci of power were uncertain, and the future of the country might have to be decided on the streets of Berlin. Friedrich Ebert and the Majority Socialists were not secure until the middle of January. By then the Anschluss movement had gained considerable force on its own. On January 12 most of the German newspapers carried a resolution declaring that the union with German Austria was an issue upon which the whole nation could agree. The German Democratic Party, the Center, the Nationalist, and the People's Parties had taken a positive stand for the union by early January. Ludo Hartmann could confidently write to Vienna that: "No one can doubt the unity of German opinion."[19]

The desire for activity on the German side was encouraged by Wedel, who alarmed Berlin with reports that the support for Anschluss was declining in Austria. Wedel argued that the Catholic clergy

[17] Ibid., pp. 33–45; Solf to Wedel, October 28, 1918, AA 3270/7418/ H187509.

[18] Solf memo, November 28, 1918, quoted in Meyers, "Germany and Anschluss," p. 165. See also Edward Keleher, "Deutschland, Deutschösterreich und die Anschlussfrage in den letzten Wochen des Ersten Weltkrieges," Österreich in Geschichte und Literatur 12 (1968): 132–43.

[19] Hartmann to Bauer, January 5, 1919, quoted in ibid., p. 214.

were opposed to joining the Protestants of the North. Industrialists and bankers feared German competition, and aristocrats were still loyal to the monarchy. The German Ambassador feared that the food shortages in Vienna might drive Austria into the camp of the entente. These fears were not only expressed by the Germans. The mounting foreign and internal opposition as well as the lack of direction from Berlin caused the generally optimistic Bauer to admit on January 3: "In view of this situation, I do not believe that *Anschluss* is a settled matter."[20]

Buttressed by a unified public opinion and fearing that Austria might be lost, the provisional government at Weimar lost no time in taking a stand. Ebert had already stated in a press interview that the first phase of foreign policy was over and that the Germans would no longer mark time on the Anschluss question. True to his promise, Ebert accepted the provisional presidency on February 11 with an address to the new Assembly in which he proclaimed, "We have solemnly renounced the principle of force between nations; no one shall be driven into union with the Republic but no one shall be forced and pulled away from joining it."[21] The new German foreign minister, Count Brockdorff-Rantzau, would repeat the government's position on February 14. Rantzau told the same body: "We are only undertaking a belated correction of an error in the establishment of the Reich which the Peace Conference will certainly not refuse to accept."[22] These remarks followed and were succeeded by the reading of telegrams from various Austrian organizations, municipalities, and states asking for union with the Reich. There was also a parade of party leaders declaring in favor of the right of German Austrians to unite with Germany. All these statements were greeted with cheers, but the largest ovation went to Friedrich Naumann of the German Democratic Party when he turned to the hall and shouted: "We greet our Austrian brothers. Come, we are waiting."[23]

The Assembly moved to action on February 21 in its unanimous reply to the Austrian Provisional Assembly's resolution of November 12. The document called attention to the common nationality of Austrians and Germans and stated that the negotiations for Anschluss should "find recognition by all powers of the world."[24] Led by Naumann and his fellow democrat Hugo Preuss, German politicians continually brought up the matter of Austria in the discussions of the

[20] Bauer to Hartmann, January 3, 1919, quoted in ibid., p. 204.
[21] *Verhandlungen der Verfassungsgebenden Deutschen Nationalversammlung*, I: 41. For *Neue Freie Presse* article see AA 2411/4665/E218821.
[22] *Verhandlungen* I: 69.
[23] Ibid. I: 59.
[24] Ibid. I: 258.

Provisional Assembly's Constitutional Committee. On February 24 the government's draft for a permanent constitution mentioned the inclusion of Austria in the Reich. Naumann had desired to go further and provide the explicit mechanism for the union. He had been out-voted in the committee; the majority had thought that this was an issue of foreign policy to be settled by the two governments. Still the final draft of the constitution stated in Article 2, Paragraph 1 that provinces could be added to Germany if their populations approved. This would pave the way for the union with Austria. Article 61, Paragraph 2 of the constitution read: "German Austria shall receive after its union with the German Reich the right of participation in the Reichsrat with a number of votes which shall be in proportion to its population. Until that time the representatives of German Austria shall participate in an advisory capacity."[25]

The events of February in Germany were paralleled by elections in Austria to the Constituent Assembly on February 15. This was the first test of the popularity of the Anschluss. Until then all was a matter of conjecture. The socialists and the nationalists considered Anschluss one of their principal issues. Both Bauer and Ludo Hart-mann were in the thick of the fight.[26] The Christian Socialists favored the Anschluss in principle but argued that it should be a long-term goal. The opposition to the union was particularly strong among the Christian Socialists in Salzburg and Tyrol. Many of these believed that the Anschluss was simply a "sell-out to Germany."[27] Despite such opposition, the results of February 16 were a clear mandate for the Anschluss. The socialists got 40.8 percent of the vote and the various nationalist parties 18.4. Of the 170 seats in the Constituent Assembly, 95 were held by these two groups. There were enough supporters of an immediate German union among the Christian Socialists to assure an overwhelming majority on any vote to unite with the Reich.[28]

With both governments assured of popular support, diplomatic negotiations could begin. Bauer journeyed to Weimar on February 26, and returned with an agreement signed on March 2. This secret treaty provided for an Anschluss on very favorable terms for Vienna. The name of Austria would be preserved as a federal state in the unified Reich. The German president would take up residence and the Reichstag would meet in Vienna for part of every year. Germany

---

[25] M. Margaret Ball, *Post-War German-Austrian Relations* (Stanford University, 1937), p. 17; Theodor Heuss, *Friedrich Naumann* (Stuttgart, 1937), p. 485.

[26] Frederick Dumin, "Background of the Austro-German *Anschluss* Movement, 1918–1919" (dissertation, University of Wisconsin, 1963), pp. 149–54.

[27] Ibid., p. 90.

[28] Ibid., pp. 175–81.

agreed to take a certain stipulated number of Austrian civil servants into the newly amalgamated central government, postal service, and railways.

There were both long- and short-term economic advantages in the treaty. Germany promised to build a Rhine-Main-Danube canal to connect the commerce of Austria with the rest of the Reich. Austria was granted the right to conclude special economic arrangements with the old lands of the Habsburg monarchy during a special transitional period. For the same period the Austrians would be allowed to place a special surcharge upon the unified tariffs for a limited number of items. An amount equal to this surcharge would also be levied on German goods coming into the former Austrian lands. Germany agreed to accept all Austrian debts that were undertaken as part of the functions of central government, leaving only those debts that would accrue to Austria if it had been a state within Germany since 1870.[29]

All these negotiations had an air of unreality. The governments in Berlin and Vienna could not exercise all the accoutrements of sovereignty. They were defeated powers awaiting the verdict of the allies on their individual and collective futures. They were under blockade and threat of occupation. Moreover these negotiations were conducted in a diplomatic vacuum. Germany and Austria did not have ambassadors in the capitals of the victors and were thus robbed of the normal day-to-day intelligence essential for the conduct of diplomacy. The decision to sign the treaty of March 2 was no more than an act in a diplomatic game of blind-man's buff. Perhaps the allies would choose to forbid the Anschluss; that was more than likely. Yet who could know? The fear of retaliation that had made the Germans timid in December might have been legitimate. Still the more aggressive policies in February could have led to a completion of the union. The treaty of March 2 might have been truly the work of both the lion and the fox.

There was more support for the Anschluss in the capitals of the entente than might have been expected. As early as 1916 Arthur Balfour, British foreign minister, favored the amalgamation of the German lands of Austria. The memorandum of the British Foreign Office experts in late 1918 was pro-Anschluss. It argued that Austria could not be allowed to exist as a satellite state that would be the natural core of a German-dominated Danubian union. Furthermore the inclusion of the Austrian Germans in the Reich would finally destroy the Bismarckian system and "restore the balance between the Catholic south and the Protestant north."[30] In any case, the British

[29] The agreement can be found in SA 25.
[30] Harold I. Nelson, *Land and Power* (London, 1963), p. 106.

experts believed that the destruction of Austria-Hungary would make the union inevitable. A French memorandum drafted by parallel experts in Paris surprisingly agreed with all these points. It argued that German nationalism could not forever be ignored. Instead of instituting a policy of opposition to the union, the French government should negotiate concessions from the Reich in exchange for the inclusion of Austria. The French memorandum went even farther than considerations of *Realpolitik*. It argued that all German national goals were not evil and that France could support legitimate aims based upon "aspirations for national unity, not upon a desire for conquest."[31]

Expert opinions are more often than not rejected by their governments. Clemenceau had no intention of increasing the size and population of the German enemy. And the French government apparently communicated these views to the Germans in December through the neutral capitals of Bern and Stockholm. The French press was almost united in opposing Anschluss. On December 29 Foreign Minister Stephen Pichon expressed these views as government policy in a debate in the Chamber of Deputies. Pichon argued that Austro-German union would offer Germany compensations for its territorial losses in other areas and allow Germany to gain control over the other German minorities in Southeastern Europe. He concluded: "It is necessary that, in the first place, this victory be translated into all its just consequences and that we exercise our rights over the vanquished to avoid their raising the possibility of imperilling the security and liberty of the world." (*Applause.*)[32]

Pichon came under attack from the Left because such a statement seemed to violate Wilson's Fourteen Points for a just peace. He was accused of violating Wilsonian principles and using the language of Bismarck. Ironically, the British government and the French Left were far more willing to accept the logic of the Wilsonian position than Wilson himself. When Wilson had enunciated the Fourteen Points, he had no thought of applying them to German-speaking people. The American position was unsure and indecisive. This ambivalence can be found in the definitive memorandum explicating the Fourteen Points that was prepared in late October by Frank Cobb, editor of the *New York World*, and Walter Lippmann. Cobb and Lippmann contended that the Austrians had the right to control their own destinies, but did not advocate any resistance to French objections. Certainly there was no attempt to reply to the Austrian initiative of November 16 which appealed: "You, Mr. President, have championed the right of the Poles, Italians, and Yugoslavs to unite with

---

[31] Ibid., p. 114.
[32] *Débats parlementaires, Annales du Chambre des Députés, 1918*, I: 3334.

their national states outside Austria. We are convinced that you will also concede the same right to the German people of Austria."[33]

In contrast to France and Great Britain, the American experts soon would take a position against the union. The allied intelligence of the defeated powers was just as bad as the intelligence that the defeated had of the victors. The principal American source of information on Austria was the head of the American mission to Vienna, Professor Archibald Coolidge. Coolidge reported in January that only the socialists were committed supporters of the union. He argued that it was impossible to gauge public opinion in Vienna, which "is still in a rather fluid state and may be turned one way or the other by the course of events."[34] Coolidge's reports were accepted in a memorandum drafted in February by Alan Dulles, F. D. Dolbeare, and Ellis Dresel, chief of the section on Current Diplomatic and Political Correspondence. The main thrust of this memorandum was to support the French contention that the union would compensate Germany for other territorial losses to be sustained in the forthcoming treaty.[35]

On March 1 the American commissioners plenipotentiary discussed the question. Dresel favored an American action to institute an Anschluss prohibition in the forthcoming treaty. Robert Lansing, secretary of state, was opposed. Lansing stated that "any idea of preventing an eventual union between the German peoples was a dream."[36] He believed any American initiative on this question could be viewed as a repudiation of Wilson's policy on self-determination. With the delegation deadlocked, no recommendation could be made until President Wilson returned from the United States.

The return of Wilson on March 14 coincided with an effective anti-Anschluss position. It is doubtful that this was the result of a carefully formulated American policy; Wilson apparently never viewed the Austrian question as important enough for a full-scale exploration. It had a low priority in the President's list of objectives. Thus Wilson could be influenced by the course of events. And by mid-March the tide had turned against the position of the Austrian and German governments. The Americans were daily becoming more aligned with

---

[33] United States, Department of State, *Papers Relating to the Foreign Relations of the United States: The Paris Peace Conference, 1919*, II: 190. The Cobb-Lippmann memorandum can be found in *Foreign Relations, 1918*, supplement I, vol. 1: 411.

[34] *Foreign Relations, Peace Conference* XII: 244.

[35] The memorandum is discussed in Dumin, "Background of the *Anschluss* Movement," pp. 310–16.

[36] *Foreign Relations, Peace Conference* XI: 88.

the French. On March 15 the American and French representatives on the Central Committee for Territorial Questions suggested that Germany be compelled to recognize the political and economic independence of Austria. The Italian and British representatives were reluctant to take such a step and the committee could do no more than transmit the joint Franco-American suggestion.[37] However that was enough. It gave Clemenceau an opening which he would later use with Wilson.

The final resolution of the Anschluss question attests its minor importance to Wilson. With very little discussion, the Franco-American position on Anschluss was accepted by the Council of Four on April 22. It is uncertain whether Clemenceau believed he was achieving a *quid pro quo* for his concessions on the Rhineland during the previous weeks. It is even more uncertain whether Wilson understood that Clemenceau was thinking of more than a temporary prohibition in line with time limits put upon the French occupation of the Saar. Clemenceau did raise the question of a permanent guarantee of Austrian independence in the Council of Four on May 2. For the first time, Wilson seems to have connected the Anschluss question with the right of Austrian independence. Wilson still supported the decision of April 22 as a necessary expedient, but he argued that no people could be permanently prohibited the exercise of their rights of self-determination. Finally French aims and American principles seemed to be in conflict. But Wilson almost immediately hit upon an ingenious solution to resolve the problem. The treaty would declare the independence of Austria to be inalienable unless the League Council would decide otherwise. Clemenceau agreed, since any decision of the Council could be vetoed by France. "Very good," exclaimed the French Premier.[38] French self-interest no longer contradicted the American principles.

The end was clearly at hand. All that remained was to clear away some of the loose ends. The Treaty of March 2 was invalid; only its secrecy protected Germany from being forced to issue a formal renunciation. When the Weimar Constitution was formally adopted on August 11, the French immediately demanded that the German government strike Article 61, Paragraph 2 from the document. The German delegation replied that the Peace Conference had no legal right to change a constitution, and, furthermore, that Article 178 of the constitution already declared invalid any provisions in conflict with

[37] Nelson, *Land and Power*, p. 308.
[38] Paul Mantoux, *Les délibérations du conseil des quatre* (Paris, 1955), I: 462.

the Versailles treaty. But Clemenceau would have his way. On September 22 the German delegation declared the paragraph null and void.[39]

The Austrians were forced to make the same concessions. The French even desired to place Austria under stronger obligations than Germany. Angered by the inclusion of Article 61, Paragraph 2 into the constitution adopted at Weimar on August 11, Clemenceau proposed a severe draft to the Council of the Heads of Delegations on August 25. The draft demanded that Austria "not tolerate on her territory any action whether of propaganda or any other sort by Austrian subjects or by foreign subjects with a purpose subversive of Austria as an independent state."[40] This draft went on to prohibit specifically any preparation for the union. If adopted it would have made the Anschluss movement of the 1920s impossible. However Clemenceau was forced to yield to British objections and withdrew the draft proposal. Article 88 of the Treaty of Saint Germain uses almost the same language as Article 80 of the Versailles treaty in declaring "the independence of Austria is inalienable otherwise than with the consent of the League of Nations."[41]

There still remained one more concession for the German Austrians to make. On May 29 Jules Cambon, chairman of the Committee for the Verification of Credentials at Versailles, refused to accept the Austrian credentials unless the name German was stricken from the title of their state. This was the result of a French initiative supported by the Yugoslavs and Czechs. The delegations believed that the inclusion of the German in the new state's title would be a perpetual reminder of Austria's ties to the Reich. The Austrian delegation temporized until the crisis over the Weimar constitution in August brought renewed pressures. Finally on October 31 the Austrian Constituent Assembly resolved in a certain ungraceful language that "German Austria within its frontiers defined by the Treaty of Saint Germain is a democratic republic under the denomination of 'Republic of Austria.' "[42]

The immediate German and Austrian response to the Anschluss prohibition was a refusal to accept the reality. On May 11 and 12 Hartmann and Renner addressed mass meetings in Vienna affirming

---

[39] Nina Almond and Ralph Lutz, eds., *The Treaty of St. Germain* (Stanford University, 1935), pp. 630–43. See also Wedel to Weimar, September 6, 1919, AA 5440/K1184/K304497–K304501.

[40] Dumin, "Background of the *Anschluss* Movement," p. 377.

[41] Almond and Lutz, *Treaty*, p. 631.

[42] Ibid., p. 252.

their commitment to Austro-German union. Hartmann urged the government at Weimar to take a firm stand against this provision in the treaty. Brockdorff-Rantzau was apparently responsive. On May 9, just three days after the public announcement of the prohibition, the German Foreign Minister still claimed total allegiance to the treaty of March 2. He attacked rumors that Germany would bargain with the allies over the fate of Austria as "nothing more than low libels."[43] Rantzau drafted a reply to the allies that again reaffirmed German support for the union. The German reply to the Versailles treaty on May 29 argued: "The right of self-determination of nations cannot be utilized universally and in all cases to the detriment of Germany."[44]

Bauer was still full of hope in May. He even believed that Austria might still take some diplomatic initiatives on the Anschluss question. Austria could pledge to remain neutral if Germany went to war again. If the political Anschluss was impossible, perhaps an economic amalgamation might be substituted. On May 26 Bauer wrote Renner, who was chief of the Austrian delegation at Versailles, a long letter envisioning a number of possibilities by which the entente might change its position. There could be a revolution in the entente states that would bring less nationalistic governments to power. Events in Southeastern Europe, particularly Yugoslavia, might change allied foreign policy vis-à-vis Austria. Perhaps a piecemeal Anschluss with the South German states would be allowed. Perhaps the entente would see it was cheaper to permit the Anschluss than to support Austria economically.[45]

Despite the wholesale reversals, the Germans still continued to hope. On July 24 German Chancellor Gustav Bauer and his foreign minister, Herman Müller, engaged in a long discussion about the Austrian problem with Finance Minister Mathias Erzberger and Hartmann. They considered a series of alternatives that would keep the hopes for Anschluss alive. They desired to accelerate the propaganda movement for union as well as call for an immediate plebiscite in Austria and Germany over the issue. Although Erzberger could represent the Center Party and Bauer and Müller the Social Democrats, this group believed that a broader organization should be formed. On July 26 an interparty commission subcommittee was set up to initiate large-scale propaganda for the union. During all this

[43] Rantzau (Weimar) to Vienna, May 9, 1919, SA 25.

[44] Almond and Lutz, *Treaty*, p. 632.

[45] Viktor Reimann, *Zu Gross für Österreich: Seipel und Bauer im Kampf um die Erste Republik* (Vienna, 1968), pp. 295–315.

Hartmann was intimately involved in the construction of the Weimar Constitution in which the goal of Anschluss was explicitly stated.[46]

By August the reality of the situation had become apparent to the Austrians. Austria's economic situation in early 1919 was critical. The value of the krone was constantly sinking. Between January 1 and June 30, government expenditures had exceeded revenues by over 200 percent. Unemployment reached 186,000 in May in a country of less than seven million. Subsidies for food, the unemployed, and failing private enterprise threatened to bankrupt the economy.[47] Bauer had hoped to forestall the crisis with assistance from the United States given on moral grounds and with massive German assistance to their common nationals in Vienna. In November he appealed to both Wilson and Haase for assistance. The Germans responded guiltily that they could not even provide for their own people.[48]

The American response was considerably better. Under United States aegis, an Inter-Allied Commission on the Relief of German Austria was set up in December. Under the direction of Herbert Hoover American foodstuffs began to arrive in Vienna. On March 5 the British, French, and Italian governments responded to the American initiative and earmarked $30,000,000 in credits for foodstuff purchases. Moreover on March 7 the Council of Four directed that all states of the old Austrian empire be required to furnish rolling stock to get this relief to Vienna. It was a tremendously successful operation. Between December 1, 1918 and August 31, 1919, 508,000 tons of supplies valued at over $108,000,000 had been delivered to Austria.[49]

The very success of the relief effort was an obstacle to the union with Germany. It made Renner cautious. He told the Germans in January: "German Austria depends upon the Entente so that it at this time can make no precipitate step toward the union."[50] It was for this reason that Renner refused Bauer's suggestion to publish the Treaty of March 2. Nor would Renner wage an adamant pro-German campaign when he moved to Versailles as head of the Austrian dele-

[46] Memo of meeting held in Weimar between Pfeiffer, Mittelmann, Brentano, and Foreign Office representatives, July 1919, AA 2411/4665/E218753–E218755; Müller (Weimar) to Hartmann, July 17, 1919, AA 2411/4665/E218757; Meyers, "Germany and Anschluss," pp. 397–404.

[47] Leo Pasvolsky, Economic Nationalism of the Danubian States (New York, 1928), pp. 98–102; Karl Renner, Österreich von der Ersten zur Zweiten Republik (Vienna, 1953), p. 22.

[48] Die Regierung der Volksbeauftragten (Düsseldorf, 1969), I: 45. A similar request was acceded to by Prince Max; see Die Regierung des Prinzen Max von Baden (Düsseldorf, 1962), p. 390.

[49] Almond and Lutz, Treaty, pp. 86–111; David Strong, Austria 1918–19 (New York, 1937), pp. 241–73.

[50] Wedel to Berlin, January 30, 1919, SA 25.

gation. The Chancellor did not follow his Foreign Minister's advice to talk the French to death. This had been Bauer's policy toward France since early January. In reply to the idea of a Danubian union for Austria and the other successor states, Bauer had responded: "My policy is to reject the idea of Danubian federation *a limine* but to negotiate it *ad absurdum*."[51] Renner was under enormous pressure to give in to the entente. In the first place, he realized that a moderate Austrian position was a *sine qua non* for continuing assistance. Second, the allies had posed a new threat to the economy by declaring Austria a belligerent and subject to substantial reparation payments. Third, he needed allied support to achieve the territorial integrity of Austria against encroachments from all sides. The Italians desired part of Tyrol; the Yugoslavs wanted most of Carinthia. Renner also wished to detach the German-speaking area of Burgenland from Hungary. He also needed allied support against the separatist movements in Austria. The Voralberg government contemplated a union with Switzerland. There were stirrings in both Tyrol and Salzburg for each province to unite with Germany in a separate pact of union. This so-called "artichoke theory" by which Anschluss would be carried out leaf-by-leaf would have further weakened the Austrian economy as well as creating even more of a rump political entity.[52]

But the failure of the German economy to respond to the Austrians was the crowning blow to any pro-Anschluss policy. Bauer had known from the beginning that hunger in Vienna might destroy the Anschluss movement. On November 16 he had asked Haase to provide foodstuffs for Vienna. Despite reports of an affirmative answer in the press, the German Council of People's Commissars was not even able to supply German, let alone Austrian, needs. In February Bauer renewed his demands. He desired that Germany support the sagging Austrian krone. Bauer pleaded that the Germans recognize that any sacrifices made now were not for foreigners but for co-nationals who would soon become fellow citizens. He argued that German egotism might wreck the move toward amalgamation and urged that political guidelines be set so that experts would not sabotage any talks for narrow economic gain. But the Germans would not accept such a policy. They brought Bauer to Weimar for talks that would end with the treaty of March 2, a treaty that promised only long-term eco-

[51] Bauer to Hartmann, January 3, 1919 quoted in Meyers, "Germany and Anschluss," p. 195.

[52] Griesinger to Weimar, July 10, 1919, AA 5440/K1184/K304342; for the general surveys, see Renner, *Österreich,* pp. 30–42; Ball, *Relations,* pp. 26–44; Goldinger, "Geschichtliche Ablauf," pp. 60–116; Meyers, "Germany and Anschluss," pp. 308 ff.

nomic advantages. All the hard decisions were to be left to commissions composed of experts. And Bauer must have known what little action would be forthcoming from such groups. The experts in the Reichsbank had already sabotaged any support for the krone. Now the Germans and Austrians could never come to agreement in the various commissions. By mid-April, German and Austrian experts were at odds. Bauer could sadly proclaim: "In not a single point has a definite agreement been achieved."[53] The Anschluss was really dead.

Bauer's hopes and illusions carried him through early June. But then he resigned as foreign minister. He was a one-issue minister; the failure of the Anschluss movement made him no longer useful to the cabinet. Bauer urged Hartmann to stay on and fuel the fires in Berlin, although he must have known such agitation was doomed. Renner went about organizing the new state, accepting Austrian independence, and arranging peaceful relations with the successor states. The Anschluss movement seemed at an end. Only the unforeseen resurrection of German influence would re-kindle it. Until then German and Austrian Anschluss supporters were reduced to echoing the Austrian politician Ferdinand Skaret's pious hope that "the chains of injustice now being forged will soon be broken."[54]

[53] Quoted in Meyers, "Germany and *Anschluss*," p. 316; see also Wedel to Weimar, March 18, 1919, AA 3270/7479/H187523. For intransigence in Reichsbank and Trade Ministry see memo of a meeting between representatives of these ministries and the Foreign Office on February 24, 1919, AA 5426/K1152/K294360–K294361.

[54] *Stenographische Protokolle die Sitzungen der Konstituierenden Nationalversammlung* I: 533. See also unsigned memo, Bern, April 2, 1919, AA 3270/7479/H187549.

SYMBOLS OF DIVISIVENESS AND UNITY

CHAPTER II GERMAN DEMOCRACY
AND THE ANSCHLUSS

IN 1919 FRIEDRICH MEINECKE wrote that the task before the new state was to complete the work of Bismarckian unification by creating a common political culture and by bringing Austria into the Reich.[1] It was a task rooted in exaggerated expectations. But even these contain a kernel of truth. Meinecke knew the two goals were interrelated. The Anschluss movement and the forces of German democracy were interlocked in numerous ways. The Anschluss would have provided a welcome sign of the republic's strength in foreign affairs. It would have meant enormous gain in prestige for the weakened Germany to complete a unification that Bismarck had not been able, or even wished, to achieve. It would have buttressed the strength of the democratic forces at the polls.

For these reasons, German democrats were thoroughly committed to the Anschluss. They dominated the largest of the Anschluss organizations. They conducted the most intensive propaganda campaigns. Yet such strong involvement had an unforeseen effect. It aroused the suspicions not only of the far Right but some of the liberal middle-class as well. Middle-class German leadership became concerned lest the socialists reap advantage from such an amalgamation. In addition, German democracy gained the traditional enmity of parochial interests that struggled against the centralizing efforts of any government in Berlin. Centralization not only became associated with democracy but, in some minds, with that part of the democratic Anschluss movement directed from the capital. Both of these forces could be considered renewed attempts at Berlin's domination and were opposed as such.

But before the divisions within the Anschluss movement can be discussed, some proof must be offered that German democrats of all hues were more closely connected with the Anschluss question than middle-class conservatives. Constructing a convincing proof is hampered by the fact that almost all Germans favored a union with

[1] Friedrich Meinecke, *Nach der Revolution* (Munich, 1919), p. 4.

Austria, that this issue found support from the Right, Left, and Center. Yet there is no doubt that the Anschluss was more closely identified with democratic than with conservative or radical politics. Middle-class democrats and the socialists were the most active propagandists for Austro-German union. The Austro-German amalgamation found ready acceptance in the pages of the press controlled by members of the German Democratic Party (DDP) and the Social Democratic Party (SPD).

There are additional means for attesting the popularity of Anschluss within the democratic camp. It was no accident that Wilhelm Marx sought to mobilize democratic support for his election as president in 1925 by advocating the Anschluss. Such a statement seemed expected from a democratic candidate; none certainly was forthcoming from his opponent, Hindenburg.[2] Marx could read the party platforms of the DDP and the SPD. They both considered the Anschluss as a fundament of a democratic foreign policy, guaranteed by the principles laid down in Wilson's Fourteen Points. Thus the 1925 Heidelberg program of the SPD could agitate for Anschluss under the general statement: "We demand the right of self-determination of peoples."[3] A more explicit statement can be found in the 1919 DDP program: "In no case can we accept the dictates of power as a binding legal principle. In no case do we recognize the splintering of Germanic groups from the fatherland. In no case do we relinquish the right of self-determination, and we strive on the basis of this principle for the unification of all Germans."[4]

The most sanguine of foreign observers were astounded by this democratic activism in foreign policy. The French nationalist deputy and future foreign minister, Paul-Boncour, had always considered the Anschluss as simply another instrument for German expansion to the east. Boncour was accustomed to annexationist demands from the conservative camp. However, he could not understand the strong commitment manifested in circles he had hitherto considered free of extreme ambitions. He feared that annexationist sentiment in Germany would be reinforced by the prestige of democracy. Boncour told his fellow Frenchmen: "In Germany the question of *Anschluss* is posed in a paradoxical form. It is not the parties of the Right (Pan-Germans, nationalists and racists) that are favorable to the annexation of Austria but the parties of the pacifist Left (socialists, democrats, the

---

[2] *Vorwärts* (Berlin), April 18, 1925, edition B; *Neue Freie Presse* (Vienna), April 18, 1925, a.m.

[3] Wilhelm Mommsen, *Deutsche Parteiprogramme* (Munich, 1960), p. 468. See also *Vörwarts*, April 25, 1927, edition B.

[4] Mommsen, *Deutsche Parteiprogramme*, p. 510.

Catholic Center) who see the acquisition of Austria as the first priority of their political program."[5]

Even the symbolism of democracy was caught up with the demands for the Anschluss. Republican Germany had to search hard for an adequate tradition. The elaborate national symbols of the Wilhelmine Reich would not do. These were intertwined with the Prussian monarchy and buttressed by Prussian heroes. The republicans had to break with such traditions; they had to resurrect the half-forgotten struggles of an earlier generation. Before 1914 the Progressive Party, the lineal ancestor of the DDP, and even some Social Democrats had appropriated the symbols of the 1848 democrats. After the war, these democrats came to be considered the predecessors of the Weimar republic.[6]

Although these symbols would become ingrained in the mythology of the new republic, their first inclusion was of an almost accidental nature. If the Weimar flag, with its black-red-gold colors, had been the banner of the 1848 republicans, it was only interjected into Hugo Preuss's early constitutional proposals at the demand of the Austrian ambassador, Ludo Hartmann. Preuss, whose original draft formed the basis of the Weimar constitution, had earlier decided to carry on with the black-white-red flag that symbolized the *kleindeutsch* solution achieved by Bismarck. But Preuss bowed before the arguments of the Austrian Ambassador. Hartmann desired the new flag to remind all that the democrats in 1848 had desired to include the Austrian Germans within their planned *grossdeutsch* republic. He also contended that the new flag was necessary to make the contemporary Austrian feel comfortable within a unified *grossdeutsch* Reich. Also Hartmann believed that any flag of the Hohenzollerns would frighten his countrymen into opposing the Anschluss.[7]

During the 1920s this same argument was advanced by liberal historians such as Friedrich Meinecke and Hans Delbrück. Meinecke and Delbrück hoped that the new German flag would come to symbolize not only democracy but union with the Austrians. They were not to be disappointed. The Reichsbanner, the democratic paramilitary

[5] *La Depêche* (Toulouse), January 19, 1926, clipping in NPA Fasz. 111, 10329 pr. 22 I 1926.

[6] Karl Rohe, *Das Reichsbanner, Schwarz Rot Gold* (Düsseldorf, 1966), p. 234.

[7] Ibid., p. 237; Theodor Heuss, *Friedrich Naumann* (Stuttgart, 1949), pp. 485–86; M. Margaret Ball, *Post-War German-Austrian Relations* (Stanford University, 1937), pp. 14–17; Stefan Grossmann, "Die Anfänge der Anschlussbewegung," *Österreich-Deutschland* 6 (November 1929): 6; Friedrich Kleinwaechter, "Deutschösterreichs Kampf um das Selbtsbestimmungsrecht bis zur Genfer Protokollen," ed. Kleinwaechter and Heinz von Paller, *Die Anschlussfrage in ihrer kulturellen, politischen und wirtschaftlichen Bedeutung* (Vienna, 1930), pp. 71–72.

organization, adopted the new German colors as its emblem in part
to symbolize national unity with the Austrians. The Austrian Minister
to Berlin in 1924 reported that the new flag was flown in democratic
political meetings to show how a forthcoming Anschluss would be a
victory for German democracy. Wilhelm Marx used this same juxtaposition of symbols in an address to a massive rally in the Berlin
Sports Palace during the 1925 presidential campaign. Marx proclaimed:

For Austria, for ourselves, before the whole world, we in no manner dis-
honor the old black-white-red flag. The German people fought with pride
under this banner of *kleindeutsch* unification. Our memories of what is
worthwhile and true are woven into it. But the new flag of the Reich means
more. . . . Black-red-gold is not only the flag of the Weimar Republic. It
is not only our legal duty to honor these colors. They are for us the
symbol of a united, free, culturally progressive and peaceful *Grossdeutschland*.[8]

There were a number of reasons why democrats supported the
Anschluss so ardently. German democracy benefited from the fact
that the Anschluss could best be achieved by a republican form of
government. The Anschluss would also bring votes to the democratic
camp. Perhaps advocating Austro-German union might allow the
democrats to win the confidence of conservative Germans and become
trusted members of the national community.

They were all good arguments. Even while opposing the Weimar
system, Gustav Stresemann reluctantly admitted that a republic was
necessary if Austro-German union were to be completed. Stresemann
believed that only German democracy had the power to overcome the
obstacles rooted in the dynastic quarrels between the Hohenzollerns
and the Habsburgs. A return to the Prussian ruling house would have
frightened the Austrians away. Stresemann never even thought of the
other alternative, a Habsburg restoration.[9]

If this were true, then the forces of democracy and national unification had become interlocked. A victory for one reinforced the
other and vice versa. Democrats argued that any weakening of the

---

[8] *Vorwärts*, April 18, 1925, edition B. For the relationship of the 1848 symbolism to the Anschluss movement, see the report of the Volksbund rally, Frankfurt to Vienna, NPA Fasz. III, 3911 pr. 4 I 1923; *Neue freie Presse*, August 31,
1925, a.m.; *Vossische Zeitung* (Berlin), March 27, 1926; Rohe, *Das Reichsbanner*,
pp. 227–44. For historians and the flag, see Meinecke, *Werke* (Stuttgart, 1957–
62), II: 338, and Hans Delbrück, *Vor und nach dem Weltkrieg* (Berlin, 1926),
p. 418. For the use of the new flag in political campaigns, see also Berlin
Chargé to Vienna, December 3, 1924, NPA Fasz. 110, 142038 pr. 10 XI 1924.

[9] Gustav Stresemann, *Reden und Schriften* (Dresden, 1926), I: 263. See a
discussion of this speech in Turner, *Stresemann and the Politics of the Weimar
Republic* (Princeton, 1963), pp. 37–38.

republic would disturb the Austrians and threaten the Anschluss. German socialists used this contention as ammunition in their campaign against Hindenburg during the 1925 presidential elections. The official socialist organ, *Vorwärts*, argued that Hindenburg's victory would force the Austrians to have second thoughts about uniting with Germany. As if to give credence to this view, the Viennese *Arbeiter Zeitung* expressed doubts about joining a Reich led by the old Marshal. The Social Democratic press in both lands argued that his election would damage Stresemann's foreign policy, since it would reawaken allied fears of an expansionist Germany. All in all, the *Arbeiter Zeitung* declared: "Who wants the Anschluss must cast out Hindenburg; who votes for Hindenburg works against the union of all the German people in one unified Reich."[10]

If the republic was a necessity for the Anschluss movement, the actual Austro-German union would provide the German democrats with a much more concrete bonus in return. In the event of union, substantial political gains would accrue to two of the parties most committed to the Weimar system. The SPD and the Center would each add between 1.3 and 1.5 million voters to their rolls. These are the minimum and maximum votes given to the Austrian Social Democratic Party and the Catholic-oriented Christian Socialist Party in the elections of 1923 and 1927. This meant a total of 2.8 million votes in any given election. These voters would have more than overbalanced the roughly 500,000 addition to the ranks of the German Nationalist People's Party (DNVP). It might have made the difference in the 1925 presidential elections where Hindenburg had won by 900,000 votes. Assuming that Christian Socialists voted for the Center candidate, Wilhelm Marx, this would have defeated Hindenburg by 1.4 million votes.[11]

There are, of course, some difficulties in such speculation. In 1925 the Christian Socialists were more conservative than the Center; they might have refused to join in an electoral coalition with the socialists. After all, a Center affiliate, the Bavarian People's Party, took just such a course and supported Hindenburg over Marx. There can be no debate about the Social Democrats. The Austrian socialists would have easily fitted in the framework of the SPD. They would not only have supported Marx in 1925 but also have added between 22

[10] *Arbeiter Zeitung* (Vienna), April 19, 1925. See *Vorwärts*, April 11, 1925, edition B, and Theodor Müller, "Das Ebert-Urteil und die Österreicher," *Österreich-Deutschland* 2 (January 1925): 2.

[11] Mommsen, *Deutsche Partieprogramme*, pp. 828–29; Rodney Stiefbold et al., *Wahlen und Parteien in Österreich* (Vienna, 1966), III: 70–94. The calculations are the author's. For similar calculations see Richart Mischler, "Die Reichspräsidenten-Wahl," *Österreich-Deutschland* 2 (May 1925): 5.

and 26 members to the SPD Reichstag delegation. If the former Christian Socialists had voted with the Center, the Anschluss would have produced a net gain of over forty seats for the supporters of Weimar. These votes could have been decisive in creating a safe parliamentary majority for pro-republican forces, especially between 1924 and 1928.[12] For this reason, a liberal Austrian journal argued that only Anschluss would permanently assure a democratic majority in the Reichstag. It contended: "Without the Anschluss there can be no German democracy."[13] Or as a German socialist publication maintained: "The German Republic . . . will be *grossdeutsch* [i.e., include Austria] or it will not be."[14]

Right-wing politicians could count votes just as well. Even pro-union papers worried that the Left would be the principal beneficiary of the Anschluss. The *Deutsche Allgemeine Zeitung*, which stood closest to Stresemann's own party, declared that socialists favored union only for political reasons. These suspicions were expressed even more strongly in the circles of the German Nationalist Party—especially in the old conservative newspaper, *Kreuzzeitung*. A more radical rightest publication could also inveigh against "the puny courage of some political parties that consider what the Anschluss would mean for presidential and Reichstag elections as well as for coalition-building."[15]

But there was more involved than mere votes. The Anschluss movement presented an even more important advantage for German democrats. It legitimized their position as German nationalists. This hardly seemed necessary for a party that contained such incontestable patriots as Friedrich Naumann and many of his followers. Naumann, Theodor Heuss, Wilhelm Heile—all saw the demands for Anschluss as a vindication of their prewar program for merging social and political reform with nationalism. Apparently blessed by Wilsonian principles, the Anschluss also could be construed as proof that democracy and nationalism were compatible. Yet the DDP could never escape the suspicions of the German conservatives. After all, it also inherited the antimilitarist traditions of Eugen Richter; it was the party of Walther Rathenau, who had been murdered for taking

[12] These calculations were also made by the author using the sources cited in n. 11. Since the Christian Socialists ran on a unity list with the Grossdeutsch Party in 1927, it is impossible to do more than estimate their strength.

[13] *Der österreichische Volkswirt* 16 (1925): 828.

[14] Rohe, *Das Reichsbanner*, p. 234.

[15] Karl Massmann, "Grundsätzliches zur Anschlussfrage," ed. Hermann Ullmann, *Werdendes Grossdeutschland* (Berlin, 1926), p. 6. The *Deutsche Allgemeine Zeitung* was quoted in France, Ministère des Affaires Étrangères, *Bulletin périodique de la presse allemagne*, Nr. 325, pp. 10–11. See also *Der Stahlhelm* (Berlin) 9 (May 8, 1927): 2–3.

a moderate stand on the reparations question. For German conservatives, the DDP was further tainted by its agreement to the Dawes Plan and by its wholehearted acceptance of Stresemann's policy at Locarno. Perhaps its demands for Anschluss could lessen this antagonism and convince more of the opposition that the policy of the DDP was in the interest of the entire national community.[16]

The Social Democrats needed the Anschluss question even more than did the DDP. Their national commitments were under far greater suspicion. As a political subculture, cut off from the main stream of Wilhelmine society, German Social Democrats were constantly on the defensive. Their rulers had often called them the equivalent of traitors for refusing to support the military budget. Even before 1914, the party leadership tried to combat this antagonism. They claimed that the socialists were the only true German patriots, striving for a just national community based upon the principles of parliamentary rule and social reform. But they could not convince their opponents. Only their votes for war credits in August 1914 legitimized their party. Hans-Ulrich Wehler explains this dilemma:

Through education, army service, the entire environment, the German national state was impressed into the inner recesses of the Social Democrat's mind. . . . Also permit us to ascribe as a law of mass psychology for the bourgeois national state that such a state causes a deep, penetrating demand from the socio-cultural personality for participation in the national prestige as shown by being recognized as part of the national community or, vice-versa, the anguish of being shut out of it. The August 1914 days show how the terrible burdensome feeling of isolation that the Social Democracy felt gave way to the overpowering desire to belong, once and for all, to this national community.[17]

The suspicion of the socialists did not die after the war. It was fed by the circumstances of the German defeat and the myth that

[16] Theodor Heuss, *Friedrich Naumann* (Stuttgart, 1937). Both Heuss and Heile were on the executive council of the most important pro-Anschluss organization; see n. 35. Both spoke at mass meetings for the Anschluss, and Heile waged propaganda for the union when he succeeded Naumann as editor of *Die Hilfe.*

[17] Hans-Ulrich Wehler, *Sozialdemokratie und Nationalstaat* (Würzburg, 1962), pp. 196–97. See also Hermann Heidegger, *Die deutsche Sozialdemokratie und der nationale Staat* (Göttingen, 1956), pp. 186–87, 326–27, 369–87; Gunther Roth, *The Social Democrats in Imperial Germany* (Totowa, New Jersey, 1963), pp. 119–27; Carl Schorske, *German Social Democracy* (New York; paperback ed., 1965), pp. 59–87; Wilhelm Maehl, "The Triumph of Nationalism in the German Socialist Party on the Eve of the First World War," *Journal of Modern History* 24 (1952): 28–41; John Snell, "Socialist Unions and Socialist Patriotism in Germany, 1914–1918," *American Historical Review* 59 (1953): 66–75. See also the memoirs of a future leader of the Anschluss movement in Paul Löbe, *Erinnerungen eines Reichstagspräsidenten* (Berlin, 1949), pp. 10–11, 42.

Germany had been stabbed in the back by the trade unionists who struck in 1917 and 1918. The socialists still needed some issue which would assure their fellow Germans of their commitment to the nation. The Anschluss was such an issue.

But would their support of union be enough by itself to legitimize German democracy? German democrats would have to do more than simply agree with conservatives about the Anschluss. They would have to be accepted by these conservatives in specific pressure groups designed to speed the arrival of the union. If this were accomplished, then German democrats could demonstrate a set of common interests with the entire national community. Then German democracy might have been successfully legitimized.

Such an attempt was made in the most important of the German Anschluss organizations, the Austro-German People's League (Österreichisch-Deutscher Volksbund). The Volksbund made a serious effort to unite all aspects of German society behind the Anschluss movement, and it was partially successful. This success was not to be measured in great numbers. Volksbund chapters were never large. It is true that in 1925 one group in Altenessen had 300 members, but in 1926 the five chapters in Baden and Württemberg had an average membership of only slightly more than 70. Even taking the former figure of 300 as an average would have given the Volksbund 21,600 members by 1929.[18]

The real strength of the Volksbund lay in its power to move large sections of the German elite. An analysis of the executive council's composition in 1927 shows a membership scattered among key professions. The Volksbund executive council presented a profile of the professions that appealed to middle-class intellectuals. It therefore had ready access to the opinion-making centers of German society. Only three artisans or shopkeepers, one financier, and one manufacturer sat on the executive council. There were seven lawyers and the same number of professors, twenty journalists, writers, and editors, twenty-two politicians, twenty-three present or former civil servants.[19]

A count of the politicians on the executive council shows an even wider representation. As early as 1920 the executive council contained Reichstag members from the Social Democratic, Democratic, Center, People's and Nationalist parties. Reichstag delegates from all these groups were present at the various mass meetings of the Volksbund.

---

[18] The author has found no compilation of Volksbund chapters. It has been necessary to construct one from the published reports appearing in *Österreich-Deutschland* 1 (January 1924): 18–20; 2 (January 1925): 18–23; (February 1925): 19–24, and passim.

[19] Volksbund 1927 list, ARk R43I/109, p. 53.

Ludo Hartmann, its first president, and his successor, Paul Löbe, were proud of this accomplishment. Hartmann could proclaim that this attendance at a 1920 meeting "shows the unity of all German parties represented in the Reichstag."[20] This supra-party structure continued throughout the Weimar republic. Lists of the executive council from both 1925 and 1927 support this contention. The 1927 list contains six socialist Reichstag delegates, four from the DVP, three each from the Center, DDP, and DNVP. Among others readily identified by party were two DDP and two SPD newspaper editors as well as two whose politics were closest to the People's Party.[21]

But appearances are often deceiving. A broad-based executive council was necessary for lobbying and propaganda, but an organization such as the Volksbund is run by only a few men. And these came from the democratic Left. It is true that the nationalist leader, Otto Hoetzsch, was a vice-chairman. However Hoetzsch was hardly an unreconciled monarchist. He voted for the Dawes Plan as well as for cooperation with the other middle-class parties. And the most outspoken proponent of compromise within the DNVP, Hans-Erdmann Lindeiner-Wildnau, was a member of the executive council.[22] Yet even if Hoetzsch had been an unreconstructed monarchist, he would have been more than balanced by the DDP vice-chairman, Wilhelm Heile, and the SPD chairman, Paul Löbe.

Löbe was definitely in command. Utilizing his prestige as Reichstag president, he became what Hermann Kienzl called "our General Field Marshal."[23] Löbe continued Hartmann's appointment, Richart Mischler, as executive secretary. Along with Mischler, he dominated the central organization of the Volksbund, especially the contents of its publication, *Österreich-Deutschland: Heim ins Reich.* And this magazine was definitely sympathetic to a democratic foreign policy. This view spilled over into the public meetings that the Volksbund initiated. At such a meeting in Berlin, Professor Martin Hobhom of the executive council declared: "We are not the Pan-German League or a similar organization. We are not annexationists."[24] Vice-Chairman

[20] Post (Berlin) to Vienna, November 23, 1920, NPA Fasz. 110, 4916 pr. 30 XI 1920. See chapter VI for discussion of supra-party nature of Volksbund demonstrations.

[21] See Volksbund list in n. 19 as well as 1925 list in ARk R43I/109, p. 113.

[22] See Lewis Hertzman, *DNVP, Right-Wing Opposition in the Weimar Republic, 1918–1924* (Lincoln, 1963), pp. 215–18; Werner Liebe, *Die Deutschnationale Volkspartei, 1198–1924* (Düsseldorf, 1956), pp. 94, 168–70.

[23] Hermann Kienzl, "Unser erster Vorsitzender," *Österreich-Deutschland* 3 (January 1926): 2.

[24] *Österreich-Deutschland* 3 (March 1926): 4.

Kienzl called the Volksbund "an army without weapons that fights for the peace of Europe."[25] Löbe reiterated this proposition to a mass meeting in Karlsruhe: "No one in Germany," he contended, "thinks of disturbing our lands by a new conflict or Europe by a new war. The battle for self-determination can be waged by legal means. We will achieve our goals through the free will of a German-Austria that pursues the unification of the two states."[26]

Was such democratic rhetoric the best device for creating a supra-party organization? This method relied upon a consensus that democratic goals were best for the entire society. General agreement on this proposition was impossible. The Anschluss movement may have, in some sense, legitimized the nationalism of German democrats, but the reverse was not necessarily true. The prestige of German democracy was never so high that it could buttress the Anschluss movement. In fact, the Volksbund was damaged by being too closely associated with democratic aims. It seemed to be merely an instrument of the democratic Weimar coalition, composed of Center, SPD, and DDP. If this were true, then it was composed of groups that too often could only command the allegiance of a minority of citizens and Reichstag delegates.[27]

The democratic Volksbund faced other serious problems. Its supra-party nature was also endangered by its narrow base—caused by overrepresentation of Austrians, middle-class democrats, and socialists and by underrepresentation among Bavarians and conservatives. Designed to bring about Anschluss, the Volksbund was paradoxically a victim of Germany's failure to achieve this task. As long as Austria was not integrated into the Reich, Austrians who lived in Germany would seek security in an organization that, by its very nature, would make them welcome. The Volksbund was always in danger of becoming simply an Austrian countryman's organization. This was particularly true in the first years of its existence. The preponderance of Austrian members in these years raised the question: how could the Volksbund represent all areas of German society when it often seemed most concerned with the fate of the Austrians living in the Reich?

This weakness could be and was partially overcome. The goals of the Austrians could be merged into the democratic rhetoric as practiced by Löbe. This was scarcely the case for German federalism.

[25] See n. 23.

[26] Der Anschluss (Vienna), May 30, 1929.

[27] See the discussion by Karl Dietrich Bracher in Deutschland zwischen Demokratie und Diktatur (Bern, 1964), pp. 63–71; and Sigmund Neumann, Die Parteien der Weimarer Republik (Stuttgart, 1963), pp. 37–39.

Weimar democracy was almost always associated with the centralizing tendencies in German politics. It often came into conflict with the strong regional loyalties that prevailed in many areas of the Reich. This regional chauvinism was translated into suspicion of the central government or any national organization directed from Berlin. In the Rhineland, especially in Bavaria, competing Anschluss organizations were founded to preserve the independence of these regions from Berlin and to bolster the commitment of these areas to more autonomous government.

Most important, German democracy was founded on the premise of accepting the socialists as an integral part of the political culture. Only minority governments or coalitions with anti-republican forces were possible without the cooperation of the Social Democratic Party. Yet the German middle class was sharply divided on this issue. Many middle-class and rural Germans remained convinced that socialism was some foreign importation. Economic conflicts played a relatively minor role in this distrust. In many ways, the problem was much more fundamental than the struggle over control of society's productive capacity. It involved the inability of the national community to absorb all its members without friction. Certainly this failure was apparent in politics. Middle-class politicians could not agree whether socialists should be included in the national cabinet. With this fact in mind, it is hardly surprising that some middle-class leaders would be suspicious of an Anschluss organization led by two socialists—Hartmann and Löbe.

It was no accident that Hartmann, the Austrian ambassador, was the first president of the Volksbund. The Volksbund grew out of the Austro-German Working Committee (Arbeitsauschuss) founded immediately after the war by the Austrian colony in Berlin. In its early days, the Volksbund was dominated by Austrians living within the Reich. As late as 1925, an Austrian diplomat contended that 80 percent of the Berlin membership was Austrian. In the same year, a Volksbund vice-chairman stated that for the first time the Rhenish chapters had more German than Austrian members. This meant practically the whole, since 70 percent of the Volksbund chapters were located in the Rhineland and Westphalia, a region in which one out of four of the 125,000 German-speaking former nationals of the Habsburg empire lived. Greater numbers were only to be found in Bavaria, where particularism worked against the Volksbund. The statistics for Sudeten Germans are even more revealing. Like the Austrians, the Sudetens settled heavily in the Rhineland. They also immigrated to neighboring Silesia where two-thirds of the Volksbund chapters precariously hugged the Czech-German border.[28]

Because the Volksbund was composed of so many foreigners, it naturally attempted to represent their interests. The Volksbund leadership wanted to allow Austrian citizens the vote in Reichstag elections. They demanded an end to the treatment of Austrians as foreigners. It especially rankled that Austrians were subject to the same passport and working-paper requirements as Frenchmen. These demands fitted well with the organization's final goal—Anschluss. A union of Austria and Germany would solve these problems, at least for Austrian citizens. As Richart Mischler, the executive secretary of the Volksbund, stated: "Only through the Anschluss can they [the Austrians] obtain all the rights of citizenship. Only through it can they obtain their legal welfare benefits and the security for their economic existence."[29]

The Volksbund jealously guarded its status vis-à-vis these foreigners. It sought to become the exclusive agent for German-speaking foreigners. In Stuttgart the Volksbund worked to dissolve all other associations of Austrian natives. In Frankfurt it warned that the multiplicity of organizations weakened the Anschluss movement. However, the Volksbund was unsuccessful in these attempts. The Austrian government founded a group to represent all its citizens in 1926. There were a number of strong local associations in Munich, Nuremberg, and Stuttgart. And the societies representing the German-speaking citizens of the successor states had proliferated even more. There was also an umbrella organization for citizens of all states that had once composed the Habsburg monarchy. It included sixty-one groups of which sixteen represented Austrian nationals.[30] Still the Volksbund did not give up its struggle. A typical article in its journal asked:

Why should our countrymen be splintered here in the Reich? In the Rhineland, in Westphalia, in Berlin, in Frankfurt and Silesia, our countrymen have been united until now in the Austro-German Volksbund. However, besides this group, there is the Austrian Union, the Sudeten German Heimatbund, the Egerländer and other organizations. Since they all pursue the same goal, why don't they unite under one banner? The broad mass

---

[28] Günther (Munich) to Vienna, April 16, 1925, NPA Fasz. 57, Zl. Pol. 15. For the Rhineland see *Österreich-Deutschland* 3 (January 1926): 5. For list of chapters, see n. 18; the population statistics are drawn from *Statistik des Deutschen Reichs*, CMI, Teil I, 384–85.

[29] Mischler letter to Vienna, October 7, 1920, NPA Fasz. 110, 4099 pr. 11 X 1920. See an earlier letter in ibid., 2359 pr. 9 VI 1920, and *Österreich-Deutschland* 3 (January 1926): 14–20; (February 1926): 18; 4 (June 1927): 17.

[30] See reports in NPA Fasz. 234 and 240.

of the Reich German population considers these problems as the collective question "German-Austria." . . . Be united! We will win if we are united.[31]

The early foreign domination of the Volksbund determined much of its character. Even after the chapters in Berlin and Frankfurt had lost their original Austrian flavor, many of the others still retained their function as gathering places for the Austrian community. The Breslau chapter's schedule for early 1926 typifies one whose members were far more interested in socializing than in politics. They celebrated the twelfth night of Christmas with a party and the singing of carols. On January 17 they held an Austrian goulash supper and dance at the Hotel Rome. Similar activities continued throughout the spring. There were a number of poetry readings to break the monotony, but scarcely any mention of foreign policy, economics, or even Anschluss. The winter season closed with a gala Viennese ball on March 20.[32]

Many chapters were led by men who did have a political conscience. They held programs in order to agitate for an Austro-German union. Typical of these was a meeting at Gleiwitz, Silesia in 1929. A lecture was given on the goals of the Volksbund and the indispensability of union. But the greatest attention was directed toward "the wonderful slides that accompanied the lecture and showed the beauties of Austria, a sight that awakened for many memories of their homeland and for others further widened their knowledge of the brotherland."[33] The formal program was followed by a dance recital, and the evening concluded with the company enjoying waltzes.

But there were other more promising signs for the Anschluss movement. By 1925 these specifically Austrian tasks had become tangential to the main purpose of the Volksbund. "We are no longer an Austrian countryman's organization," proclaimed Vice-Chairman Hermann Kienzl in 1926.[34] He stated that the Volksbund had finally become a full-fledged pressure group designed to bolster the movement for Anschluss. This influx of Germans can be explained. Undoubtedly some of it was gradual, but the date 1926 is significant. This was the year that Germany entered the League of Nations. The Anschluss appeared feasible in post-Locarno Europe. This renewed hope certainly encouraged many German citizens to join the Volksbund. These new members certainly accepted many of the demands

[31] Karl von Elberfeld, "Die sudetendeutsche Sprache im Reich ins Stammbuch," *Österreich-Deutschland* 3 (January 1926): 7.

[32] *Österreich-Deutschland* 3 (March 1926): 26.

[33] Ibid. 6 (January 1929): 23.

[34] Ibid. 3 (January 1926): 5.

emanating from the Austrians within the organization. After all, the fulfillment of such demands would be viewed as a preparation for Anschluss. Both could be subsumed under the rhetoric of a democratic foreign policy. Witness the following excerpt from the Volksbund bylaws:

The Volksbund strives for the *Anschluss* with German-Austria on the German Reich based upon the principle of self-determination of peoples and peace treaties. . . . Further the Volksbund demands the unrestricted right of self-determination and the protection of minority rights of that part of the German people, especially in the Alpine and in the Sudeten lands, that live under foreign rule. In the realm of political goals, it undertakes to look after the interests of those former Austro-Hungarians who live in the German Reich. This task especially concerns the questions of common citizenship and equal legal rights with the people of the German Reich.[35]

The fear of socialism could not be so easily washed away. This problem persisted throughout the entire history of the Volksbund. In 1921 Hoetzsch complained to the Austrian Chargé d'Affaires that the Volksbund was recruiting politically unripe people, translated as socialists. The Chargé himself commented that "the better circles of the [Austrian] colony as well as the local society stand completely aloof from the activities of the Volksbund."[36] And this viewpoint continued throughout the Weimar republic. As late as 1931, the Austrian press attaché and Volksbund executive council member, Erwin Wasserbäck, reported that his fellow middle-class members worried about socialist domination of the group.[37]

Class divisions were often complemented by regional animosities. Berlin was not only red but also the seat of the Prussian and central governments. Rhenish Catholics had always worried about domination from Berlin. It is truly remarkable that the Volksbund's Gau Rhineland-Westphalia accepted Löbe's rule without any strong protest. But the Cologne chapter dragged its heels. Organized in 1925 and predominantly under the influence of conservative Centrists, the Cologne group feared the Social Democratic leadership in Berlin. It remained aloof from Löbe and Mischler.[38]

The attitude in Cologne inspired fears that the Volksbund might become involved with Rhenish separatism. There were rumors of a

---

[35] Volksbund bylaws, ARk R43I/107.

[36] Post to Vienna, June 26, 1921, NPA Fasz. 110, 29966 pr. 2 VII 1921.

[37] Wasserbäck (Berlin) to Vienna, October 31, 1931, NPA Fasz. 234, 6322 pr. 30 XI 1931.

[38] Wildner (Cologne) to Vienna, April 14, 1926, NPA Fasz. 234, 11961 pr. 16 IV 1926. See also same to same, April 15, 1926, 11989 pr. 17 IV 1926; November 30, 1929, 24944/13/29.

deal between Austrian and Rhenish Catholics to build a state composed of Austria, the South German lands, and the Prussian Rhine provinces. The fomenters of such an alliance were reputed to have been Ignaz Seipel, then between Austrian chancellorships, and Konrad Adenauer, mayor of Cologne. Of course these speculations were pure fantasy. Seipel denied any knowledge of the scheme, and he was undoubtedly telling the truth. Such action was improbable because Seipel was a foe of the Volksbund. The former Austrian Chancellor told his own Foreign Ministry that the Volksbund was a purely Social Democratic organization in whose mass meetings no prominent Centrist could be comfortable. Also Seipel stated that Adenauer was too clever to engage in unprofitable adventures. The Mayor of Cologne was simply not a fool. On the contrary, Seipel thought Adenauer was "a very great man who belongs to the future."[39]

Separatism was not confined to the Rhineland. The strongest desire for apartness came from Bavaria. The German democratic press worried that these Bavarian separatists would create a Catholic German political amalgamation with Austria in order to exclude Berlin. French newspapers, even the Soviet Foreign Office, seriously considered rumors of an alliance between Wittelsbach and Habsburg legitimists for the purpose of creating this new South German state. During the Ruhr crisis, both Masaryk and Mussolini thought such a possibility realistic. Even in 1929 Stresemann still humorously referred to it.[40] In that year the Bavarian legitimist and Eisner assassin, Count Arco-Valley, asked: "Why can't Bavaria become a part of Austria?"[41]

Yet Arco-Valley was hardly the man to put such a plan into action. The fears of and hopes for separatism were equally groundless after 1925. Heinrich Mataja, a leading Austrian politician, could exclaim without much worry the contradiction that "our especially close ties with Bavaria have nothing to do with separatist ideas."[42] But he could not do the same for the federalist movement led by Bavaria but prevalent in other areas as well.

The federalists attempted to turn the near unanimity on the Anschluss question to their own advantage. They sought to play upon the real Austrian anxieties over the fate of this small land within the larger Reich by contending that a centralized Germany would swallow up the small Alpine state. Then they pleaded with Germans

---

[39] Seipel letter to Peter (Vienna), April 18, 1926, NPA Fasz. 402, 12.147/13. 1926.
[40] See chapter XII for discussion of this problem.
[41] *Der Anschluss*, May 16, 1929.
[42] Ibid.

to support federalism as the only method for reassuring the Austrians and making the Anschluss possible. This was the argument of Johannes Rathje, who was head of the Reichsarbeitsgemeinschaft der Deutschen Föderalisten, an organization composed mostly of Bismarck's old Hanoverian enemies. The federalists also hoped to mobilize Austrian traditional enmity against Prussia in order to destroy the state built up by the Hohenzollerns. Like many federalists, Rathje made little distinction between the two governments in Berlin, the national and the Prussian. He saw both as interdependent and advocated breaking up Prussia into its constituent parts as the surest safeguard against the power of the central government. Rathje expressed these views in a letter to the anti-Anschluss Viennese newspaper, *Die Reichspost*:

The German Hanoverian leaders have declared that they feel . . . the responsibility for Anschluss lies solely with the Austrian people. Certainly it is their wish that the Anschluss be completed. But it is unthinkable that the overwhelming majority of Austrians would demand the union as long as they recognize that the Reich is really an enlarged Prussia, before it is certain that no German land need fear to bear the same sad fate of Hanover.[43]

The democrats, the entire Anschluss movement, launched a counterattack. Democrats opposed the demand for state's rights because they believed a strong central government was necessary to insure a true national community. They were contemptuous of federalism as the last vestige of German particularism. They claimed that the federalist argument was made up of whole cloth and that the Austrians would be treasured in the new Reich whether the state was constructed in a federalist or unitary form. Yet even the democrats were unconvinced by their own arguments. Meinecke wrote that one of Weimar's most important constitutional tasks was the need to complete the Anschluss "without endangering the unitary state we desire and, on the other hand, without frightening the Austrians away."[44]

The democrats recognized that the federalist movement had a strong attraction for the Austrians, especially in the rural strongholds

[43] *Die Reichspost*, May 30, 1926. For supporting views, see Rudolf Henle, *Kleindeutscher Einheitsstaat oder grossdeutsches Reich* (Cologne, 1929), pp. 15–16. A general discussion of federalism can be found in Gerhard Schulz, *Zwischen Demokratie und Diktatur* (Berlin, 1963), I: 405 ff.; Karl Schwend, *Bayern zwischen Monarchie und Diktatur* (Munich, 1954), pp. 316–85; Heinrich Otto Meisner, "Preussen und der Revisionismus," *Forschungen zur brandenburgischen und preussischen Geschichte*, 43 (1930): 253; Hajo Holborn, "Prussia and the Weimar Republic," *Social Research* 22 (1956): 331–42.

[44] Meinecke in *Neue Freie Presse*, September 29, 1927, a.m.; Franz Klein, "Deutscher Einheitsstaat und Deutsch-Österreich," *Die Hilfe* 34 (1928): 200–3; Karl Renner, "Der Staat der deutschen Nation," *Gesellschaft* 4 (1927): 97–107.

of Tyrol and Styria. They closely watched the meetings between Seipel and the Bavarian Chancellor Held in 1928 and 1929. The *Berliner Tageblatt* believed that these visits would be used to further federalist agitation in the Reich. With such evidence in mind, German democrats worried that the addition of Austria might raise insuperable obstacles to the completion of the unitary state.[45] The democratic *Kieler Zeitung* could exclaim:

Under the present condition, the *Anschluss* with Austria could lead to a strong underscoring of the Main line in German politics and very substantially limit, if not completely stop, the movement already underway for a unitary state. If we today view the question without ideological or sentimental predelictions while realistically considering the contemporary South German situation, we cannot dislodge the fear that *Anschluss* will become a threat to German unity.[46]

Given such a situation, any Anschluss organization formed in Bavaria was certain to raise suspicions. Thus the creation of the Deutsch-Österreichische Arbeitsgemeinschaft in 1925 initiated a flurry of reports from Munich to Berlin. The Arbeitsgemeinschaft was ostensibly designed to complement the Volksbund by preparing special studies on the problems an eventual union would confront. It denied any conflict of interest with the Volksbund, since its purpose was neither to lobby nor propagandize. Evidently Paul Löbe accepted this argument. The small membership of the Arbeitsgemeinschaft seemed to substantiate this contention. Even by 1928 it had only 392 members in all of Germany. These were drawn from the elite, principally civil servants who could hardly be considered experts in political propaganda.[47]

But Löbe did not understand the full set of circumstances behind the founding of the Arbeitsgemeinschaft. Its first chief, Freiherr von Branca, admitted to the Austrian Consul in Munich that his group desired to challenge Berlin's heretofore unquestioned leadership of the Anschluss movement. And this organizing effort fell upon fertile ground. The German South had always been suspicious of the Volks-

---

[45] *Berliner Tageblatt*, December 9, 1928, a.m.; *Der Anschluss*, May 16, 1929; *Münchner Neueste Nachrichten*, January 10, 1927. Lerchenfeld to Berlin, December 13, 1928, AA 4492/K920/K229406–K229408; Haniel to Bülow, December 14, 1928, ibid., K229434–K229436.

[46] Quoted in *Österreich-Deutschland* 4 (June 1927): 10.

[47] Haniel (Munich) to Berlin, September 25, 1925, AA 2345/4576/E171857; January 9, 1926 AA 4495/K922/K231681; January 28, 1926, ibid., K231686–K231691; *Der Anschluss*, January 15, May 15, 1928; *Deutsche Einheit* (Vienna), December 31, 1927; Paul Löbe, "Die deutsch-österreichische Anschlussbewegung im letzten jahre," ed. H. Freiherr von Richthofen, *Jahrbuch für auswärtige Politik* (Berlin, 1929), I: 165.

bund; Branca played upon these suspicions. The Reich's Representative in Munich feared that the Arbeitsgemeinschaft would be drawn into the struggles between Berlin and Munich. He thought that the Bavarian government's financial support would overwhelm Branca's little group and, therefore, create a regional split in the Anschluss movement. To avoid control by the Bavarian federalists, the Reich's Representative in Munich appealed to the Foreign Office for subsidies.[48] By 1927 he had achieved this goal. The Arbeitsgemeinschaft received 6,000 marks, only 4,000 less than the established subvention for the Volksbund. And to forestall Bavarian domination, two-thirds of this money went to the newly formed Arbeitsgemeinschaft chapter in Berlin.[49]

This subsidy worked; the Foreign Office was no longer receiving alarming reports. The Arbeitsgemeinschaft had expanded safely beyond its narrow Bavarian base. There were chapters in Frankfurt, Hanover, Cologne, Stuttgart, Dresden, and Berlin. Its Bavarian flavor had been reduced by Branca's resignation in 1927, the result of objections raised by the Hessian and Rhenish chapters. At the suggestion of the Reich's Representative in Munich, he was replaced by Erich Emminger.[50] But this group was certainly not turning to Berlin for leadership. Emminger may have been acceptable to the Foreign Office, but he was still a Bavarian political leader, a Reichstag delegate for the Bavarian People's Party.

As was often the case, regionalism was reinforced by anti-socialism. Branca, a leader of the DNVP, told the Austrian Consul in Munich that his organization was attempting to provide alternative leadership to the Berlin socialists. He complained that the Austrian Arbeitsgemeinschaft too freely admitted socialist leaders.[51] Yet even Branca felt impelled to construct a supra-party organization. The concept of a united front for Anschluss was too attractive a symbol to be discarded. Unfortunately for Branca, he was searching for executive council members at the wrong time. The Arbeitsgemeinschaft was founded in October 1925, while Munich was in an uproar over what was to become known as the "stab-in-the-back trial." The *Süddeutsche*

[48] Haniel to Berlin, September 25, 1925, AA 2345/4576/E171858; January 30, 1926, AA 4495/K922/K231692, and ARk R431/107, p. 208; Günther to Vienna, January 22, 1927, NPA Fasz. 57, Zl. 1 Pol.

[49] Foreign Office memo, May 30, 1927, AA 3692/K55/K006319. For Volksbund subsidy see memo of July 14, 1926, ibid., K006413, and throughout serial K56.

[50] Köpke memo, February 17, 1926, AA 4495/K922/K231695–K231696; Branca letter to Foreign Office, May 12, 1926, ibid., K232712; Haniel to Berlin, December 6, 1926, ARk R431/108, p. 240.

[51] Günther to Vienna, November 14, 1925, NPA Fasz. 57, Zl. 2 Pol.

Monatshefte had accused the socialists of disrupting the home front and assuring defeat in 1918. This was very old dirty linen and a patently false charge as well. A Munich socialist sued for libel. The emotionally charged atmosphere of the Bavarian capital during this trial was not conducive to constructing a supra-party constellation. Three Social Democrats withdrew their names after agreeing to be members of the executive council. At last Wilhelm Sollmann, a former interior minister, agreed, but the damage had been done.[52]

In any case, these socialists were only intended as showpieces. Branca's final executive council did include every major German party, but it was unquestionably constructed in a conservative cast. Besides Branca, there was the moderate DNVP Reichstag delegate, Lindeiner-Wildau; Count Lerchenfeld from the BVP; Karl Jarres, the former conservative presidential candidate; and Karl Hepp, head of the Reichslandbund—both from the Right-wing of the DVP. With the addition of Count Lerchenfeld from the BVP, this grouping tended to overwhelm the democrats, composed of Sollman, Heuss of the DDP, and the centrist Adam Stegerwald. And Stegerwald was very often displeased with socialist methods, especially those Löbe used in leading the Volksbund.[53] By 1927 this movement to the Right was reinforced by the addition of three bankers and Wilhelm Cuno, former chancellor and president of the Hamburg-American Line. Perhaps these men were included to facilitate raising money, as the Arbeitsgemeinschaft was always short of funds.[54] However their inclusion gave this organization a distinct business-oriented complexion that was lacking in the socialist-led Volksbund.

Ultimately ideological divisions fragmented the Anschluss movement. In this instance, national goals did not provide a focus around which disparate groups could unite. The interests of social class, region, and political parochialism proved stronger than the common pursuit of a national goal. And this would be true of Austria as well.

[52] Haniel to Berlin, November 3, 1925, ARk 4618/1064/K272694. For importance of trial, see *Egelhaafs historisch-politische Jahresübersicht für 1925* (Stuttgart, 1926), pp. 260–61.
[53] Fischer letter to Vienna, October 1, 1925, NPA Fasz. 110, 16393 pr. 13 XI 1925. For list of executive council, see ARk R2 Zg 1955ff/1622; and Haniel to Berlin, January 28, 1926, AA 4495/K922/K231689.
[54] Ibid., K231691.

CHAPTER III   IDEOLOGICAL CONFLICT
IN AUSTRIA

THE AUSTRIAN ANSCHLUSS movement was just as troubled by ideological conflict, but there seemed to be more hope of its resolution in Vienna than in Munich or Berlin. In the first place, the Anschluss was a far more important issue for the Austrians than for the Germans. In the Reich, the Austro-German union was only one of many foreign policy goals within a system of unclear and constantly shifting priorities. This was not the case for most Austrians who saw union with Germany as the single prerequisite for their salvation. Thus Richart Mischler could conclude in a classic understatement: "The *Anschluss* is certainly much more of a living question for Austria than for Germany."[1]

For this reason, the Austrian Anschluss movement involved more of the political community than that of the Reich. The struggles for Austro-German union were harder and more meaningful. Because the stakes were higher, there was also considerably more effort to construct a political coalition that would subsume conflicting groups under the aegis of German patriotism. The aim of this coalition was also different from any that could be built in the Reich. The German Volksbund believed that constant propaganda was necessary to keep the Anschluss question alive. The Austrian Anschluss supporters, on the other hand, claimed that their fellow countrymen did not need to be prodded to consider German union as their salvation. Therefore the Austrian Anschluss movement was not constructed for internal political reasons; it was designed as an instrument of foreign policy to show the allies that, in Vienna, national loyalties took precedence over their domestic quarrels. The middle-class publications, especially the influential *Neue Freie Presse*, clearly enunciated this view. An editorial in *Der österreichische Volkswirt* declared: "We must successfully build a circle of representative men from all parties who are

[1] Richart Mischler, "Reichstagswahl und Anschluss," *Österreich-Deutschland* 5 (May 1928): 1.

42

prepared to tell the entire world the truth about an Austria that here lives as a piece of the German nation . . . that sees its political and economic future alone assured by union with the German Reich."[2]

Founded in 1925, the Austrian branch of the Volksbund was determined to fulfill this task. The supra-party Volksbund was designed to disprove the allegation that the entire Anschluss movement was directed from Berlin. A pronouncement of 1925 declared: "The Austro-German Volksbund fights for the *Anschluss* with Germany; it includes all occupations and classes; it believes in a community of fate between ourselves and the Reich Germans. One people, one state! The Volksbund is above party politics; it excludes all political questions but one. With a knowledgeable and sharp one-sidedness, it only separates the nation into two groups—those for or against the *Anschluss*."[3]

At first glance, the Austrian Volksbund seemed ideally structured to achieve this goal. Unlike its German counterpart, the Austrian organization was not content merely to conduct drives for individual members. Its rules allowed the addition of whole associations in one stroke, bringing in 94,000 railway workers or 45,000 Catholic trade unionists. These associations did represent all classes of Austrian society from socialist unions, to handcraft workers' and employers' groups, to men's choral societies, and even to the teaching corps of many schools. Also aiding its supra-party image was the fact that the Austrian Volksbund was more geographically dispersed than the German. There were chapters in the capitals of all the Austrian states, with the exception of little Voralberg. And, as the most important piece of evidence, all major political parties were represented at its meetings and in its executive council.[4]

However, as with Germany, signs can be misleading. The Volksbund prepared a list of Nationalrat delegates who were members as of 1930. From this document, it is a relatively simple task to calculate the political composition of the Volksbund and compare this with the strength of the parties in the Nationalrat elected in 1927. Seipel's party, the Catholic-oriented Christian Socialists, and the Social Democrats had roughly equal numbers in the Nationalrat, yet the Volksbund included fourteen Nationalrat delegates who were socialists and only

[2] *Der österreichische Volkswirt* 17 (1925): 501. See *Neue Freie Presse*, March 26, 1926, p.m.

[3] Österreichisch-Deutscher Volksbund, *Warum fördern wir den Anschluss* (Vienna, 1926), p. 16.

[4] Volksbund 1931 statement, NPA Fasz. 402, 2076 pr. 9 II 1931; *Der Anschluss*, June 15, 1927; Hermann Neubacher, "Die Organisation für den österreichische-deutschen Zusammenschluss" (eds.) Kleinwaechter and Paller, *Die Anschlussfrage in ihrer Kulturellen politischen, und wirtschaftlichen Bedeutung*, pp. 611, 614.

four who were Christian Socialists. Even the much weaker nationalist groups—the Grossdeutsch Party and the Landbund—contributed seven delegates to the Volksbund. The president of the Austrian Volksbund, Hermann Neubacher, was an avowed supporter of the Grossdeutsch Party.[5]

The Christian Socialist representatives partially made up in influence for the numbers they lacked. They included two men who had been Austrian chancellors in the 1920s—Rudolf Ramek and Ernst Streeruwitz. Certainly Ramek and Streeruwitz must have envisioned their participation in the Volksbund as a move designed to create a national coalition for pursuing the Anschluss. It is no accident that both these leaders appeared willing to think about the so-called "great coalition" with the Social Democrats.[6] Nor were tireless Christian Socialist workers such as Professor Hans Eibl and Bundesrat delegate Professor Karl Hugelmann adverse to sitting on the same platform with Austrian and German socialists. The same phenomenon was apparent in the Austrian section of the Arbeitsgemeinschaft. Its executive council contained four Social Democrats, two Grossdeutsch Party members, and only two from the Christian Socialists. And one of the Christian Socialists was Karl Drexel, long considered an advocate of accommodation with the Austrian Marxists.[7]

Thus the minority of Christian Socialists who actively worked for the Anschluss were often also advocates of internal accommodation with the Social Democrats. It was no accident, either, that the strongest opponents of Anschluss within the party were also antagonistic to cooperating with the Austrian Social Democrats. After all, a "great coalition" with the socialists would only add to the pressures for Anschluss within the Austrian government. Thus an antisocialist internal policy was more than compatible with an anti-Anschluss foreign policy.

This was certainly the attitude of Ignaz Seipel, twice in the 1920s chancellor and party leader after 1926. In a letter of 1926, Seipel wrote: "I am unsympathetic to the whole German-Austrian Arbeitsgemeinschaft, and I hold myself aloof from it. But I have no pressing reason to demand the same from all my party colleagues. However I completely reject the Austro-German Volksbund. . . . Naturally we must wait for the right time to make this position public."[8] Why did the Volksbund merit such a different approach from the Arbeits-

[5] Volksbund statement, n. 4.

[6] Wirth letter to Foreign Office, June 6, 1928, AA 2347/4576/E173477; Ernst von Streeruwitz, *Springflut über Österreich* (Vienna, 1937), pp. 395–96.

[7] Pfeiffer to Berlin, April 30, 1925, AA 4495/K922/K231661–K231663.

[8] Chapter II, n. 39.

gemeinschaft? Why did not the latter bring forth the same con-
demnation? Despite the fact that the Volksbund was headed by a
Grossdeutsch sympathizer and had strong support from middle-class
nationalists, despite the fact that its publications were definitely conservative in tone, the Volksbund was tainted by its socialist membership.
Even a Foreign Ministry memorandum could contain the statement:
"The Volksbund is commonly considered to be tinged with red in
contrast to the Austro-German Arbeitsgemeinschaft that bears a distinctly national character."[9] Seipel implied the same in the letter
mentioned above. He called attention to the large numbers of socialists who participated in Volksbund demonstrations held in August
1925. The Christian Socialist organ, Die Reichspost, made similar
statements.

This antipathy to Social Democratic participation was not confined
to the Christian Socialist opponents of Anschluss. The radical rightist
newspaper, Die Deutschösterreichische Tageszeitung, complained
that one of these August 1925 demonstrations was dominated by 4,000
members of the socialist paramilitary Schutzbund who arrived with
their insignia prominently displayed. As usual this newspaper's account
was exaggerated. A Viennese police report mentioned a reception on
August 28 attended by 200 Schutzbund members in civilian clothing.[10]
Yet these exaggerations did have a kernel of truth. The Anschluss
movement was troubled by real ideological divisions that could never
be totally submerged in the rhetoric of German patriotism. At another
meeting on August 30, these divisions erupted following the traditional
singing of the German national anthem. A small group of communists
began to sing the "Internationale" in protest. This brought about a
massive reaction from the greater part of the audience which
answered with the socialist "Song of the Workers." Adding to the
confusion, another little band began to sing the so-called "Stahlhelm
Song" to show its sympathy with the nationalist Right.[11]

Divisions along ideological lines were again stronger than any
possible consensus on foreign policy. However these divisions were
not altogether destructive of Austro-German cooperation. They only
undermined attempts at organizing across party lines. The Austrian
and German middle class could work together, as long as socialists
were not involved. Witness the long and fruitful meetings between
the Austrian and German sections of the Arbeitsgemeinschaft. In
fact, fear of socialism could unite various groups in these lands that

[9] Foreign Ministry report, see Volksbund statement, n. 4.
[10] Police report, August 28, 1928, NPA Fasz. 234, 15052 pr. 28 VIII 1925;
Deutschösterreichische Tageszeitung, August 31, 1925.
[11] Police report, August 31, 1928, NPA Fasz. 234, 15072 pr. 31 VIII 1925.

would not readily cooperate on other issues. If the Bavarian government was always willing to talk to the Austrians, it was reluctant to give up any advantage for Austria's sake. As shown in chapter VII, Bavaria refused to grant any but the smallest concessions to bolster the weakened Austrian economy. Yet in 1924 the von Kahr government offered to unite with their Tyrolean neighbors against the socialist trade unions and to run the Tyrol railway in the event of a strike. The succeeding Held cabinet was more circumspect. But during a 1927 general strike the Bavarian section of the Reichsbahn was prepared to send trains across the border to Innsbruck, the capital of Tyrol. Only Foreign Office intervention stopped this action. And this intervention was only successful because the Bavarian government feared Italy would follow their lead.[12]

Ideological warfare was not confined to governments. Both Left- and Right-wing paramilitary organizations were in close communication with similar groups on the other side of the border. For the moment, let us consider only the armed Right. After World War I, Tyrol and Styria had been fertile ground for cooperation between Austrian and German paramilitary formations, as the Austrian Heimwehr received assistance from various German Free Corps.[13] By the late 1920s the post of chief of staff for the entire Heimwehr movement had been given to a German who had first joined the organization in Tyrol. He was Waldemar Pabst, an ex-Kappist, whom the German government considered a traitor after 1920. However Stresemann realized that Pabst could be of value to the German Foreign Office. The Reichsminister not only worked to quash the indictment against Pabst but put the Heimwehr leader on the payroll at a salary of 12,000 marks a year.[14]

Despite the efforts of Pabst, the Heimwehr would become an instrument of Seipel's policy, more dedicated to Austrian independence than to Anschluss, more willing to work with Mussolini than with Stresemann. Yet the fear of socialism could still drive Austrian statesmen into the arms of conservative Germans. Ex-Foreign Minister Heinrich Mataja belonged to the wing of the Christian Socialist Party

---

[12] Immelen (Innsbruck) to Berlin, November 10, 1924, AA 1483/3086/ D613967–D613969; Maltzan (Berlin) to Immelen, November 11, 1924, ibid., D613970–D613971; Redlhammer (Munich) report to Berlin, July 17, 1927, AA 2346/4576/E172853; Saller (Innsbruck) telephone report to Berlin, July 18, 1927, ibid., E172855–E172856.

[13] Walter Goldinger, "Die geschichtliche Ablauf der Ereignisse in Österreich von 1918 bis 1945" (ed.) Heinrich Benedikt, Geschichte der Republik Österreich (Vienna, 1954), p. 149.

[14] Gatzke, Stresemann and the Rearmament of Germany (Baltimore, 1954), pp. 51–52.

that distrusted Germans and looked for alternatives to the Anschluss. Mataja had striven in 1926 to organize a Christian Socialist boycott of a Volksbund meeting, even when the principal speaker was a fellow Catholic politician from the north. Mataja always hated socialists more than middle-class Germans. He called the Schutzbund a group of red fascists; he attempted to found an international paramilitary combination to undermine the armed Viennese socialists.

Mataja urged the Heimwehr leaders to form a Catholic paramilitary organization in conjunction with their German counterparts, a *Zentrumskammeradschaften* it was to be called. He even envisioned this organization paving the way for the unification of the two Germanic states under a conservative, authoritarian government. It was a typical plan for Mataja who was often guilty of grandiose hopes and hyperbolic statements. The extent of his delusion is attested by the fact that he hoped not only to include various Free Corps leaders such as Georg Escherich but also Catholic democratic politicians like Josef Wirth. With his typical luck, the former Foreign Minister was never able to arrange a meeting with Escherich who expressed some interest in this plan. He did meet with Wirth, but the interview was a disaster.[15]

Mataja's suggestion was taken up by a group that was totally repugnant to the Heimwehr movement. Hitler's National Socialists had always believed in uniting with their Austrian counterparts. Between 1920 and 1923 Hitler attempted to amalgamate with the Austrian National Socialists, arguing that an international coalition was necessary to undermine an international Jewish conspiracy. In 1923 the Austrian party split into three groups, one of which accepted the direction of Hitler. By 1926 the party had been refounded under the domination of Munich. Hitler announced the supremacy of the Reich organization at a large rally in Passau on the Austro-German border. The party organ stated: "He had previously not meddled in the situation of the Austrian party, but now he would concern himself with it . . . since the movement must have total leadership. The principal task lies with the German state region. From this will come the great impulse that will make them one by *Anschluss* with Austria."[16]

The National Socialists were never important in the 1920s; they

[15] Pabst to Stresemann, August 11, 1926, Stresemann Nachlass 3143/7313/H158838–H158839; same to same, September 29, 1926, ibid., H158846–H158849; Lerchenfeld (Vienna) to Berlin, November 10, 1926, AA 4491/K920/K228722–K228723; *Die Reichspost,* November 11, 1926.

[16] *Völkischer Beobachter* (Munich), August 15/16, 1926. For a discussion of the first years of Austrian National Socialism, see Franz Langoth, *Kampf um Österreich* (Wels, 1951), pp. 29–30; Otto Reich von Rohrwig, *Der Freiheits-*

could only garner 30,000 votes in the 1927 elections. Yet the idea of an anti-Semitic union to create the Anschluss was appealing to a great many people outside of the Hitler movement. Count Reventlow, the racist political leader in North Germany, and *Deutschöster-reichische Tageszeitung* (Vienna) agreed that the Jews were not German nationalists and that the destruction of Jewish financial power was the *sine qua non* for completing the Anschluss. As a propagandist for Anschluss stated: "In Austria, for the most part in Vienna, there are 300,000 Jews. . . . Austrian Judaism is coming more strongly under the influence of Zionism. He [the Jew] is in agreement with the British Protectorate over Palestine. For this reason, he supports British world policy and is irrevocably opposed to the *Anschluss*."[17]

Ultimately it was not capital but labor that the middle class feared. The strength of the Austrian Social Democratic Party stimulated fears of revolution. These fears would eventually turn Anschluss supporters away from their original goal. Middle-class and rural German nationalists would forget their patriotic rhetoric in order to isolate the Social Democratic Party. To assure a permanent antisocialist majority in the Nationalrat, the Grossdeutsch Party in 1922 accepted a political alliance with the Christian Socialists whose credentials as German patriots were certainly tainted. The Grossdeutsch Party leaders were willing to ignore Seipel's coolness toward the Anschluss. They overlooked the anti-German editorials in the leading Christian Socialist newspaper, *Die Reichspost.* They were willing to accept the Christian Socialist Party platforms at face value when these advocated the union. Interestingly the Grossdeutsch Party's leadership seemed less concerned with Christian Socialist opposition to Anschluss than the position the Catholic party took on church schools.[18]

The Grossdeutsch leaders justified their agreement to a coalition because it increased the strength of the pro-Anschluss forces in the government. The party chief, Franz Dinghofer, argued that their action had decisively changed Austrian foreign policy. "Anschluss is

---

kampf der Ostmark-Deutschen von St. Germain bis Adolf Hitler (Vienna, 1942), pp. 56–73; Andrew G. Whiteside, "Nationaler Sozialismus in Österreich vor 1918," *Vierteljahrshefte für Zeitgeschichte* 7 (1961): 353–59; Adam Wandruska, "Österreichs politische Struktur," ed. Benedikt, *Geschichte der Republik Österreich,* pp. 406–10.

[17] Siegmund Schilder, *Der Streit über die Lebensfähigkeit Österreichs* (Stuttgart, 1926), pp. 10–11; Count Reventlow is cited in *Österreich-Deutschland* 4 (January 1926): 13; *Deutschösterreichische Tageszeitung,* August 3, 1928.

[18] Friedrich Funder, *Von Gestern ins Heute* (Vienna, 1953), pp. 386–400; Oskar Kleinschmied, *Schober* (Vienna, 1930), p. 194; Adam Wandruska, "Österreichs politische Struktur," ed. Benedikt, *Geschichte de Republik Österreich,* pp. 659–65.

on the march," he proclaimed.[19] However there is little evidence to support this contention. There is only the one lone fact, that the Grossdeutsch Party seemed to have gained permanent control over the diplomatic post in Berlin by some sort of gentlemen's agreement. Certainly the party's electorate was not lulled by the proclamations of their leaders. In the 1920 Nationalrat elections, the Grossdeutsch Party had gained 12.3 percent of the vote and 20 seats. Then came the coalition in 1922. In the following year, the party's share of the vote fell to 7.8 percent. Penalized by a decrease in the number of seats in the Nationalrat and a new electoral law, its delegate strength fell to only 10. In 1927 the *Grossdeutsche* agreed to form a unity list with the Christian Socialists. Seipel's generosity saved them from even further embarrassment by so favorably placing them on the electoral lists as to gain two seats. In the same elections, the nationalist agrarian party, the Landbund, more than doubled its vote, proving that nationalist parties did much better in opposition than in the government.[20] It was apparent to all that the Grossdeutsch Party's influence was declining. The democratic Anschluss supporters viewed this situation with equanimity. *Der österreichische Volkswirt* stated in 1925: "As for the *Grossdeutsche*, they no longer present a fit subject for conversation. One wonders whether this party will survive the next elections. The body cannot live anymore because the spirit is unwilling."[21]

Yet this decline did not stop other nationalists from joining the coalition. After refusing to participate in the unity list of the 1927 elections, the Landbund finally became part of Seipel's coalition in the same year. Their presence was necessary to form a firm antisocialist block. More vigorous in their demands for Anschluss, more insistent on a pro-German foreign policy, the Landbund even worried Chancellor Seipel. The Austrian Chancellor did seem to make some rhetorical concessions to the Landbund, but, on the whole, his fears were unjustified. When the Social Democrats attacked Seipel, Landbund chief Ernst Schönbauer defended his Chancellor. Hatred of the socialists had effectively removed much of the venom from the Landbund.[22]

---

[19] *Neue Freie Presse*, May 25, 1925, p.m.; Leopold Waber, "Zehn Jahre Arbeit der Grossdeutschen Volkspartei," ed. Wilhelm Exner, *10 Jahre Wiederaufbau* (Vienna, 1928), pp. 19–21.

[20] See chapter II, n. 8.

[21] *Der österreichische Volkswirt* 18 (1925): 473. See also Otto Bauer, *Die österreichische Revolution* (Vienna, 1923), p. 267.

[22] Schubert memo on discussion with Seipel, May 30, 1927, AA 2346/4576/E172890; *Stenographische Protokolle über die Sitzungen des Nationalrats*, III Gesetzgebungs Periode, I: 32.

The bourgeois and agrarian Anschluss movement was not unique in compounding the Anschluss problem by vigorously upholding internal political divisions. The July, 1927 issue of the socialist *Der Kampf* carried an explosive article on the Anschluss question by Otto Bauer. Bauer argued that the Austrian Social Democrats had consistently favored the Anschluss. He believed large elements of the middle class remained monarchists in 1918 because they had not wished to unite with a revolutionary Germany. He admitted that the Austrian middle-class had changed its opinion, but only after Germany became dominated by bourgeois governments. The Austrian middle class had since come to view the Anschluss as the best method available of undermining the Viennese socialists who would be less powerful in a middle-class dominated Reich.

In any case, Bauer believed that this middle-class union was a chimera. Bourgeois politics could never overcome the national animosities that were characteristic of the capitalist state. The legitimate rights of the Austrians would go unrecognized as long as the middle class dominated France and the fascists, Italy. He argued that only a proletarian revolution could overcome these entrenched hatreds by alleviating the legitimate fear among foreign statesmen that Anschluss was an instrument of German aggression. Therefore, until this revolution had spread to Germanic countries, the Anschluss would remain uncompleted. Yet this was not an insurmountable task. Bauer stated: "We do not have to fear the bourgeoisie whom we see today in the Reich. The Anschluss will be completed in time when revolutionary changes will bring forth another Germany. It will not be the Reich of Hindenburg and the middle class that we shall join."[23]

Bauer would never retract these statements, even when under the severest criticism. Yet he claimed to have been misunderstood because he had explicitly rejected force in both domestic and foreign affairs. This revolution, so glibly discussed, was to be achieved by democratic means. The *Kampf* article really seems to be an outgrowth of a campaign conducted among his fellow Democratic Socialists in the Second International. In 1927 the Austrian Social Democrats approached their French, Belgian, and Czech comrades about the Anschluss problem. The Austrians hoped, somewhat naively, to transform international socialism into a vehicle for diminishing the European opposition to the Anschluss.[24]

Yet the revolutionary rhetoric remained to be explained away. Brilliant, impulsive, totally committed—Bauer appeared to many as

[23] *Der Kampf* (July 1927) quoted in *Zentral Archiv für Wirtschaft und Politik* 6 (1927): 850. See Bauer's reiteration in *Arbeiter Zeitung*, July 7, 1927.
[24] Marek (Prague) to Vienna, July 14, 1927, Fasz. 64, Zl. 94 Pol.

an Austrian version of Trotsky. His revolutionary rhetoric outdistancing his political goals, Bauer gave the bourgeoisie enough evidence to feed their suspicions. He accepted the ballot box as the sole means for gaining power, but he could not envision governing in conjunction with the middle class. He never agreed with Karl Renner that the Social Democrats should form a "great coalition" with the Christian Socialists. Renner and more contemporary historians have contended that Bauer's intransigence helped wreck the republic. Certainly it made a coalition of all pro-Anschluss forces even more difficult. What middle-class leaders could work with a man who still thought a "dictatorship of the proletariat" might have to be used by an elected socialist government against counter-revolutionary elements? This is intellectual confusion of the highest order, yet Bauer was able to exert enough influence to insert this phrase in the Linz party program of 1926. He had not thereby intended to subvert the Anschluss movement. Bauer, after all, had resigned from the Renner cabinet in 1920, stating that Anschluss-supporter Renner was not taking a strong enough pro-German course. Bauer would even greet the Anschluss of 1938. As the *Kampf* article stated, Bauer saw the victory of international socialism and the German union as compatible causes to be pursued together. He rejected the proposition of the German Communist Party that proletarian revolution took precedence over Anschluss. He could never accept the view of the German Otto Reichenberger who stated: "We Communists cannot join the bourgeois and Social Democratic Anschluss movement, but we must use the political convulsions and battles which it would unleash to bring forward the cause of revolution."[25]

The Christian Socialist leadership hoped to confuse Bauer's statements with those of the communists. It was not a difficult task. They could play upon the Austrian Social Democratic leader's intransigence and the fears he engendered. Mataja, whose anti-German propensities were well known, could argue that the socialists would have to choose between bourgeois unification and revolution. Actually he wanted neither. But certainly the Austrian middle-class Anschluss movement

---

[25] Otto Reichenberger, "Die Deutschefrage und der Anschluss Österreichs," *Die kommunistische Internationale* 8 (1927): 2329. Bauer's views were, however, less in conflict with the statements of Johann Koplenig, Austrian communist leader; see Koplenig, *Reden und Aufsätze* (Vienna, 1950), p. 10. For the Linz Program's support of Anschluss, see *Protokoll des sozialdemokratischen Parteitags, 1926*, p. 194. For the struggles with the Austrian socialist party, see Julius Braunthal, *Otto Bauer* (Vienna, 1961), pp. 36–75; Charles Gulick, *Austria from Habsburg to Hitler* (Berkeley, 1948), I: 113 ff.; Karl Hannak, *Karl Renner und seine Zeit* (Vienna, 1965), pp. 381–84, 473–78; Karl Renner, *Österreich von der Ersten zur Zweiten Republik* (Vienna, 1953), pp. 79–80.

was disturbed by the fears that Mataja voiced. Part of this opinion was simply due to the ideology of immutable class conflict present, to some extent, in every bourgeoisie. The middle-class press was more than willing to place all the blame upon the Social Democrats, although even an antisocialist newspaper like the *Neues Wiener Tageblatt* understood the implications of such a break when it wistfully called attention to "the tragic line of demarcation between the Anschluss politics of the bourgeoisie and the proletariat."[26]

On July 15, 1927, only a few days after the publication of Bauer's article, this tension erupted into violence on the streets of Vienna. On July 14 a federal court had acquitted a number of Heimwehr members who were accused of killing two socialists during a confrontation in Schattendorf, Burgenland. The Viennese workers marched in a protest that ended in conflict with the police. By evening the *Reichspost* offices, a police station, and the Palace of Justice were in flames. There were casualties on both sides. Austria was on the brink of civil war, but both the Christian Socialist and Social Democratic leadership eventually gained control and gradually moved their followers away from a collision course. Still, after 1927, the threat of armed conflict always was present—a threat that would finally be realized in 1934.[27]

The Austrian civil disturbances were certain to involve Germany. With the possibility of an armed conflict always at hand, the socialist paramilitary organization, the Schutzbund, became more important. And any discussion of the Schutzbund necessarily called attention to its close ties with the German democratic paramilitary group, the Reichsbanner. The Reichsbanner and the Schutzbund had consistently maintained their identity of interests. The Austrian group sent representatives to the important Reichsbanner meetings that celebrated the anniversary of the Weimar constitution, where they were greeted with the warmest of welcomes. In Berlin in 1925 they were received by the local Gau leader with the following statement:

Tomorrow morning we will participate in the entire German nation's celebration of the Weimar constitution. (*Cries of bravo! Hand clapping.*) We consider you already a part of the whole German nation and will document this fact by enrolling you in our formations. In this spirit, I again welcome you and hope that these days of friendship will strengthen

---

[26] *Neues Wiener Tagblatt*, July 10, 1927, quoted in *Bulletin périodique de la presse autrichienne*, Nr. 183, p. 23; *Neue Freie Presse*, July 4, 1927, p.m.

[27] Gulick, *Austria from Habsburg to Hitler*, I: 717–77; Lerchenfeld to Berlin, July 1927, AA 4491/K920/K229027–K229029.

you in the fight that we have in common to create a real *Grossdeutschland* that is built upon a democratic foundation.[28]

The democratic rhetoric of the Reichsbanner and Schutzbund sounded hollow to the German and Austrian middle class. Although self-proclaimed, supra-party organizations, the Reichsbanner was dominated by the SPD, and the Schutzbund was drawn almost totally from the ranks of the Austrian Social Democrats. Thus, to many, the democratic rhetoric of these paramilitary groups scarcely seemed to veil the speech of class solidarity. Witness the words of the Schutzbund leader, Julius Deutsch, as he welcomed Reichsbanner chief Friedrich Hörsing to Vienna in January 1926:

In this brotherhood, we have already completed the *Anschluss*. The German working classes and their battle are already a piece of German unity that cannot be lost. We fight against National Socialism and Fascism. . . . We have heard that the Wittelsbachs [of Bavaria] would again like their crown. We are convinced that, in such a case, the Bavarian workers would use their fists as well. We want to create a *grossdeutsch* republic from the North Sea to the Karawanken and Burgenland.[29]

The Austrians were particularly anxious about such statements. Mataja believed that the socialists were working to create the same kind of international paramilitary organization that he had desired for the conservatives. He carefully watched these joint Reichsbanner-Schutzbund demonstrations and protested when the Austrian Consul at Nuremberg attended such a meeting. What Mataja did not know was that this same Consul had issued a report unfavorably comparing the discipline at Reichsbanner demonstrations with that of the National Socialists.[30] The Austrian and German governments themselves became worried that these promises of cooperation would be translated into action after the July 15 disturbances in Vienna. There was talk in Munich of Bavarian Reichsbanner bands crossing the border to aid the socialist strikers in Tyrol. While such action never materialized, the situation was complicated by a manifesto issued by Hörsing and purporting to explain the situation. Hörsing criticized the Austrian police and claimed that only the Schutzbund had effectively maintained order throughout the rioting. The Austrian Minister to Berlin protested. Stresemann's vacation had to be interrupted on this account.

[28] *Vorwärts*, August 8, 1925, edition A.

[29] *Österreich-Deutschland* 3 (January 1926): 8.

[30] Foreign Ministry memo, August 17, 1927, NPA Fasz. 240, 14.052/13/26; same, August 24, 1927, ibid., 14.127/13/26; Pacher (Berlin) to Vienna, August 25, 1927, NPA Fasz. 240, 24016 pr. 29 VIII 1927.

Hörsing, who was provincial president of Upper Saxony, was put under enormous pressure. He eventually resigned from the Prussian civil service, announcing publicly that this action was caused by his struggles against international reaction.[31]

There is still one footnote to this story. Hörsing's action provided an ideal excuse for German Chancellor Wilhelm Marx to resign from the Reichsbanner. Marx had entered this organization in 1925 when he had been running for president as head of a democratic coalition. In 1927 he was chancellor in a right-of-center cabinet whose members were naturally suspicious of an organization led by socialists. Marx needed some pretext to exit from the Reichsbanner with his honor intact. The situation in July 1927 was ready made for his purposes.[32] There were other issues involved in his resignation as well, but Marx's action shows how political conflict between socialist and middle-class interests substantially weakened the Anschluss movement.

[31] Redlhammer to Berlin, July 18, 1927, AA 2347/4576/E172959; Schubert memo, July 21, 1927, ibid., E172862; Stresemann to Pünder, July 21, 1927, ibid., E172864; Frank (Berlin) to Vienna, July 19, 22, 1927, NPA Fasz. 11, Zl. 166 Pol, Zl. 172 Pol.

[32] Karl Rohe, *Das Reichsbanner, Schwarz Rot Gold* (Düsseldorf, 1966), pp. 292–303.

CHAPTER IV FINDING A PLACE FOR
AUSTRIA IN
GERMAN NATIONAL
SYMBOLISM

THESE IDEOLOGICAL STRUGGLES were carried over into the one serious attempt at finding a common ground from which all Germans could pursue the Anschluss. Thus each German envisioned uniting only with those Austrians of complementary belief and life style. These contradictory visions would undermine the creation of a single set of symbols to describe the national experience. Yet there was one centripetal force that pulled these divergent opinions together. Each ideological grouping would have to grapple with very similar views of the past. Therefore their solutions would prove strikingly similar in outline, if not in details.

After all, the fears were the same. Even the most fervid Anschluss supporter could be suspicious of Austria. Theodor Heuss worried that the Bismarckian solution itself might have irremediably severed the Austrians from the main stream of German experience. He saw an Austria that had been politically divided from the rest of Germany for fifty years. "The Viennese thus sank out of the common German state of mind and became Austrian specialists."[1] The DDP chairman, Erich Koch-Weser, was apprehensive that postwar Austrians might truly reject German nationalism for a cosmopolitanism more in keeping with their experience of living in a multinational empire. This cosmopolitanism was best expressed in a United States of Europe. "The longer Austria and Germany are separated," he wrote, "the more they will think separately. If unification is not completed soon I fear it will never be."[2]

Gustav Stresemann understood such fears of Austrian uniqueness; he had them himself. He strongly supported the Anschluss even at the expense of his relations with other states. Yet he could not fully suppress a latent anti-Austrianism.[3] He believed that Anschluss would

[1] Theodor Heuss, "Die grossdeutsche Frage," Der Kunstwart 39 (1926): 20.
[2] Diary, March 8, 1927, Bundesarchiv Koblenz, Koch-Weser Nachlass, Nr. 36, p. 147.
[3] An interesting series of anti-Austrian statements can be found in Stresemann Nachlass, Col. U. 3.

severely test the fabric of the German state and could undermine its cultural and political equilibrium by strengthening the Catholic South vis-à-vis the Protestant North. Sometimes the German Foreign Minister despaired of anyone overcoming these dangers; at other times, he seems to have thought that he could personally carry out this task. Stresemann was hardly humble; he undoubtedly envisioned himself in a role that "would require a great statesman to work these problems out."[4]

The main task of resolving these doubts fell upon German historians, who were remarkably well equipped to institute such a change of opinion. In the first place, they were not particularly bothered by internecine strife; they were an essentially homogeneous group regardless of political affiliation. There were no socialists among the major historians, and the few democrats, such as Meinecke, were hardly Left-wing liberals. In the second place, they were never out of touch with their middle-class constituency. Like most middle-class Germans, they were unwilling to free themselves from their prewar veneration of the nation-state.[5]

Third, they were committed to the Anschluss, since any change in the composition of the state was of prime importance to them. When in 1919 Friedrich Meinecke gave the highest priority to a "union with our Austrian brothers," he was not alone in the historical profession.[6] Yet implicit in this demand was a new political role for the Austrians that was scarcely thought possible before 1918. This political conception quite naturally influenced historical writing. "The *Anschluss*," wrote Hans Herzfeld, "was one of the strongest forces in Weimar historical thought."[7] This was true although the acceptance of Anschluss seemed to violate the heretofore preponderant *kleindeutsch* tradition in German historiography. This chapter traces in detail the attempt of these new forces to undermine the old kleindeutsch history.

It was not an easy task. Kleindeutsch historians were well en-

---

[4] Stresemann memo on conversation with d'Abernon, June 4, 1925, AA 2344/4576/E171648. The same statement was made to the Italian Ambassador and the German Crown Prince; see Bosdari to Mussolini, March 8, 1925, *I documenti diplomatici italiani*, serie VII, vol. II: 558 and Stresemann letter to Crown Prince, September 7, 1925, Stresemann Nachlass 3168/7318/H159872. This letter to the Crown Prince is discussed in Anneliese Thimme, "Gustav Stresemann, Legende und Wirklichkeit," *Historische Zeitschrift* 181 (1956): 331 ff.

[5] See Georg Iggers, *The German Conception of History* (Middletown, Conn., 1966), pp. 229–38; Fritz Ringer, *The Decline of the German Mandarins* (Cambridge, Mass., 1969), pp. 63–64.

[6] Friedrich Meinecke, *Nach der Revolution* (Munich, 1919), pp. 63–64.

[7] Hans Herzfeld, "Staat und Nation in der deutschen Geschichtsschreibung der Weimarer Zeit," *Veritas-Justitia-Libertas, Festschrift zur 200-Jahrfeier der Columbia Universität* (Berlin, 1954), p. 141.

trenched. Not only had they made substantial contributions to the Prussian-led unification movement but they had also played an important part in the development of the newly created Reich. Treitschke, Droysen, Sybel, and others of their school provided not only a justification for the actions of Bismarck, they taught a veneration for past Hohenzollerns that certainly accrued to the benefit of the current occupant of the throne. William II readily grasped the utility of such an education. He expanded it beyond the confines of the university. During his reign, a whole generation of German youth was trained in Prussian hagiography. German civics education was rooted in kleindeutsch thought—Protestant, Prussian, anti-Austrian, anti-Catholic, contemptuous of its *grossdeutsch* opposition. And this indoctrination was successful. What could provide clearer proof of the German historian's worth? Armed with this knowledge, pre-World War I historians quite naturally tended to exaggerate their own importance. Historical scholars often thought of themselves as more than mere academicians. They had the potentiality to become "educators of the nation."[8]

Yet suddenly, after the war, kleindeutsch history became embarrassing. Austria had become overnight a sister German state whose people longed to join the Reich, as witnessed by a decision of the Provisional Assembly as early as November 12, 1918. It could no longer be maligned as the sinister force that had hindered German unification. Reich citizens could no longer consider Austria as an entity separable from the main stream of national society and history. The fall of the Habsburg and Hohenzollern dynasties had paved the way for ending the conflicts that had come from German dualism. Only allied prohibitions stood in the way of completing this aspect of national unification.

And there would be a great number of advantages accruing from this Anschluss. The completion of the Austro-German union would give Germany an enormous victory over the Versailles system as well as an enhanced geographic position from which to penetrate South-

[8] Lenz applied this term to Ranke in *Kleine historische Schriften* (Munich, 1922), II: 295; his neo-Rankean colleague, Erich Marcks, surprisingly also awarded this accolade to Ranke's severest critic, Treitschke, in *Männer und Zeiten* (Leipzig, 1911), I: 310-11. The best single introduction to the nineteenth-century problem is still Eduard Fueter, *Geschichte der neueren Historiographie* (Munich, 1936), pp. 535–49. In addition to the standard works, see Walter Langsam, "Nationalism and History in the Prussian Elementary Schools," *Nationalism and Internationalism*, ed. Edward Meade Earle (New York, 1950), pp. 242 ff.; Horst Schallenberg, *Zum Geschichtsbild der Wilhelmischen Ära und der Weimarer Zeit* (Ratingen bei Düsseldorf, 1964), pp. 55 ff.; Hans-Heinz Krill, *Die Ranke Renaissance* (Berlin, 1962), pp. 80 ff.

eastern Europe. The union also raised other hopes. Many historians believed that an Anschluss would awaken the lost faith in a purposive national community and thus restore some sense of security to the individual German. It seemed to offer the surest way to surmount the difficulties resulting from the 1918 defeat. As a leading historian of nineteenth-century Germany, Erich Marcks, stated, it was "something new with the promise of a future."[9]

But before these promises could be fulfilled, historians would have to undo the kleindeutsch myths they had so laboriously fashioned. A commitment to kleindeutsch historiography implied a belief in the separateness of the Austrian. If such an attitude persisted, would the citizens of the Reich continue to desire a union with Austria? Would the Austrians not be deterred from demanding it? The young Catholic historian, Martin Spahn, expressed an urgency even his elders shared. Spahn contended that if the Germans "retained their kleindeutsch mentality, then the Anschluss will never be completed."[10] Friedrich Meinecke, Hermann Oncken, Willy Andreas—many of the most respected leaders of the profession—were committed to replacing symbols of Hohenzollern statecraft with those more in conformity with the new reality. By expanding the concept of the nation to include Austria, these historians sought to restructure the middle-class conception of German nationalism, to lay the groundwork for accepting the Austrians as partners in the enlarged Reich.[11] It was an unabashedly political task, but there was no suggestion that this work would conflict with academic integrity. German and Austrian scholars were prepared with strong arguments against any narrow conception of their professional role. The Viennese professor, Heinrich von Srbik, urged his German colleagues to consider history as more than a mere technique for explaining the past; they were to judge their work by standards derived from the goals of the national community. Erich Keyser went even further and enjoined the professional historian to

---

[9] Erich Marcks, "Auf- und Niedergang im deutschen Schicksal," *Archiv für Politik und Geschichte* 8 (1929): 13. Meinecke's enthusiasm for the same future was expressed in *Strassburg/Freiburg/Berlin* (Stuttgart, 1949), p. 267. See the discussion of Austria's importance for German historical writing in Heinrich von Srbik, *Geist und Geschichte* (Munich, 1951), II: 15 ff., and Hans Herzfeld, "Staat und nation in der deutschen Geschichtsschreibung der Weimarer Zeit."

[10] Martin Spahn, "Die Anschlussfrage und die Zukunft des Reich," *Volk und Reich* 2 (1926): 50.

[11] Willy Andreas wrote prolifically on the Anschluss; see his 1922 essay in *Kämpfe um Volk und Reich* (Stuttgart, 1934), pp. 216–41; idem, *Die Reichspost*, June 6, 1930, and *Österreich und der Anschluss* (Berlin, 1927), pp. 14–18. Hermann Oncken's 1924 essay was reprinted in *Nation und Geschichte* (Berlin, 1935), pp. 15–42. Meinecke's works are cited throughout the chapter.

withhold evidence that might hinder the achievement of national aims.[12]

At first glance, this reinterpretation did not seem to present insurmountable difficulties. The way had already been prepared by the movement for a German-dominated *Mitteleuropa* in World War I. The promise implicit in such a construction turned academicians from an exclusive interest in a Prussian-centered Reich. And these hopes did not die with the end of war. In the 1920s Vienna still seemed an ideal base for the German economic and political penetration of Southeastern Europe. This view necessitated a reappraisal of the Austrian Germans who would become partners in this newly formed Mitteleuropa.[13]

The opposition to such a reevaluation was also eased by a changing of the guard within the historical profession itself. By 1919 the founders of the kleindeutsch school were dead. There were, it is true, still supporters of Hohenzollern-centered history in the succeeding generation of scholars, but their numbers were diminishing. The most important loss was Reinhold Koser, the definitive biographer of Frederick the Great, who died in 1914. Most scholars of this new generation did not feel impelled to create pro-Prussian historical myths after 1918. The most successful prewar defender of Hohenzollern traditions, Otto Hintze, had a genuine conversion to Europe as a whole and rebuked his colleagues for their single-minded attention to Germany. The influential popularizer, Erich Marcks, found pressing political reasons to reevaluate Austria's role. Kleindeutsch historical writing suddenly became out of fashion and its proponents suffered the rebukes of nonconformity. The standard work on German historiography brushed this interpretation aside as untenable. And a young scholar could confidently declare that "Droysen's Prussian historiography belongs to a period that lies behind us."[14]

---

[12] Heinrich von Srbik, *Gesamtdeutsche Geschichtsauffassung* (Leipzig, 1932), p. 5; Erich Keyser, *Die Geschichtswissenschaft, Aufbau und Aufgaben* (Munich, 1931), p. 167. Srbik's views had already been articulated by Georg von Below in *Die deutsche Geschichtsschreibung von Befreiungskriegen bis zu unsern Tagen* (Munich, 1924), p. 114.

[13] For *Mitteleuropa*, see Theodor Heuss, *Friedrich Naumann* (Stuttgart, 1937), pp. 307 ff.; Henry Cord Meyer, *Mitteleuropa in German Thought and Action* (The Hague, 1955), pp. 196–205; Paul Sweet, "Recent German Literature on Mitteleuropa," *Journal of Central European Affairs* 3 (1943): 1–24.

[14] Felix Gilbert, *Johann Gustav Droysen und die preussisch-deutsche Frage* ("Beiheft XX der Historischen Zeitschrift"; Munich, 1931), p. 4. The standard historiographical work cited is Georg von Below, *Die deutsche Geschichtsschreibung*, p. 49. The most thorough discussion of Hintze can be found in Gerhard Ostreich's foreward to Otto Hintze, *Gesammelte Abhandlungen* 2 (Göttingen, 1964). For Erich Marcks, see n. 9.

Yet this view was too optimistic. The Prussian victory of 1866 was still eulogized by a whole school of unreconstructed kleindeutsch historians, such as Erich Brandenburg, Dietrich Schäfer, and Albert von Hofmann. Brandenburg was the best scholar of the group, but he was difficult, stubborn, and rigid. "It is hard to talk to Brandenburg," wrote Friedrich Meinecke. "He is hard of hearing and hard-headed."[15] Refusing the lead of other professionals, Brandenburg hardly changed a jot of his Hohenzollern nostalgia. He rejected Droysen's teleology as naive, but still managed to find a miraculous correspondence between Prussia and German destiny. He claimed that while the Prussian rulers had not actively pursued a conscious German policy, they had achieved the same results by following a policy of raison d'état. "They were forced by the situation of the state itself to represent German interests even if their motives were only the protection and the increase of their own state's power."[16]

As with Treitschke and Droysen, Brandenburg's Prussian teleology was accompanied by attacks against Austria. Yet, surprisingly, despite his view of Austrian history, Brandenburg favored the Anschluss. He did not undergo a transformation similar to that of his colleagues. He remained convinced that the Austrians had been irremediably ruined by Habsburg rule, and he did not relish adding these people to the Reich. Brandenburg only supported the Anschluss for reasons of Realpolitik. It could be used as a lever with which to budge the entire Versailles system.[17]

Brandenburg's position was extreme only when viewed within the perspective of the historical profession. Almost all historians had made some accommodation to the postwar reality, but a small minority of Germans did not. There were die-hard Hohenzollern loyalists who refused to accept Austria on any terms. True to its eighty-year tradition of Prussian conservatism, the Kreuzzeitung argued that both Prussia and Austria could never be included in one Germany. If Bismarck had wanted the Austrians, he would have added them in 1866! But Bismarck had recognized the impossibility of overcoming the North-South dualism deeply rooted in German history, present at the battles between Maria Theresa and Frederick II, derived from

[15] Friedrich Meinecke, Werke (Stuttgart, 1957–62), VI: 173.

[16] Erich Brandenburg, Die Reichsgründung (Leipzig, 1923), I: 95. See also Albert von Hofmann, Politische Geschichte der Deutschen (Stuttgart, 1928), V: 15, 457; Dietrich Schäfer, "Oesterreich, Preussen, Deutschland. Deutsche Geschichte in grossdeutscher Beleuchtung," Deutschlands Erneuerung 10 (1926): 400.

[17] Brandenburg, Die Reichsgründung, II: 463; "Bismarcks Reichsgründung und die Gegenwart," Süddeutsche Monatshefte 18 (1921): 262. Similar views were expressed by Hofmann, "Die Wege der deutschen Geschichte," Deutschland: Die natürlichen Grundlagen seiner Kultur (Leipzig, 1928), p. 362.

an obscure struggle between forgotten tribes in the first century.[18] Few Germans were convinced by this argument and the *Kreuzzeitung* was universally denounced. Even such Prussian conservatives as Count Kuno Westarp and Gottfried Treviranus were forced to repudiate the editorial publicly.[19]

Both Brandenburg and the *Kreuzzeitung* editors fundamentally accepted a permanent German dualism that never could be fully resolved. Was this assumption correct? A recognizable Austrian culture might not have survived the Anschluss. Many Austrians, such as the historian Viktor Bibl, accepted the Anschluss as the ultimate victory for the kleindeutsch idea, and such views were not confined to the Austrians. Heinrich Wolf, a racist historian, who argued that Austria could have easily been absorbed into the Bismarckian Reich, was even more contemptuous of Austrian character than Brandenburg. He believed that the Austrians had betrayed their weakness as unsatisfactory soldiers at the front during the war. Yet Wolf still maintained that the Anschluss could cleanse Austria by totally submerging the Alpine and Viennese ways of life into the kleindeutsch-Prussian stream.[20]

Adolf Hitler was just the politician to put these ideas into practice. Hitler had early adopted the kleindeutsch mythology and viewed Frederick the Great as an eternal symbol of national resurrection, while attacking the Habsburgs as traitors. Remembering his youthful frustrations, Hitler railed against the Viennese, whom he considered as either "theatrical babblers of the putrid bourgeois elements" or the "Marxist enemies of Germany."[21] Such contempt meant rejecting a large role for Austrians in his party. It even could be seen in other party leaders. As early as 1923, some Bavarian Nazis protested against the influence of what they thought of as a *Junker*-oriented, Prussianized, anti-Catholic faction in the party. These disputes grew out of an already superheated atmosphere in the émigré circle in Austria after the failure of the Munich *Putsch*. They were a response to Alfred Rosenberg's attacks on Catholicism which seemed to show the dominance of a Prussian-Protestant teleology at the Munich headquarters during Hitler's absence.[22]

[18] *Kreuzzeitung*, July 23, 1927.

[19] *Der Anschluss*, August 15, 1927; *Münchner Zeitung*, August 21, 1927; *Österreich-Deutschland* 4 (August 1927): 6.

[20] Heinrich Wolf, *Angewandte Geschichte* (Berlin, 1920 ff.), I: 431–32; V: 250-54.

[21] *Hitler's Secret Book* (New York, 1961), p. 192. See also *Mein Kampf* (Boston, 1943), pp. 68–74.

[22] The attempted assumption of control over the Austrian party is discussed in chapter III. For the events of 1923, see Ernst Hanfstaegl, "Erwiderung auf die von Kapt. Lt. A. D. Erklärung. . . ," pp. 7–8, NSDAP Hauptarchiv, Reel

Although a tenaciously held opinion, unreconciled kleindeutsch historiography was not the major obstacle to forging a unified scheme for German history. The real problem lay with the lingering kleindeutsch belief present even in those historians and politicians who were ostensibly committed to a reevaluation of Austria's role. German historians had been trained to admire Prussia as the lifeblood of German idealism, as representative of the genius of the German state, and they showed little intention of undermining these Prussian traditions. Sometimes this view was stated stridently: "I was born a Prussian," wrote Erich Marcks, "and I intend to die a Prussian."[23] Sometimes this commitment was made almost apologetically. Friedrich Meinecke recognized that Prussia had left an ambiguous heritage— "at the same time the strongest particularist and the strongest champion of the need for Germany unity."[24] But even he did not advocate a complete break with the past by turning his back upon the Hohenzollerns' accomplishments.

Very few historians had Meinecke's sophistication. They could not elaborate the contradictions in their own thought between their kleindeutsch training and their new interpretations. Young nationalist scholars, such as Wilhelm Schüssler, defended the necessity of creating the kleindeutsch empire of 1866. Thus he enunciated a thinly disguised version of Brandenburg's hypothesis on the connection between Prussian *raison d'état* and national destiny. Similarly, Adolf Rapp of Tübingen argued for the elimination of Germanic particularism, while underrating the possibilities of a German confederation under Austrian leadership before 1866. Even Franz Schnabel, who undertook the principal revision of Treitschke, was suspicious of Austria. Schnabel's sympathies were quite clearly with the Napoleonic-era Prussian reform movement rather than with conservative Austria. Moreover he seemed to associate Austria with tasks of a European rather than a purely German nature.[25]

33, Folder 636; Hanfstaegl, *Hitler: The Missing Years* (London, 1957), p. 81. The Bavarians especially objected to the editorial policy of the *Völkischer Beobachter*, by then in Rosenberg's hands although Dietrich Eckart held *de jure* control until December, 1923; see Serge Lang and Ernst von Schenck, *Portrait eines Menschheitsverbrechers* (St. Gallen, 1947), pp. 74, 102–3.

[23] Erich Marcks, *Geschichte und Gegenwart* (Stuttgart, 1925), p. 153.

[24] Meinecke, *Werke* V: 460. See also ibid. II: 304–5; Meinecke in *Neue Freie Presse*, September 29, 1927, a.m.

[25] Wilhelm Schüssler, *Oesterreich und das deutsche Schicksal* (Leipzig, 1925), p. 211. Schüssler was attacked by grossdeutsch Austrians in *Das Neue Reich* 7 (1926): 1061. Adolf Rapp, *Der deutsche Gedanke* (Bonn, 1920), pp. 82, 163–64; idem, *Das österreichische Problem in den Plänen der Kaiserpartei von 1848* (Tübingen, 1919), pp. 3 ff.; idem, *Grossdeutsch und Kleindeutsch*, p. xxii and passim. Franz Schnabel, *Deutsche Geschichte im neunzehnten Jahrhundert* 2

The academicians' failure to provide an unambiguous leadership affected another critical area—primary and secondary education. In the long run, the reindoctrination on Austria could be carried out most effectively through the schools. As one prominent textbook writer commented: "A truly good historical education is the best preparation for Anschluss."[26] While the educational establishment favored Anschluss, it could not uproot the lingering kleindeutsch interpretations. A recent analysis of German history texts illustrates this dilemma. Although paying lip service to the goal of Anschluss, these textbooks were still built on Prussian foundations. If William I was no longer venerated as a dynast, his personal qualities were praised and his chancellor remained the epitome of German accomplishment.[27] Franz Eggersdorfer, a Bavarian professor of education, feared that this teaching would permanently undermine the Anschluss movement.

All grossdeutsch revisionist oratory will mean little if the historical teaching remains kleindeutsch, if the study of one's native land (*Heimatkunde*) and of geography considers the borders of Germany as the national frontier, when the textbooks and class lectures only recognize the great men of Reich Germany. Are not today in the Reich German schools the victories of Frederick the Great over Maria Theresa fought joyfully from the standpoint of the conquerer without thinking that the human and German greatness of his opponent could also deserve the same admiration? Is not the war against Napoleonic oppression considered as the definitive movement for German national freedom while the preceding lonely struggle of Austria receives scant attention?[28]

Historians had to eradicate this remnant of kleindeutsch thought. But what method could they use when kleindeutsch historiography was so embedded in the whole interpretative framework of German history? At first glance there were two alternatives open to them, both labeled grossdeutsch although rooted in vastly different traditions.

German democracy had already found the Anschluss an especially propitious question, the one area of national policy in which democrats had clearly taken the lead. As shown in chapter III, in 1848 democrats had been grossdeutsch; they had demanded the inclusion

(Freiburg, 1933), passim; idem, "Die politische Entwicklung" (eds.) W. Hofstaetter and F. Panzer, *Grundzüge der Deutschkunde* (Leipzig, 1925), II: 19–64.

[26] Bernhard Kumsteller, "Fragen der Angleichung, Anschlussarbeit der Geschichtslehrer," *Österreich-Deutschland* 7 (July 1930): 9.

[27] Schallenberg, *Zum Geschichtsbild*, pp. 168–76, 195–203.

[28] Franz Eggersdorfer, *Das reichsdeutsche und österreichische Bildungswesen im Vergleich zu einander* (Munich, 1927), p. 12. For confirmation of lingering Hohenzollern nostalgia in the German schools see, R. H. Samuel and R. Hinton Thomas, *Education and Society in Modern Germany* (London, 1949), pp. 80–81.

of the German-speaking Austrians in the Reich. Yet these democrats provided a basis for political rhetoric more than for historical interpretation. Only a handful of democratic writers undertook any extended refutation of Hohenzollern legends; none of them were academicians. The historical profession was unprepared to accept such a radical departure. It stigmatized these works as propaganda masterpieces but horrors of interpretation.[29]

The main body of historians also attacked another form of grossdeutsch thought centered around Bismarck's old opponents who continued the traditions of nineteenth-century grossdeutsch historiography. These opponents were Catholics who identified both contemporary and historical Prussia with Protestant materialism and Bavarian and Hanoverian legitimists who still sustained their ancient dynastic quarrels with Prussia. The professional historians generally dismissed such views as vestigial, but they still feared the possible political consequences of such opinions.[30] Accordingly, while reviewing a book by an Austrian historian of this grossdeutsch school, Wilhelm Schüssler maintained:

It is important to bridge these contradictions [based on tradition and religion] as much as possible, to set aside what separates and emphasize the common. It is unfortunate that . . . the so called "grossdeutsch" historical writing again recalls the old contradictions and considers the past in a false historical perspective. . . . This is especially unfortunate because of the changes which have occurred since the 1918 collapse . . . when we stand in far-reaching agreement about the immediate future—namely the Anschluss with Austria.[31]

[29] See the revisionist works by a Bavarian poet and a displaced architect: Herbert Eulenberg, *The Hohenzollerns* (New York, 1929), pp. viii ff.; Werner Hegemann, *Frederick the Great* (London, 1929), pp. 303–13. These works were reviewed in *Historische Zeitschrift*, 138 (1928): 604–14, 626–32. For a discussion of these books and their reviews, see Oscar Hammen, "German Historians and the Advent of the National Socialist State," *Journal of Modern History* 13 (1941): 175–77, and S. D. Stirk, *The Prussian Spirit* (London, 1941), pp. 125–35.

[30] Hans Rost, "Die vierhundertjährige Zerstörung des grossdeutschen Gedankens," *Das Neue Reich* 9 (1926–27): 109–11, 174–76, 430, 452–54, 522; Albert von Ruville, "Die politische Bedeutung und positive Leistung des Hauses Habsburg in der Geschichte," *Schönere Zukunft* 6 (1930): 1105; *Hannoversche Landeszeitung*, December 13, 1924; Rudolf Henle, "Deutsche Geschichte, Gegenwart und Zukunft," *Schönere Zukunft* 4 (1928): 248; Heinrich Triepel, "Der Föderalismus und die Revision der Weimarer Reichsverfassung," *Zeitschrift für Politik* 14 (1925): 412–24; Heinrich Otto Meisner, " Preussen und Revisionismus," *Forschungen zur brandenburgischen und preussischen Geschichte* 43 (1931): 252–89.

[31] *Historische Vierteljahrschrift* 24 (1928): 289. The book reviewed was Raimund Friedrich Kaindl, *Oesterreich, Preussen, Deutschland* (Vienna, 1926). For similar comments see, H. Ruider, " Aus Oesterreich," *Historisches Jahrbuch* 47 (1927): 766–70; Dietrich Schäfer, *Österreich Preussen, Deutschland*," pp. 389–400.

There were still other alternatives for overcoming kleindeutsch thought, alternatives that sprang from neither republican nor monarchist traditions. A younger, more flexible generation of historians began to see the dichotomy as simply another consequence of German dualism rather than an adequate tool for reconstructing the past. These younger historians rejected both sides of the dichotomy, of course, but they were particularly effective in straightforwardly attacking the whole edifice of fact upon which the kleindeutsch interpretation had been built. Schnabel (born in 1887) debunked the Prussian claims of national leadership before 1840. Wilhelm Mommsen (born in 1892) thought that the grossdeutsch-kleindeutsch dichotomy had been exaggerated. He believed that the Frankfurt Parliament in 1848 had supported Prussian leadership out of political necessity rather than anti-Austrianism. In reality, "the large mass of kleindeutsch politicians were grossdeutsch in their hearts."[32] Egmont Zechlin (born in 1896) maintained that Prussia and Austria had simply been bound by their position within the European state system; both national policies had been motivated by *raison d'état*; neither had been inherently superior. While occasionally succumbing to nationalist rhetoric, Hans Rothfels (born in 1891) dealt the final blow to the mythic structure of *Kleindeutschland*. He depicted Bismarck as the product of East Elbian society, as a particularistic Prussian and a cosmopolitan European but never a narrow German nationalist.[33]

Dualism could be overcome by other methods more philosophical in origin and more propagandistic in intent. These methods did not seek to minimize the kleindeutsch-grossdeutsch contradictions but rather were designed to build upon them. By retaining the old dichotomies, the historians were able to restructure the German national mythology without appearing to break with the past. Since they could concern themselves with familiar themes, they did not have to undertake a complete reeducation of their audience. Such an approach is probably the most effective propaganda. It accords with the social scientists' contention that propaganda works best when it appears to reinforce existing opinion rather than cause a fundamental change in attitude.[34]

These methods also had another advantage. They were complemented by the impulse of German philosophy to resolve opposites

<hr/>

[32] Wilhelm Mommsen, "Zur Beurteilung der deutschen Einheitsbewegung," *Historische Zeitschrift* 138 (1928): 542.

[33] Egmont Zechlin, *Bismarck und die Grundlegung der deutschen Grossmach* (Stuttgart, 1930), pp. 2–8; Hans Rothfels, *Bismarck und der Osten* (Leipzig, 1934), pp. 7–14, 34–37, 71.

[34] Bernard Berelson and Gary Steiner, *Human Behavior, an Inventory of Scientific Findings* (New York, 1964), pp. 541–42.

through strife. Thus Erich Marcks could enthusiastically proclaim: "North and South, lands of old and new faith push against each other full of life, full of contradictions. Such was and is the German world."[35] By making these conflicts an inherent part of history, he had robbed them of any meaning. Then both Frederick and Maria Theresa could be unambiguously Germanic; the battles of the Seven Years' War need never be refought. Reinhold Schneider praised the greatness of both rulers, strengthened by equally viable dynastic traditions. Willy Andreas went even further and installed the two old enemies in the Pantheon of German heroes.[36]

If such statements served to reduce tension, they were only partial amelioratives. The acceptance of two coequal traditions precluded any synthesis that would eliminate both as unnecessary contradictions. Wilhelm Bauer, the Viennese historian, and Moritz Bonn, the Berlin political scientist, were representative of a group that demanded more than mere toleration. They saw the Anschluss as the instrument for molding a new Germanic man who would combine Prussian thoroughness with the Austrian understanding for everything human.[37] But even such statements were not strong enough for völkisch historians who saw this new man as more than a pale composite of Austrian and German characteristics, his whole more than the sum of his parts. He could only gain strength by evolving organically as part of the nation. And this organic unity would be achieved through a mystical union between German man and his soil. Germans were therefore directed to become at one with their landscape and region.[38]

There was to be a truly völkisch history designed to restore the proper relation between man and his region, man and his landscape. Völkisch history was by no means as sympathetic to the state as kleindeutsch history had been. It tended to consider many states as artificial elements which distorted the natural relationship between man and his landscape. Using these standards, it often viewed the absolutism of princely houses as divisive foreign encrustations on Germanic soil. Erich Keyser, the Danzig historian, redefined methodology on

[35] Erich Marcks, "Auf- und Niedergang," p. 28.

[36] Reinhold Schneider, Die Hohenzollern, Tragik und Königtum (Leipzig, 1933), p. 191; Willy Andreas, Geist und Staat (Munich, 1922), pp. 88–128.

[37] Wilhelm Bauer, Oesterreich in dem reichsdeutschen Geschichtsschulbüchern (Berlin, 1927), p. 12; Bonn's views were expressed in the Neue Freie Presse, May 31, 1925, a.m. For a view that the South was absolutely necessary for German salvation, see Bavarian press reports, Haniel to Berlin, May 18, 1927, AA 4491/K920/K228322–K228333.

[38] See Philipp Funk, "Weg der Geschichtsrevision," Hochland 25 (1928): 637–43. For a definition of landscape and its connection with the Volk, see George Mosse, The Crisis of German Ideology (New York, 1964), pp. 15–17.

the basis of population, space, and culture, while slighting traditional dynastic politics. Josef Nadler, a Prague-trained philologist, believed that German culture resulted from the creativity of regional groupings which only incidentally corresponded with dynastic boundaries. Both recognized a power in the *Volk* to overcome all contradiction and melt away political animosities. The North-South opposition was caused by a princely inspired dualism and appeared unimaginably small when viewed from the heights of völkisch purpose. A new German whole, built on regional diversity, could include Austrians as well as Prussians.[39]

A typical example of this viewpoint can be found in the work of the Viennese musicologist, Robert Lach. Lach believed that the differences between North and South German musical styles were caused by variation in the landscape. "The melancholy heaths and moorlands, the dusty grey clouds" of the typical North German landscape found expression in the intensity of Bach and Handel, while "the mild landscape of the Vienna woods" engendered the more classical and lyrical styles of Mozart and Haydn.

Both groups are separate, yet both are part of each other through the German spirit that lives in them. Do not Bach, Handel and Schubert, Haydn and Mozart, belong to each other as Germany and Austria? Are they not unified in the common living German spirit as Beethoven united German and Austrian music? And is not Beethoven a symbol of this unification of the German and Austrian soul, a symbol that will eternally stand?[40]

A Viennese professor, Heinrich von Srbik, coined the name for this supradynastic history—*gesamtdeutsch*. While most historians were willing to designate their unified history as grossdeutsch, Srbik desired a complete terminological break with the past. Grossdeutsch could be confused with Habsburg legitimism. In any case, old names recalled old animosities, implicitly led historians into old argumentative traps, and succeeded in fixing allegiances to one of the great Germanic houses. Gesamtdeutsch interpretations replaced dualistic quarrels with an attempt to assess impartially both Habsburg and Hohenzollern contributions. Austria had been the bearer of the old supranational imperial ideals and the newer faith of Mitteleuropa. Prussia had been the prime example of strong national government. Yet these

---

[39] Keyser, *Geschichtswissenschaft*, pp. 87–105; Josef Nadler, *Literaturgeschichte der deutschen Stämme und Landschaften* (Regensberg, 1913), II: ii, iv–v, and passim. See Hammen, "German Historians," 182–84.

[40] Robert Lach, "Die grossdeutsche Kultureinheit in der Musik" (eds.) Kleinwaechter and Paller, *Die Anschlussfrage*, pp. 294–95.

areas of competence were not mutually exclusive; they were concentric circles of human experience and need never conflict. Not only had Srbik learned to live with Germanic contradictions; he had made them compatible. "In the co-existent, in the successive, in the reciprocal relationships of the universal, the Central European (mitteleuropäische), and the nation-state movement, I see the most profound problem for German history, the present and the configuration of the future."[41]

Srbik's magnum opus, *Deutsche Einheit*, was more than a contrivance to end the tension and provide the intellectual ammunition for Anschluss. It was a moral tale designed to overcome the defeatism of collapse and to serve as the restorative for German psychological wholeness. Having diagnosed the most painful of German neuroses, Srbik sought to overcome them with an impassioned, personal statement, a work of "love and sorrow."[42] Even after thirty years and despite its hopelessly opaque style, *Deutsche Einheit* can still move the reader by its sophistication and by the complexity and emotion of its vision. *Volk*, landscape, region, culture, power, space, ideology—all were at last molded into a final, if somewhat abstract, whole. Srbik was constructing a radical reinterpretation of the past to be used as the basis for a radically changed and more promising future. Despite its scholarly appurtenances, *Deutsche Einheit* was aimed directly at this future, at influencing the malleable youth who would undo the dualistic work of the previous generations.

This new generation takes up the obligations placed upon it by the needs of the Volk. It must consider the individual action in a total völkisch relationship, construct an organic unity for overcoming old quarrels, broaden the meaning of loyalty to include the Volk as well as the state and Reich. The task of German history is to help build a new German house on this foundation.[43]

Certainly the young were confronted by their less flexible elders, many of whom were Habsburg and Hohenzollern loyalists and thus Srbik's fiercest critics.[44] But these views seemed hardly to have influ-

---

[41] Heinrich von Srbik, *Deutsche Einheit, Idee und Wirklichkeit von Heiligen Reich bis Königgrätz* (Munich, 1935 ff.), I: 9. Srbik's early adhesion to National Socialist Germany has caused some historians to identify all of *Deutsche Einheit* with Hitlerian historiography; Jacques Droz correctly maintains that at least volume I of this work was a product of postwar and not post-1933 collapse; *Les révolutions allemandes de 1848* (Paris, 1957), pp. 17–18.

[42] Srbik, *Deutsche Einheit*, I: 7. Meinecke testified to the impassioned nature of Srbik's work: *Werke* VI: 152–54.

[43] Srbik, *Gesamtdeutsche Geschichtsauffassung*, p. 2.

[44] The two most devastating reviews by kleindeutsch historians were Fritz Hartung, "Preussen und die deutsche Einheit," *Forschungen zur branden-*

enced the young. Whatever their private doubts, the educational establishment was committed to the Anschluss. If textbooks showed lingering kleindeutsch attitudes, there were still numerous signs of agreement with the ideal of an Austro-German union.

The leaders of the professional educators' organizations were more responsive to change. The semiofficial *Preussische Lehrerzeitung* called for the instruction of all Germans in Austrian truths. As the historical journal linking university scholarship with the Gymnasium, *Vergangenheit und Gegenwart* continuously emphasized Austria's role in Germanic culture. The executives of the German Philological Association organized a meeting in Vienna where the membership was requested to recognize the unity of Northern and Southern German literary and artistic styles.[45]

At this point, the democratic grossdeutsch historiography could become merged with the more restrained academic variety. If the academicians would not totally accept the banners of the grossdeutsch democrats, they could agree with the central proposition of these democrats that Austria was a part of Germany. Thus, the sophisticated attempts of historians to deal with their lingering kleindeutsch belief were more of personal and professional than educational importance. For elementary and secondary education, the simple assertion—Austrians are Germans—was enough. Grossdeutsch republicans worked easily with academic historians and professional educators who were often more conservative in their politics. Led by a Prussian school official, the Volksbund Educational Committee organized student exchanges, planned for a future common educational system, and submitted a series of demands to reshape German textbooks even further by stressing Austrian contributions, especially those in the wars against the Turks, Louis XIV, and Napoleon.[46]

Since the public's near unanimity for Anschluss had made it a politically appealing issue, there was no reason why revisionist propaganda could not bear fruit. The Reichstag's Budget Committee asked the Interior Ministry to inspect textbooks in order to ascertain whether "the statement of Austrian history is not present in a manner

burgischen und preussischen Geschichte 49 (1937): 1–21; and Erich Brandenburg, "Deutsche Einheit," *Historische Vierteljahrschrift* 30 (1936): 757–70.

[45] *Preussische Lehrerzeitung*, quoted in *Österreich-Deutschland* 4 (September 1927): 18; *Vergangenheit und Gegenwart* 14 (1924): 154–56; 15 (1925): 193–251; 17 (1927): 325–54, 405–22; the position of the Philological Association was reprinted in Felix Behrend (ed.), *Das grössere Deutschland, Deutsche Zukunft* (Leipzig, 1929).

[46] Alois Bradl, "Der Schulauschuss des österreichisch-deutschen Volksbunds," *Österreich-Deutschland* 3 (January 1926): 2; ibid. 8 (January 1930): 8–9.

unfavorable to the grossdeutsch ideal and the goal of Anschluss with Austria."[47] However the central government in Berlin could do little; education was the province of the federal states. But even decentralization of authority could scarcely complicate such a popular issue. If Bavarian curricular instructions emphasized only participation in the völkisch community without specifically mentioning Anschluss, their next door neighbor, Württemberg, directed teachers to create an understanding for the fate of German-Austria. And Prussia, most important of all, demanded that an understanding of Austria's importance be awakened in the young.[48]

With such authority on its side, supradynastic history would eventually prevail in the schools, but an entirely successful gesamt-deutsch education would have to reach the adult as well as the pupil. Here the central government could take positive action through its information service, the Reichszentrale für Heimatdienst. Operating directly under the chancellor, the Reichszentrale financed the publication of pro-Anschluss historical works, supported over 136 lectures in all parts of Germany, provided financial subvention for pro-union meetings in Austria. It also arranged functions in Germany at which Schüssler and Löbe were the principal speakers. More typical, however, were eight lectures given during January 1929 in Thuringia and Saxony by a certain Frau Pokorny on Austrian and South Tyrolean art or the thirty lectures of her fellow Viennese, General von Einem, delivered all over Germany in 1926 and 1927 on "How can the Reich Germans learn to know German Austria?" The Reichszentrale expressed satisfaction with the success of its efforts, even offered to extend its functions into Austria, and proclaimed that "a good part of the growing German understanding for Austria goes back to the steady and planned propaganda work of the Reichszentrale."[49]

The official apparatus was supplemented in many ways; the strongest unofficial efforts were made by the Anschluss lobby. The

---

[47] *Verhandlungen des Reichstags*, CCCCXIV, *Anlagen zu den stenographischen Berichten*, Nr. 3095, p. 9.

[48] *Amtsblatt des Bayerischen Staatsministeriums für Unterricht und Kultur*, LX, Nr. 16, December 29, 1926; *Amtsblatt des Württembergischen Kulturministeriums*, February 18, 1926; Walter Landé, *Richtlinen für die Lehrpläne der höheren Schulen Preussens* (Berlin, 1925), p. 65.

[49] Reichszentrale für Heimatdienst report to Chancellor, 1929, ARk 4619/K1064/K273350. The information service's files were never microfilmed in sequence; however, many documents pertaining to Austria can be found in Reichskanzlei microcopy and in the Reichskanzlei files, Bundesarchiv Koblenz, especially Folders R43I/109 and R43I/110. The most effective book subsidized by the Reichszentrale was Heinz von Paller, *Der grossdeutsche Gedanke* (Leipzig, 1928). For subvention to the Right-wing organized Grossdeutsche Tagung, see Foreign Office memo, May 5, 1927, AA 4491/K920/K228815.

Volksbund was committed to reeducating the Germans by emphasizing Austrian culture in its journals, by introducing slide lectures on such topics as "Gay Vienna," by printing thousands of pamphlets entitled *German-Austria's Contributions to German Literature*, by calling attention to Austria's musical preeminence, by supporting tours of the Vienna a capella choir and the Vienna philharmonic.[50]

In the long run, this concerted effort would certainly become successful. The German historical profession had created a new set of symbols to explain Austria's role in German history. These symbols were transferred from the lecture room to elementary, secondary, and adult education. It would only be a matter of time before the educational institutions eradicated their lingering kleindeutsch thought. Brandenburg and the unreformed kleindeutsch historiography had become effectively isolated; Hitler's kleindeutsch views seemed to have little following. Yet such a revision did not touch the fundamental propositions that most Germans held about their nation; it did not transform the several views of the good society into one. As in the political side of the Anschluss movement, differing forces could cooperate for fixed and purposive goals even when they could not agree as to the final disposition of the nation. Thus democratic grossdeutsch historiography could be put in harness with the far more conservative opinions of the German historical establishment, so that Austria might be saved for the Reich. What kind of Reich was Austria being saved for? This question was still open to dispute.

[50] *Österreich-Deutschland,* the official journal of the Volksbund, carried a series on "German Austrian Literature" from its first issue, 1 (January 1926): 19 and passim; see also ibid. 3 (April 1926): 20–21; 5 (April 1928): 19–20; 6 (January 1929): 23.

THE ANSCHLUSS QUESTION IN
GERMAN FOREIGN POLICY

CHAPTER V   THE POSSIBILITIES OF ACCOMPLISHING THE ANSCHLUSS

IT WAS EASIER for Germans to fit Austria into their national symbolism than to annex the land itself. Germans might almost unanimously agree upon the final aim of national unification, but the problem still remained of completing the Anschluss. Prohibited by the allies, the Anschluss could not be achieved without a new war or a diplomatic revolution. It was to the latter that the hopes of the Anschluss movement turned.

After all, Wilson had promised to reconstruct Europe upon the principle of national self-determination. Wilson believed in the necessity for each people to control its own destiny through the democratic process. Such an assumption was certainly acceptable to German socialists and democrats. The SPD and DDP bemoaned the fact that self-determination was applied to all the other nations but their own. They claimed to be demanding only what had been granted to these other nations.

Implicit in self-determination is the acceptance of democracy as a political system. Yet conservatives who opposed democracy could still use this principle to justify the restitution of the land given to Poland and the removal of obstacles against the Anschluss. Most political groups believed that these lands were German by a right which was flaunted in the allied prohibitions. Thus all political colorations in the Anschluss movement had succeeded in adopting an apparently impregnable moral position. From this bastion, they could exercise a kind of self-hypnosis by which at least the virtues of the allies were weakened and those of Germany strengthened.

The German and Austrian foreign ministries knew that no exaggerated rhetoric could possibly transform the foreign policy situation of the Reich. German diplomats believed that only time would provide the answer. They hoped that time would give Stresemann an opportunity to settle the continuing disputes with Germany's western neighbors before turning his attention eastward. They gambled that time might lessen the suspicion of Germany accruing from the war.

They hoped that, in time, the allies could consider the addition of Austria as something less than an annexation. The signs of Franco-German rapprochement after 1925 seemed to buttress the case of the diplomats. German democrats also believed Locarno had opened new avenues. They thought that proper manipulation of this opportunity could lead to an Anschluss. But these hopes proved unfulfilled.

The opposition was strongly entrenched in France, Italy, and Czechoslovakia, where few showed any disposition to change their opinions. Dominating the foreign policy of their respective countries during this period, the Czech and French foreign ministers, Eduard Beneš and Aristide Briand, were joined by Mussolini in this concern. The Italian fascist leader was unwilling to share a common border with the Reich. He believed that Anschluss would make the Reich the protector of German minority rights in South Tyrol. This was a situation he wished to avoid at all costs. Also Mussolini and a great part of the Italian press viewed the Anschluss as an instrument of German expansionism—pan-Germanism as they frequently called it. An enlarged Reich would play a more substantial role in Southeastern Europe, an area that the Italian leader had already staked out as his own.[1]

The Czech motives were somewhat similar to those of the Italians. Czech leaders recognized that the union would make the Sudeten Germans restless under Slavic rule. Even more important, these leaders saw the Anschluss as threatening the very existence of the Czechoslovak state. The enlarged Reich would surround Czechoslovakia on three sides and thus make its defense all but impossible. The post-Anschluss Germanic state would also take such a large proportion of Czech exports as to make Prague an economic client of Berlin and Vienna. It is no wonder that Beneš felt compelled to oppose the Anschluss at every turn. Desperately, compulsively, the Czech Foreign Minister repeated the same statement to diplomats, journalists, and even German politicians. He argued that the Austro-German union could only be achieved by disrupting Europe. Intimating that Czechoslovakia would oppose such a union by force, he constantly reiterated: "The Anschluss question is a question of war and peace."[2]

France possessed greater freedom of the press than Italy. Anschluss would not change the situation of France's western border. Therefore there was less unanimity in Paris than in Prague or Rome. Some Left-

---

[1] See chapters VIII and XIII.

[2] Marek to Vienna, May 31, 1928, NPA Fasz. 64, Zl. 78 Pol.; Ludwig Zimmermann, *Deutsche Aussenpolitik in der Ära der Weimarer Republik* (Berlin, 1958), p. 408. See also chapters VIII and XIII.

wing politicians were willing to accept the Austro-German union. The pacifist, Gustav Hervé, and the president of the League for the Rights of Man, Viktor Basch, did not believe that an Anschluss would endanger world peace. The communists demanded revisions in the Versailles treaty. The socialist leader, Leon Blum, summed up the opinion of many of the French Left when he contended: "Socialism has proclaimed repeatedly the right of self-determination of peoples. . . . I can find no reason why this right should not be conceded to contemporary Austria or to any other peoples."[3]

Yet even Blum worried that the Anschluss might precipitate a general European crisis. He pleaded with the Austrian Minister in Paris to be patient. He argued that the eight postwar years had seen enormous changes; he asked for forbearance until the inevitable union could be achieved.[4] Other French politicians were even more convinced that the Anschluss would be the prelude to a European conflict, since they were determined to go to war over this question. They believed that German expansion would have to be fought at all costs or the security of the French state would be endangered. There was general agreement on this point in most of the French press, including newspapers representing such diverse groups as Radical Socialists and the Action Française. Most French journalists agreed that the Anschluss would upset the European balance of power in favor of the Reich. They saw Anschluss as only "the first step in the return of Germany to hegemony over Central Europe and the development of its influence in the Balkans and the East."[5]

The maintenance of Austrian independence had become a matter of great concern for the French nation. Even rapprochement with Germany would not change this fact. The Austrian Minister to Paris commented in 1926: "One cannot make a visit to the Quai d'Orsay without being expressly told that Thoiry and the policy of reconciliation with Germany will in no way change the French position against the Anschluss."[6] At other times, Briand clearly stated that France would go to war in order to avert a unilateral German attempt at Anschluss. He opposed the application of Wilsonian principles to the Germans and saw no conflict in this view with his self-image as a

[3] Leon Blum, "Anschluss—Warum nicht?" Österreich-Deutschland 5 (September 1928): 1. See also La Liberté quoted in Der Anschluss, November 15, 1927; ibid., August 15, 1928; Deutsche Einheit, May 31, August 31, 1928.

[4] Grünberger (Paris) to Vienna, October 22, 1926, NPA Fasz. 59, Zl. 6988/33 Pol.

[5] Le Temps, August 31, 1925. See also Le Figaro, August 31, 1925; Foreign Office memo, August 21, 1928, AA 4492/K920/K22981–K22983.

[6] Grünberger to Vienna, Oct. 22, 1926, NPA Fasz. 59, Z6988/33 Pol.

man of the Left. Briand clearly outlined his position in a speech to the Chamber of Deputies in December 1928. The italicized portions represent the responses from the Chamber.

It is a very notable formula which has been solemnly proclaimed, but that does not mean I agree to the "right of suicide." (*Very good! Very good! Very good!*) And this includes such destructive political plans as the Anschluss. . . . If, in the national interest, 10 percent of the people wish to safeguard their independence, do you believe that the right of self-determination shall prevail? I do not and never shall.[7]

How could the Austrian and German Anschluss supporters overcome such a solid front? After 1918 Germany could no longer rely upon the diplomacy of power politics backed by the threat of force. Disarmed and with a woefully inadequate army and navy, the Weimar republic had to construct its foreign policy upon some other basis. The democratic Anschluss movement appeared to have the answer. It looked to world opinion as the substitute for military preparedness. Before 1914, German middle-class intellectuais had been accustomed to confusing armed might with morality. After 1918, middle-class democrats joined with the socialists in attempting to find some viable policy based upon moral principles alone. But Beneš and Briand believed they were defending moral principles as well. Established French and Czech policy was not to be easily overturned. In the end, these moral stands were only useful for establishing a self-righteous position, both in foreign and internal politics. The German democrats and socialists claimed that the foreign opponents of Anschluss were to blame, since they were untrue to their democratic heritage.

The Germans could now pose as defenders of the European moral order. *Vorwärts*, the SPD organ, feigned an inability to understand how Beneš, "an educated man with leftist tendencies," could fear the unification of Austria with a democratic Germany.[8] The journals of the Anschluss movement argued that postwar France had abandoned its traditional role as leader of the progressive elements on the continent. They claimed that France was more interested in perpetuating the psychology of war than in reconstructing Europe. Franz Roders, a Cologne journalist, wrote: "The France of the Revolution has become the most conservative land in Europe. It maintains that it alone knows progress and is the mother of civilization. Yet in political matters, it recognizes no progress and no civilized development."[9] Some Anschluss supporters went so far as to comment that French

---

[7] *Débats parlementaires, Annales du Chambre des Députés*, CXXXVI, 640.
[8] *Vorwärts*, May 5, 1925, edition B.
[9] *Deutsche Einheit*, August 31, 1928. See *Der Anschluss*, September 15, 1928.

politicians had inherited the same Latin blood that flowed through Machiavelli's veins. However Machiavellianism was apparently also acquired through the environment, since the Slavic Beneš was also accused of slavishly following the apothegms of *The Prince*.[10] Others were kinder. Stresemann simply attributed the intransigence of the French to "the bad conscience of those who emphasized self-determination in the war and remember unhappily how hard they dealt with this principle in the stipulations of their peace treaties."[11]

Conservatives could also intone these Wilsonian principles. The right of self-determination was demanded by conservative interests, particularly the publications of the Austrian Anschluss organizations. The extreme antidemocratic forces also found these Wilsonian arguments congenial with their predisposition to accept the wickedness of France and Czechoslovakia. Weaned on the wartime patriotic agitation, the members of the radical Right could picture Germany as an innocent brought to the ground by French and Czech imperialism. They could contend that the Anschluss was necessary to protect their co-nationals in Austria against this imperialism. The National Socialists would even accept the Wilsonian language and proclaim their support for "the union of all Germans on the basis of the principle of self-determination of peoples."[12]

Thus conservatives and democrats were united in their demands for what they conceived as equal justice. Both groups associated guilt with the status quo; both groups agreed that the present European borders were the work of the devil. Very often relatively mild rumors of attempts to perpetuate the status quo precipitated a massive reaction. Thus, in 1926 and 1927 there was a great flurry over the proposal that the seat of the League be moved to Vienna. The idea was so well entrenched that the German Minister to Geneva discussed it as a possibility. The German, Austrian, and even the French press were filled with rumors that the move was imminent. From the *Völkischer Beobachter* and the *Kreuzzeitung* to the *Kölnische Zeitung* and *Vorwärts*, German newspapers were alarmed. Journalists and editors almost unanimously argued that the removal to Vienna would assure Austria's neutrality and thus its independence. Seipel was always believed to be the principal culprit behind the scheme. At one time he was supposed to be working in conjunction with Beneš, at

---

[10] *Der Anschluss*, October 15, 1927; Gustav Stolper, "Der Anschluss," *Der österreichische Volkswirt* 17 (1925): 903.

[11] Gustav Stresemann, *Vermächtnis* (Berlin, 1932–33), II: 441–42.

[12] *Rot-Weiss-Rot Buch* (Vienna, 1946), p. 2. See also *Gewissen* 9 (July 18, 1927): 1; Otto Maul, "Die politische-geographische Struktur," *Zeitschrift für Geopolitik* 8 (1931): 31–44; Kleo Player, "Der tschechische Druck auf die Donau," *Volk und Reich* 2 (1926): 447–53.

another with Mussolini, still in a third instance with the French Foreign Office.

Yet these fears had little basis in reality. There were no public statements emanating from the Austrian government. And, privately, by 1928 the Austrian Foreign Ministry had rejected any consideration of this plan because its accomplishment would have embittered relations with Switzerland.[13] Yet the rumors persisted. Devils are extraordinarily hard to kill. The Anschluss supporters in general, the democratic Left in particular, had too much emotional capital invested in the hoped-for union to let the slightest threat go unheeded. *Vorwärts* tried to reason against the move. If Vienna were chosen, Briand and Chamberlain would have to travel too far. Mussolini would never agree to meet in a city dominated by socialists. Yet such objections were hardly emotionally satisfying. *Vorwärts*, more easily, lapsed into hyperbolic rhetoric at once designed to prove Germany's righteousness as well as providing a cathartic for the fears that the Anschluss might never be completed. The Social Democratic newspaper was not alone. Hermann Kienzl, vice-chairman of the German Volksbund, argued that the League would transform Vienna into a center for world espionage. "It would naturally become the meeting place for international swindlers, conterfeiters, and all groups that are enemies of society."[14] The Austrian section of the Volksbund made a great show of dispassionate toleration. Its journal stated: "We declare that the Austro-German Volksbund will not oppose the League's coming to Vienna. But, on the day it arrives, the League will be greeted by a mass meeting for the Anschluss greater than any Vienna has yet experienced.[15]

There were a few breaches in this united front for the Anschluss. These were, however, never really serious. As we have seen in chapter IV, a few Hohenzollern loyalists maintained their traditional antagonism to the Anschluss. On the Left the communists were hardly interested. Also some pacifists challenged the moral basis of revision

---

[13] Foreign Office memo, NPA Fasz. 465, 20705 15 II 1928; letter from Karl Lahm to Paul Goldmann, February 3, 1928, AA 2346/4576/E173316–E173320; Lerchenfeld to Berlin, February 13, 1928, ibid., E173322; Köpke memo, December 13, 1928, ibid., E173323–E173325; Müller (Geneva) to Berlin, February 20, 1928, ibid., E173333; Lerchenfeld to Berlin, February 21, 1928, ibid., E173343; Stresemann memo of conversation with Wirth, April 4, 1928, ibid., E173398; Stresemann, *Vermächtnis*, III: 330–31; *Berliner Tageblatt*, February 6, 1928, p.m.; *Der Anschluss*, February 15, 1928; *Kölnische Zeitung*, April 7, 1926, weekly edition; *Völkischer Beobachter*, June 15, 1925; Otto Loening, "*Wien* also Völkerbundsitz," *Österreich-Deutschland* 5 (March 1928).

[14] *Der Anschluss*, February 15, 1928. *Vorwärts* article is quoted in the same issue.

[15] Ibid., December 15, 1927.

and felt compelled to work for the European status quo. The Austrian section of the International Women's League for Peace argued that such a union would simply put another six millions under the rule of Prussian militarism. The League's arguments were echoed by another pacifist group, loosely organized around the magazine called *Die Menschheit*. Friedrich Foerster, a leader of the *Menschheit* pacifists, attacked the basic premise of the Anschluss movement. He declared that the principle of nationalism was the cause of Europe's troubles. "For Europe," he wrote, "the teaching of self-determination is dynamite and must inevitably blow up the community."[16]

Yet the *Menschheit* group was not representative of all of German pacifism. On the contrary, the most influential group of pacifists was represented by another journal, *Die Friedenswarte*. Foerster's article was bitterly attacked by Helmuth von Gerlach, an important member of the *Friedenswarte* circle. Gerlach contended that the Women's League and Foerster were really federalists in disguise who had based their whole case upon a misreading of German politics and history. He claimed that every pacifist should have supported the Anschluss since "whoever negates this right of self-determination must reckon with the necessity of irredendist movements that nourish and prolong the threat of war."[17]

As Gerlach's opinion overwhelmed Foerster's, the German members of the Pan-European movement battered down the proposition that European unification should precede any talk of Anschluss. This latter position was the view of Count Coudenhove-Kalergi, the Viennese founder of the movement, who believed that Anschluss was impossible without European integration. Coudenhove believed that Austro-German union could be achieved only when "the growth of one country's power will not be considered an unmitigated threat to its neighbors."[18] This was the view that the Pan-European Congress took in its first meeting held in Vienna during 1926. At this time, the executive council of the Austrian Volksbund asked the Congress to put the Anschluss question on its agenda. The organizers of the Congress replied in the negative. They argued that their meeting was confined to a discussion of the destruction of all European borders and simply refused to consider any rearrangement of frontiers. Needless to say, the Volksbund reacted with a flood of nationalist rhetoric.[19]

---

[16] Friedrich Foerster, "Prinzipien zur Anschlussfrage," *Die Friedenswarte* 27 (1927): 168. See also *Deutsche Einheit*, January 30, 1927.

[17] Helmuth von Gerlach, "Pazifismus und die Anschlussfrage," *Die Friedenswarte* (1927): 132.

[18] *Neue Freie Presse*, May 26, 1929, p.m.

[19] *Deutsche Einheit*, October 30, 1926.

The German democratic Left agreed with the Austrian Volksbund. Democrats and socialists suspected that European unification might only be another French scheme designed to maintain the status quo. These suspicions were reinforced when Briand became the most influential proponent of this scheme. To overcome their fears, democratic politicians were determined to turn the Pan-European movement into more familiar channels, to use it as an instrument to attack the status quo. Willi Hellpach, DDP president of Baden, argued that German democracy's task was to unite Europe. But, he proclaimed, there could be no such union without a strong German core state, one that included Austria. Wilhelm Heile was even more specific. With a hint of blackmail, Heile argued that the Anschluss would assure European unification and the peace, since it would diminish German aggressiveness.[20]

Interestingly, the German Pan-European organization and the Austro-German Volksbund had a close relationship. Paul Löbe was president and Wilhelm Heile a vice-president of both these groups. Why not? Heile and Löbe were always careful to make their priorities understood. They believed that European unification was impossible without a prior German national unification. As Löbe told a meeting of the Volksbund in Frankfurt on June 14, 1926: "For the part of us that are active in the Pan-European movement, it is out of the question to postpone our German demands until this far-reaching goal is achieved. On the contrary, our right of national self-determination takes precedence over other solutions of the European problem."[21]

The Pan-European question illustrates more than the democratic commitment to treaty revision. It shows distinctly the limits of agreement between the democratic Left and the Right. The Right could only agree with the democratic Left on the legitimacy of Germany's aims. Once the discussion moved from the need for abstract justice to diplomatic methods, an unbridgeable gulf opened between most conservatives and most democrats. German conservatives in general believed that Pan-Europe violated the principle of national sovereignty. In an extreme assertion of this position, the National Socialists could even charge Löbe with treason for his participation in the European union movement. The *Völkischer Beobachter* asked: "What

---

[20] Hellpach in *Berliner Tageblatt*, July 7, 1925, p.m.; Heile in ibid., August 15, 1925, a.m. See also *Der Anschluss*, August 15, 1929; Karl Anton, Prince Rohan, *Umbruch der Zeit* (Berlin, 1930), p. 104; Hans Eibl, "Die Widereinigung als Rechtsdanke" (eds.) Kleinwaechter and Paller, *Die Anschlussfrage in ihrer kulturellen, politischen und wirtschaftlichen Bedeutung* (Vienna, 1930), p. 105.
[21] *Deutsche Einheit*, October 30, 1926.

shall one say to this grossdeutsch heresy, to this economic-political demagoguery?"[22]

The clearest expression of this split was, of course, in the attitude of these political groupings to Stresemann's foreign policy. The Right attacked anything that smacked of compromise—the Dawes Plan, Locarno, Germany's entrance into the League of Nations. From the National Socialists to a significant number within Stresemann's own DVP, German conservatives believed that accommodation with the allies made treaty revision more difficult. Thus Stresemann's accomplishments were often considered to be of a dubious nature, hardly to be greeted as signs of a lessening of allied opposition to Anschluss. Certainly some German conservatives must have had a renewed enthusiasm for Anschluss as a result of Stresemann's policy. Their participation in the Austro-German Arbeitsgemeinschaft after 1925 illustrates this. But it was the German democratic Left that took up the demands for Anschluss with the most enthusiasm. Democrats and socialists believed that Stresemann's foreign policy had renewed respect for Germany in the world community. This meant that the Austro-German union might become a reality.

The amount of democratic and socialist agitation for Anschluss had a direct relationship to diplomatic accomplishment. It rose and fell with the prestige of the German state. The agitation for Anschluss which had been strong in 1918–19 gradually died away as the republic faced the crises of the Ruhr occupation and inflation. It was only when these difficulties were surmounted that the demands for Anschluss rose again to an appreciable level. The greatest impetus for this renewed agitation was the signing of the Locarno Accords in 1925. While the Locarno agreements were being negotiated, the German Volksbund was also being transformed into a true political pressure group, the Austrian section of the Volksbund and the Arbeitsgemeinschaft were founded. As a memorial of the Viennese Volksbund proclaimed: "Since the days of Locarno, the world situation has changed. The German people have again achieved an equal place at the side of other people. For German-Austria, a view of the future is opened."[23]

Clearly the democratic Anschluss movement viewed Locarno as

---

[22] *Völkischer Beobachter* (Munich), February 4, 1927.

[23] Arbeitsgemeinschaft, *Warum fördern wir den Anschluss*, p. 11. See also Heile in *Österreich-Deutschland* 3 (January 1926): 18; Karl Hugelmann, "Oesterreich und die Verträge von Locarno," ibid., pp. 3–5; Hans Eibl, "Zum Vertrag von Locarno," *Das Neue Reich* 8 (1925): 128–29; Ludwig Quessel, " Europa und der Anschluss Österreichs an Deutschland," *Sozialistische Monatshefte* 34 (1925): 662.

the first step toward undoing the work of Versailles. Erich Koch-Weser, leader of the DDP, cogently expressed this standpoint. He told the Reichstag: "The Locarno Treaty will be meaningless if it is meant to be a continuation of the spirit and work of Versailles."[24] The Volksbund and the Arbeitsgemeinschaft greeted Locarno in this light and looked forward to Germany's entrance into the League as the first step toward revision of the peace treaties. They demanded action. As a liberal Austrian journal, the *Volkswirt*, stated: "The silence has hurt us enough. Now is the time to talk! The Austrian problem is as unsolved as on the first day."[25]

Were these expectations ultimately realistic? Did they not simply engender false hopes? What could Germany do in the League? Even with a permanent seat on the League Council, Germany was only one of the major powers. And it required a unanimous decision of the Council to reverse the prohibitions of Anschluss in Article 80 of the Versailles treaty and article 88 of the Treaty of St. Germain. This decision could never have been reached as long as France maintained a permanent seat on the Council and could exercise a perpetual veto. Thus Germany's entrance into the League provided more of a psychological assurance of a better future than the means for assuring this future itself. It was an illusion to hope for the transformation of the League into a vehicle that would facilitate an Austro-German union. Yet the illusory nature of such a task did not stop the distinguished Viennese jurist, Rolf Wolkan, from exploring its possibilities. Wolkan argued that the requirements of unanimity could be overcome through invoking Article 5 of the Covenant. Article 5 stated that procedural matters could be decided by a simple majority vote. Wolkan had carefully calculated that the composition of the Council in 1929 would give Germany a minimum of seven votes against a maximum of six in opposition. Wolkan believed that Germany could count on the votes of Chile, Cuba, Finland, Japan, Persia, Spain, and Venezuela. How could he arrive at such a conclusion about states that had taken no public stand on the Anschluss question? He was simply guilty of the wishful thinking so common among Anschluss supporters.[26]

Another Viennese law professor, Adolf Merkl, claimed to have a more realistic proposal. But, in the end, he only replaced Wolkan's legalism with the familiar argument of Germany's moral supremacy. His prescription was simply another case of wishful thinking. With

[24] *Verhandlungen des Reichstags, Stenographische Berichte*, CCCLXXXVIII, 4524.
[25] *Der österreichische Volkswirt* 18 (1925): 437.
[26] *Wiener Neueste Nachrichten*, March 25, 1928.

its entrance into the League, Germany would become "viewed as a worthwhile and solid member of the world community."[27] Once this goal was achieved, the Germans could call the Anschluss opponents chauvinists who sabotaged the natural development of Europe based upon the right of self-determination.

Wolkan had one other argument that was not based upon any faith in the League. He explicated the difficulties in fashioning the League into an instrument for hindering Anschluss. Wolkan emphasized that unanimity was required for any League action, even that initiated by France to forestall the Anschluss. Certainly the French feared just such an occurrence. The semi-official *Le Temps* called attention to this weakness in the League's structure. The influential journalist Pertinax went so far as to maintain that Germany would disregard the League altogether and achieve the union by its own action. He believed that: "Never will there be found in Geneva a Council able . . . or willing to act against such a *fait accompli*."[28]

For the French Right and Center, Germany's new diplomatic position seemed anything but propitious. They believed the Locarno treaties would encourage German expansion to the east and the annexation of Austria. Thus French fears kept pace with German hopes. If anything, the French Right and Center placed an even higher value on Stresemann's ability than did the Germans. They thought the German Foreign Minister might catch them unaware, might achieve an Anschluss while the French were unprepared to circumvent this act. On May 26, 1925, Senator Chênebenoit addressed a plea to his colleagues in the upper chamber. He declared that France's present position was analogous to that of 1866. Then Paris had stood by while Bismarck had swallowed up the South; now it was Austria that was threatened. Chênebenoit demanded that Briand deal with the matter immediately.[29] This same fear was expressed in a 1928 editorial in the newspaper *Gaulois* that warned Frenchmen to be careful of the good manners of German statesmen. *Gaulois* claimed the Germans were determined to achieve by smiles and geniality what had been denied them by force. They had made "softness and sentimentality a subterfuge for political action."[30]

Yet, in the end, Wolkan's premises and French fears were just as unrealistic as the German reliance upon moral supremacy. The

[27] Adolf Merkl, "Das angebliche Anschlussverbot für Oesterreich und der Eintritt des deutschen Reiches in den Völkerbund," *Deutsche Juristen Zeitung* 21 (1926): 1392.

[28] *New York Times*, February 19, 1926.

[29] *Débats parlementaires, Annales du Senat*, CII, 1113.

[30] Paris to Berlin, August 21, 1928, AA 4492/K920/K229108.

Anschluss was in the distant future. German hopes for union with Austria had been put aside until more urgent problems were resolved. Before the Anschluss could be considered, the French would have to be convinced to withdraw their troops from the Rhineland, and the reparations question would have to be reopened. Stresemann clearly stated this order of priorities to the Crown Prince in 1925, to Ignaz Seipel in 1927, to Josef Wirth in 1928, to Bernhard von Bülow, then leader of the Foreign Office's section of League affairs, sometime in the late 1920s.[31] His statements were backed by Chancellor Wilhelm Marx, by Bülow, by Karl von Schubert, secretary of state in the Foreign Office.[32]

For this reason, German policy was designed just to procrastinate, to wait for better times. Any attempt at Anschluss would mobilize allied opposition to all the aims of German foreign policy, not only those concerning Austria. As Stresemann wrote to his Ambassador in Rome during 1925: "In reality we do not consider the Anschluss question is now acute, and we certainly realize how disastrous would be an attempt to bring this question to a decision."[33]

"Not acute"—this was the favorite phrase of German diplomacy; it was used indiscriminately with Frenchmen, Italians, Czechs, and Englishmen. It represented the thinking of the professional diplomats in the Foreign Office as well as their political chief. Gerhard Köpke, director of the Foreign Office's Second Department dealing with Western and Southeastern Europe, explicated this position in a 1925 memorandum. He concluded:

The German government should not be pressed by the nervous voices from the camp of the grossdeutsch ideology in both lands. It should continue the present tempo and the line of its Austrian policy heretofore followed because, considering the situation from the standpoint of *Realpolitik*, this leads in its present form from stone to stone to important, rightful and

[31] Stresemann memo on conversation with D'Abernon, AA 2344/4576/ E171648; Seipel, Stresemann, Marx conversations in Vienna, November 1927, AA 2346/4576/E173194; Stresemann memo on conversation with Wirth, April 12, 1928, ibid., E173394; Stresemann letter to Crown Prince, September 7, 1925, Stresemann Nachlass, 3168/7318/H159872; Bülow's recollection of a conversation with Stresemann can be found in *Documents on British Foreign Policy, 1919–1939*, series II, vol. 1: 46. See Bosdari's report of a conversation with Stresemann in *I documenti diplomatici italiani*, serie VII, vol. III: 558.

[32] Marx statement can be found in the Vienna conversations cited above, E173192. See also Schubert memo, March 26, 1926, AA 2345/4576/E172294; Bülow memo in F. G. Stambrook, "The German-Austrian Customs Union Project of 1931: A Study of German Methods and Motives," *Journal of Central European Affairs* 21 (1961): 20.

[33] Stresemann to Neurath for communication to Mussolini, May 15, 1925, AA 2344/4576/E171583.

careful work. This policy also performs a useful service that leads to the accomplishment of the high völkisch ideal of the German-Austrian union beckoning in the future. This is true much more than if we have made the overhasty steps which, in the present situation of European power politics, can only create serious harm to the hopes of Anschluss.[34]

The realism of this position seemed to be attested by the views of the Austrians. Seipel and others might have opposed the Anschluss, but even its proponents realized that neither German state could initiate an active policy. Vienna, like Berlin, was dependent upon the good will of the western powers, particularly considering its weak economic structure. Thus the Austrian diplomats agreed with the German. Franz Peter, secretary general in the Ministry for Foreign Affairs, expressed the same views, albeit more cogently than had Köpke. He told his Ambassador to Washington: "The Anschluss question must always be handled with the greatest care. Every kind of policy that leads toward demonstrations must be completely disavowed. We wish that evidence of a general tendency for Anschluss both at home and abroad be seen as a natural and understandable occurrence. But we wish that the Anschluss question be left in absolute peace until the time of decision comes."[35]

These views were reiterated whenever Austrian heads of government met with their German counterparts—at the visit of Austrian Chancellor Ramek to Berlin in 1926 and during the journey of German Chancellor Marx to Vienna in 1927. In 1926 there was a concerted attempt to make these opinions known beyond the closed doors of the meetings. German Chancellor Hans Luther spoke on the difficulties of achieving the union. This statement was partially conceived for foreign consumption, to calm the fears of the French and Czechs. But it was also directed against any excessive hope that might be in the minds of Austrians and Germans. Luther stated that people of both states would have to be content with only symbolic representations of union.[36] And, for a time, his lesson was accepted. Ignoring the taunts of the communist newspaper, Rote Fahne, the Germanic press agreed with Luther. This was even true for the SPD newspaper, Vorwärts, and the Grossdeutsch Party organ, the Wiener Neueste Nachrichten. Germania, speaking for the Center Party, stated that no

[34] Köpke memo, March, 1925, AA 4491/K920/K228332.

[35] Peter to Prochnik (Washington), April 1926, NPA Fasz. 111, 1193 pr. 10 IV 1926. See Austrian Foreign Ministry memorandum, 1926, NPA Fasz. 464, 11747.

[36] Luther's speech, March 28, 1926, AA 2345/4576/E172533. See also Köpke memo to various embassies, March 30, 1926, ibid., E172547.

halfway sensible man considered the two states were preparing for unification. Always in the forefront of the Anschluss agitation, the *Berliner Tageblatt* stated: "The time is not ripe for the Anschluss. Much water will flow down the Spree and the Danube before this desire becomes a reality."[37]

But there is more than one possible interpretation of German foreign policy. What passes for Realpolitik could have been defeatism in disguise. To argue that nothing could be done was to insure that nothing would be done. Perhaps the situation would have changed once the Rhineland occupation had ended, and the sword of Damocles no longer hung over Germany. However, this did not prove true when the proposed Austro-German customs union of 1931 met with the strongest opposition from France, Italy, and Czechoslovakia. Still there were unvoiced hopes that the French political structure would change. German diplomats carefully watched for signs of an impending victory of the Left. They must have speculated on what would have happened if control of French policy came into the hands of someone like Leon Blum, who was sympathetic to treaty revision.

There were some signs that these hopes might be fulfilled. Even the Czechs, who were the strongest opponents, gave some signs of weakening. President Masaryk suggested that a *modus vivendi* could be reached with Germany on the basis of German support for Czech sovereignty over the Sudetens. But Masaryk's allusions were hardly fact. Seipel, however, was convinced that Masaryk's rival, Premier Antonin Švehla, was an advocate of closer ties with Germany. Seipel believed that Švehla desired to construct an economic union between Germany, Austria, and Czechoslovakia, in contradiction to Beneš' and Masaryk's schemes for an economic combination based on the Little Entente. Švehla evidently was leader of a faction that included the Czech ambassador to Berlin, Kamil Krofta. Again the key issue was the status of the Sudeten German minority. Karl von Schubert reported on a conversation with Krofta in 1926:

He told me quite openly that the Czechs must naturally work against the Anschluss in the current political framework. But he has absolutely no understanding of those people who doubt that Germany would complete the Anschluss if she were placed in a more favorable situation. He is of the opinion that the road from Berlin to Vienna goes through Prague. When all the disputes between Prague and Berlin—and he means especially

---

[37] *Berliner Tageblatt*, March 27, 1926, p.m. See also *Rote Fahne* (Berlin), March 30, 1926; *Kölnische Zeitung*, March 31, 1926, weekly edition. For the rest of the German press opinion, see *Neue Freie Presse*, March 30, 1926, p.m., and *Bulletin périodique allemagne*, Nr. 335, pp. 9–11. *Wiener Neueste Nachrichten* is quoted in *Bulletin périodique autrichienne*, Nr. 185, p. 6.

the minority question—are settled, then he thinks that the Czechs would be able to give up their opposition to Anschluss and even greet it.[38]

Despite such statements, the solid front of opposition showed no indication of weakening. Perhaps the supposition of democratic politicians and diplomats was wrong. Perhaps the Anschluss could only have been achieved by war. The radical Right, at least, seemed interested in such a catastrophic solution. If no one in Germany believed a renewed war was imminent, still the "young conservatives" used a rhetoric that was permeated by the language of war. As one such writer stated: "The world stands in flames; the middle of Europe is a crater; the time of fairy tales is over. Thus German Austria must come into the battle line for the fate of Europe."[39] Yet the radical Right was as troubled as the democrats by the disjunction between the demands for Anschluss and their ability to be realized. The Right could indulge in fantasies just as wild and illusory as the democrats. This was evidenced by an editorial in the anti-semitic, extremist *Deutschösterreichische Tageszeitung* (Vienna). Even the mixed metaphors are striking examples of the futility of German policy. The editorial proclaimed:

We feel we cannot go any farther. Then swastika trumpets part the clouds, and milk and honey flow into the land in such bright colors that the heart palpitates with happiness. We are now in the same position as the Jews before the walls of Jericho. Because it is impossible to achieve the Anschluss through the use of force, the swastika people hope to destroy the obstacles with screeching trumpets and finally to come home to their beloved country.[40]

[38] Schubert memo of conversation with Krofta, March 26, 1926, AA 2345/4576/E172294. See also Seipel conversation with Stresemann in Vienna, November 1927, NPA Fasz. 464, 25299; Austrian Foreign Ministry memo, November 1927, ibid.; Marek to Vienna, August 1, 1928, NPA Fasz. 68, Zl. 103 Pol. For more on such possible deals, see chapter VIII.

[39] Herbert Werner, "Deutschösterreich," *Deutschlands Erneuerung* 7 (1924): 50.

[40] *Deutschösterreichische Tageszeitung*, July 8, 1925.

CHAPTER VI METHODS OF AGITATION
AND PREPARATION

THE CONSTRAINTS UPON German foreign policy may have led to un-realistic appraisals of the chances for an Austro-German union, but they could not stop the activities of Anschluss supporters. Their conscience demanded some visible effort. Their convictions impelled them to action. The only problem was to determine what kind of action should be taken. The democratic Anschluss movement, dominated by socialists, differed from the traditional middle-class movement under the aegis of the Arbeitsgemeinschaft. The first group tended toward propaganda; the second attempted to lay a careful groundwork for Anschluss by unifying laws and practices in the two Germanic states, a method called Angleichung. The first solution was often in conflict with the Foreign Office's desire for the Anschluss question to remain dormant; the second seemed more compatible with Stresemann's aims. Yet the Foreign Office could do little more than give moral support to the efforts of the Arbeitsgemeinschaft. Bound by exigencies of foreign policy, the German government was forced to remain in the background and allow other agencies—some private, some parliamentary—to carry the burden of Angleichung. Despite this problem, the Arbeitsgemeinschaft could point to some positive accomplishments. In the end, however, these accomplishments were less important than the visibility given to the Anschluss movement in the attempt to achieve them. Thus both attempts at propaganda and Angleichung were not so far apart in their final result—to show that there was strong and consistent support for the Anschluss, to keep the Anschluss question alive.

Of the two alternatives, propaganda was considerably more dramatic. It seemed to fulfill the needs of the Volksbund leadership as no other course of action could. The Berlin leaders willingly traveled to mass meetings, where they delivered major speeches for Anschluss. They included Hermann Kienzl, Wilhelm Heile, Richart Mischler, and, of course, Paul Löbe. As Reichstag president, Löbe could often attract a large crowd. Even in Danzig, a city without a

Volksbund organization, he could draw as many as 1,200 to a meeting. In the Rhineland where there were numerous Volksbund branches, he often addressed gatherings of more than 1,000. The other speakers could not count on such large attendance. Still Mischler once spoke to over 1,500 people at a Volksbund rally in Recklinghausen.[1]

There were other occasions to propagandize for Anschluss. The Volksbund published a magazine for its membership. It sponsored tours of Viennese artists, writers, and organizations, especially that of the Vienna a capella choir, through Berlin and the Rhineland. The high point of the choir's visit occurred during a concert in the Reichstag hall where Löbe and the head of the choir both made speeches demanding the union. Anschluss supporters could go further and find propaganda even where such thoughts were not verbalized. The *Berliner Tageblatt* saw such an expression when the Volksbund greeted the Vienna Philharmonic. The newspaper claimed: "Though it was scarcely talked about from such a perspective, this meeting was arranged to further the plans of Austro-German union and to put this goal into the form of political action."[2]

The most important Volksbund demonstration occurred in Vienna during August 1925. Löbe and a delegation of 300 German Volksbund members crossed the Austro-German border at Passau on August 29. There the Germans were welcomed by their Austrian colleagues. The combined groups proceeded to Linz where they were greeted by the mayor—the Grossdeutsch Party leader—Fritz Langoth. The normal mass meeting was held, closing with a cheer for Grossdeutschland that reverberated through the hall. The Germans and Austrians then boarded a ship to take them to Vienna where an even larger demonstration followed. In Vienna they were greeted by an honor guard from the Republican Schutzbund and took part in a procession through the streets of that city. A great rally was held at the city hall. The auditorium was filled to its capacity of 3,000, so that the speeches had to be broadcast to an overflow crowd of 10,000 in the square outside.

Representatives were present from all German parties except the communists and National Socialists. The Austrian socialist and Grossdeutsch Party leaders were also in attendance. Only notable Christian Socialists were conspicuous by their absence. Thus the speakers could intone the well-worn contention that the Anschluss was desired by all Germans and almost all Austrians, that the Volksbund was above party politics. Other familiar arguments were also restated. The

[1] *Vorwärts*, June 13, 1926, edition A; *Der Anschluss*, February 15, 1927; *Österreich-Deutschland* 3 (January 1926): 16, 23; 5 (July 1928): 20, passim.

[2] *Berliner Tageblatt*, June 20, 1925, a.m. For the choir's visit see *Österreich-Deutschland* 3 (May 1926): 21.

speakers concluded that Austria was German by right of culture and history, that Austria was neither an economically nor a politically viable entity. Despite or because of such statements of doom, the air was filled with hope. The European constellation appeared to be changing. Löbe argued that the future security pact with France would mean the end of Germany's isolation. He was seconded by a number of Austrians who included the liberal economist, Gustav Stolper, and the socialist Nationalrat delegate, Karl Leuthner. Leuthner ended his speech by proclaiming: "We make for ourselves a new way and stand now at the beginning of a new era."[3] Immediately following this injunction, the meeting closed with the singing of the German national anthem.

Such statements were bound to arouse the French. If the French became convinced that the German government was interested in initiating plans for the Anschluss, then Paris would balk at signing the security pact, and the English troop withdrawals from the Rhineland would be further delayed. The international repercussions were complicated by Löbe's dual position in the Anschluss and in the European peace movement. In late August, Löbe was staying in France and preparing to address an international peace gathering. He intended to go to Vienna and then return to Paris for this other meeting. The Foreign Office feared that the interruption of Löbe's French visit would call attention to the German support of the Anschluss at a most unpropitious time. Such an act might have needlessly antagonized Paris and created the demand for guarantees against the Anschluss in the forthcoming security pact. This was substantially the argument that Stresemann had used with his chancellor, Wilhelm Marx, who had interjected the Anschluss issue into the April presidential campaign. Marx had contended that the Anschluss was a righteous demand "which we must bring up again today when the security pact is being debated."[4] Stresemann had been appalled, but he had also been able to prevail upon Marx to leave the subject alone. After all, Marx as chancellor was ultimately responsible for the success of German foreign policy.

Stresemann had no such influence with Löbe, who was much more of a free agent. At first it seemed as if there would be no need to

[3] *Vorwärts*, August 30, 1925, edition A. See also *Neue Freie Presse*, August 31, 1925, a.m.; Police report, August 30, 1925, NPA Fasz. 234, 15072 pr. 31 VIII 1925; Margaret Ball, *Post-War German-Austrian Relations* (Stanford University, 1937), pp. 62–64.

[4] See chapter II, n. 7. See also Schubert to Munich, June 5, 1925, AA 2344/4576/E171663; Stresemann to Hoesch (Paris), April 22, 1925, AA 1483/3086/D614011.

worry. Until August 21 the Foreign Minister believed that the Volks-bund demonstration would present few difficulties. He had been personally assured by Löbe that the Reichstag President had no intention of traveling to the Austrian capital. When it became obvious that Löbe was actually going, Stresemann became infuriated at this breach of faith. He requested Löbe to reconsider. Despite his anger, the Foreign Minister's letter to Löbe was a carefully reasoned statement. The Reichsminister called attention to the delicate nature of the security pact negotiations and stated: "We are all agreed about the final goal of Anschluss. It only comes down to this: What methods promise the most success? From my knowledge of the foreign policy situation, I know that every meeting for the Anschluss, especially when you attend, can only be viewed by foreign lands as having an official character and will succeed in laying difficulties in the path of realizing the Anschluss."[5]

Löbe dodged the bearer of Stresemann's letter until August 24. To emphasize the urgency of his request, Stresemann telegraphed the same message on both August 25 and the following day. Löbe answered on the 25th, but his reply was hardly encouraging to Berlin. The Reichstag President complained that he could not desert the Volksbund membership at such a late date. At the very least, he would have to travel as far as the Austrian border and apologize for not attending. Löbe promised to call the Foreign Office while passing through Munich. But Munich came and went without any communication. When the Foreign Office finally traced the missing Reichstag President, he was, to no one's surprise, in Vienna.

Löbe later apologized to Stresemann. He claimed to have been greeted by fifteen Austrians at the frontier. Naturally these Austrians would have been insulted if the Reichstag President had not gone on to Vienna. Stresemann certainly never believed this fairy tale; but he had to make the best of Löbe's *fait accompli*.[6] At least the Reichstag President did emphasize that his visit was unofficial. He proclaimed that neither the Austrian nor German governments had participated in the demonstration: "What happened here today was not brought about by any cabinet, not wished for by any cabinet—neither the Austrian nor the German. The Austrian and the German Foreign Ministers have absolutely no responsibility for this meeting.

---

[5] Stresemann to Löbe, August 21, 1925, AA 2344/4576/E171813–E171814.
[6] Ibid., Stresemann to Pfeiffer, August 29, 1925, AA 1483/3086/D614136–D614138; Löbe to Stresemann, September 5, 1925, ibid., D614163–D614165; Stresemann to Löbe, September 13, 1925, ibid., D614168–D614169; Köpke memo, August 31, 1925, AA 2344/4576/E171828–E171830.

The President of the Reichstag speaks here only as a representative of the people, of all parties."[7]

Yet Löbe knew full well that such an event would have political repercussions. In the same speech, he stated that the enthusiasm of the audience had changed the demonstration from a nonpolitical expression of German unity and thus it "was turned into a national political event because the will of the people for the union finds sympathy from us in the Reich."[8] Certainly the French interpreted the meeting in such a light. When Löbe arrived back in Paris to address the International Peace Conference, Eduard Herriot, then president of the French Chamber of Deputies, refused to be on the same platform with the Reichstag President. To soothe his fellow countrymen, Senator de Monzie, the conference chairman, was able to persuade Löbe to cancel a speech planned for the formal banquet. But this unleashed a cry of anguish from the German delegation, especially from the DDP leader, Erich Koch-Weser. Only the calming effects of the German embassy staff saved the conference from the embarrassment of Koch-Weser's withdrawal. Löbe still participated in the work of the conference, although Herriot and other Frenchmen were conspicuous by their absence from the sessions.[9]

The Reichstag President sought to make light of this matter. He claimed that Herriot had sent him a telegram promising to work amicably together in the future. But such a slight would not aid Franco-German rapprochement. Even if the incident were forgotten in Paris, the Germans would still remember. A socialist meeting in Bremen protested this insult to the Reichstag President. There were even some who welcomed any confrontation involving the Anschluss question. The Austrian *Volkswirt* editorialized that Löbe's journey from Marseilles to Paris by way of Vienna had been absolutely necessary. The French had to be taught a lesson. Until France accepted Germany's right to pursue an independent foreign policy there could be no pacification of Europe.[10]

The German Foreign Office was to have constant trouble with the Reichstag President. In August 1928, after addressing another meeting in Vienna, Löbe was preparing for another Anschluss demonstration in the Reichstag hall to commemorate the November 1918 resolution of the Austrian Reichsrat asking for union with Germany.

[7] *Neue Freie Presse*, August 31, 1925, a.m.
[8] Ibid.
[9] Rieth (Paris) to Berlin, September 3, 4, 8, 1925, AA 1483/3086/D614144–D614158, D614167, D614168.
[10] See Foreign Office report, September, 1925, Stresemann Nachlass, 3168/7318/H159886–H159887; *Der österreichische Volkswirt* 18 (1925): 1370.

The Foreign Office did not accept Löbe's explanation that he was undertaking this act as a private citizen. As Köpke wrote: "There will be little predeliction abroad to consider a Reichstag President as a private man while taking an active part in a meeting held in the Reichstag building for which he is responsible."[11]

If it were any consolation to the Germans, the Austrian government could not avoid the same problem. In May 1925 Foreign Minister Heinrich Mataja pleaded with Karl Buresch, governor of Lower Austria, to quell any public support for the Anschluss. Buresch answered through a subordinate in a manner that seemed a purposeful misunderstanding of Mataja's appeal. The letter stated that the Anschluss movement could not be eradicated as long as it did not disturb the peace. On December 13, 1926 Franz Dinghofer, the Grossdeutsch Party leader and vice-chancellor, made a pro-union address in Berlin. Dinghofer explained to Austrian Chancellor Seipel that he carefully differentiated his roles as a public figure and a private citizen. On this occasion, he claimed to be speaking in his capacity as a citizen. How Seipel received this news is not recorded. But there can be little doubt that even Dinghofer knew such a distinction was made of whole cloth.[12]

Unlike their Austrian counterparts, German conservatives did not make much trouble for their diplomats. The German middle-class Anschluss movement in general, as embodied in the Arbeitsgemeinschaft, did not stage massive demonstrations. Middle-class propaganda took a different form. There were semiprofessional propagandists on both sides of the border who wrote history pamphlets designed to prove that the Reich and Vienna had always been inseparably bound up in a common culture. There were those who wrote economic pamphlets to prove that the Austrian economy was not viable and that Anschluss was the only possible solution to Vienna's economic woes. These pamphlets were replicated in newspaper columns as well.[13]

Even such actions were not always welcomed. The Foreign Office favored this variety of pro-Anschluss propaganda in principle only as long as it did not complicate German foreign policy. This was apparent when the Reichszentrale für Heimatdienst desired to extend

---

[11] Köpke to Geneva, September 14, 1928, AA 4492/K920/K229325. See also Müller to Löbe, September 20, 1928, ibid., K229332–K229335. Invitation from Austrian colony in Berlin to Chancellor Müller, November 1928, ARk R43I/109, p. 206.

[12] Mataja to Buresch, May 24, 1925, NPA Fasz. 110; see also Dinghofer situation in documents NPA Fasz. 111, 15965 pr. 16 XII 1926, 16001 pr. 20 XII 1926.

[13] See chapters IV and XI.

its operations to Austria. At first, the Reichszentrale took up the suggestion that the Deutscher Schulverein der Südmark become the Viennese outlet for its slides and literature. But the Schulverein membership was divided as to whether to assume this task. In any case, the Reichszentrale was most eager to do the job itself. However, the Austrian government, with the exception of Transportation Minister Schürff, was indifferent and the German Foreign Office feared such an act would be interpreted as intervention in Austrian affairs.[14]

However, this was a special case. On the whole, the Foreign Office paid scant attention to slide showings and lectures. Even when middle-class groups did stage demonstrations they seemed, at first glance, less embarrassing to German foreign policy. This appeared to be the case for the gathering of the German Choral Society (Deutscher Sängerbund) held on July 19–22, 1928, to commemorate the hundredth anniversary of Schubert's death. Certainly this was a patently middle-class group. The *Arbeiter Zeitung* and *Lidové Noviny* of Prague both thought it was a *petit bourgeois* gathering. And it seemed so safe that prominent Christian Socialists such as Ignaz Seipel joined in sponsoring the event with the German Chancellor and Foreign Minister, as well as the presidents of both states. The German cabinet made no objection to Interior Minister Severing's attendance.[15]

Yet both the Austrian and German governments underestimated the ability of Paul Löbe and perhaps did not recognize that Friedrich List, the choral society's chairman, was a member of the Volksbund executive council. In any case, the emotionalism associated with the visit of over 260,000 Germans from all over the world was certain to supercharge the atmosphere, and the repeated singing of patriotic songs was scarcely able to cool the emotions. A mass meeting in a temporary hall in the Prater had over 100,000 in attendance. List closed the session by demanding a cheer for the Anschluss, "for the Grossdeutschland that we can foresee and strive toward what is

[14] Friedrich Rucker to Reichszentrale für Heimatdienst, August 30, 1926, AA 4491/K920/K228716–K228718; Mayr (of Reichszentrale) to Linder (Foreign Office), October 29, 1926, ibid., K228711–K228715; Deutscher Schulverein der Südmark to Reichszentrale, December 28, 1926, ibid., K228792–K228793; Mayr to Linder, February 7, 1927, ibid., K228788–K228790; Wettstein to Mayr, February 22, 1927, ibid., K228795; Mayr to Linder, March 2, 1927, ibid., K228791; Köpke memo, January 17, 1927, ibid., K228766–K228767; Zech to Vienna, November 18, 1926, ibid., K228719–K228720.

[15] *Lidové Noviny* quoted in *Der Anschluss*, August 15, 1928; *Arbeiter Zeitung*, July 20, 1928; see the enthusiasm of *Die Reichspost*, July 19, 1928; List of Welcoming Committee for the Schubert Festival, NPA Fasz. 454, 21846 17 IV 1928; Köpke to Vienna, July 17, 1928, AA 4492/K920/K229136.

represented by the German national anthem: Heil! Heil! Heil!"[16] The
Neue Freie Presse described the result: "Simultaneously there rose
this three-times Heil through the hall and over the square so that no
one felt it needed a radio to penetrate far and wide. Then, out of
the call, out of the waving banners, rose the song, 'Deutschland,
Deutschland über Alles, über Alles in der Welt'."[17] Löbe himself
addressed a rally at the Vienna city hall on the night of July 22 where
he claimed that the choral groups represented a unity of purpose.
Löbe's speech was an example of his usual hyperbolic rhetoric. The
Reichstag President stated:

"The meeting in Vienna has a national political importance since it stirs
up the thoughts of Anschluss. The German national anthem has served the
German unity movement before; the great massive demonstration for Anschluss will be borne by those circles who sing the anthem today."[18]

Or in the words of the *Vossische Zeitung*: "Who can hinder us now?
Europe will never allow the Anschluss, and yet it marches on with
a sure step. That is the impression we bring home from Vienna."[19]

Although the Arbeitsgemeinschaft, the bastion of the middle-
class Anschluss movement, proved more amenable to Foreign Office
policy, it did feel impelled to organize an Austrian week in Munich
during January 1927. However this week did not see any rousing
speeches by Löbe. There were instead harmless recitals or long
discussions on the technical details of the union. Under Foreign
Office pressure, Branca, the Arbeitsgemeinschaft chief, even prevailed
upon the Austrian visitors to deemphasize politics in their public
statements. It is true that the Arbeitsgemeinschaft did seek to involve
the Bavarian government in this demonstration. Yet Branca never
intended to embarrass German foreign policy. He was well satisfied
when the Bavarian governmental leaders agreed to a nonpolitical
breakfast with the distinguished Austrian guests.[20]

This was a far cry from the Volksbund rallies. But after all, the
Arbeitsgemeinschaft had different goals. It rejected the methods of
propaganda that the Volksbund used. Its stated goals were as follows: "The German-Austrian Arbeitsgemeinschaft is no mass organiza-

[16] *Neue Freie Presse*, July 22, 1928, a.m.
[17] Ibid.
[18] Ibid., July 23, 1928, a.m.
[19] Quoted in *Österreich-Deutschland* 5 (August 1928): 12. For the political
effect of this meeting see chapter VIII.
[20] Haniel to Berlin, January 7, 11, 18, 1927, ARk R43I/108, pp. 278, 283,
293; same to same, January 5, 13, 18, 1928, AA 4491/K920/K228763, K228778–
K228779, K228787. For the results of this meeting, see *Münchner Neueste
Nachrichten*, January 10, 12, 13, 1927.

tion but strives to prepare for and clarify various questions pertaining to the Anschluss through the use of small groups of experts. It will not accomplish its demands for Anschluss through mass meetings but will complete its striving quietly and without unnecessary publicity."[21]

The goal was the same as the Volksbund's; only its manner of achievement was different, being peculiarly suited to an organization principally composed of civil servants and academicians. The need to work for the Anschluss was present in the same intensity in both the Volksbund and Arbeitsgemeinschaft; only the latter group felt more at home in the quiet of committee work and away from the glare of publicity. And committees abounded to cover all aspects of life. In Vienna they were founded to prepare for Anschluss in the fields of education, art, culture, economics, law, and journalism. Each was headed by a civil servant or former official. The economics committee also included businessmen, bankers, labor leaders, and the foremost economic journalist of his day—Gustav Stolper.[22]

The Arbeitsgemeinschaft in the Reich had a far more complicated organization. Committees were scattered throughout Germany. Munich housed committees for education, the youth movement, forestry, handicrafts and handwork, physical culture, and tourism. Berlin was the center for those groups dealing with law as well as with finance and foreign exchange. Cologne held the committees for the press and women's rights; Frankfurt the group concerned with social questions. Some committees even had more than one permanent location. Art and culture were considered in both Frankfurt and Cologne. Agriculture was discussed in Berlin and Munich, energy resources in Munich and Stuttgart. The trade and industry committee was located in Frankfurt, Cologne, Berlin, Munich, and Stuttgart.[23]

The Arbeitsgemeinschaft was undoubtedly over-organized. The law committee was divided into eighteen separate subcommittees. The committee on social questions had seven subcommittees, each composed of one Austrian and one German expert. Of the fourteen named, three were college professors and eleven, in keeping with the work, were civil servants. Yet all this careful organization did not seem to impede the work of the Arbeitsgemeinschaft. On the con-

[21] See Arbeitsgemeinschaft statement of objectives, 1927, ARk zg 1955 ff/ 1622. For a similar statement of goals, January 28, 1926, see AA 4495/K922/ K231686.

[22] Lerchenfeld to Berlin, April 30, 1925, AA 4495/K922/K231661–K231664; Der Anschluss, January 15, May 15, 1928; Deutsche Einheit, December 31, 1927.

[23] See statement of objectives, ARk, n. 21; Richtlinien für die Organisation und die Arbeit der "Deutsch-Österreichischen Arbeitsgemeinschaft" im Reich, ARk, R43I/108, pp. 96–98; Deutsche Einheit, December 31, 1927, November 30, 1928; Neue Freie Presse, November 2, 1928, a.m.

trary, these subcommittees seemed to multiply the efforts of what was, after all, a little band of less than 400. There was an enormous outpouring of effort for such a small number of men. The Arbeitsgemeinschaft conducted its own studies and subsidized others. It supported the publication of many pamphlets and worked to get its viewpoint represented in professional and business groups.[24] In many ways, it was more successful than the considerably larger Volksbunds and certainly less embarrassing to German foreign policy.

The Arbeitsgemeinschaft also contended that Germany and Austria could reap immediate benefits from its work, even while the two states remained separated. It advocated an *Angleichung*—the creation of similar institutions and laws even before the Austro-German union—and the German Foreign Office supported this move. Surprisingly, not only Stresemann but even Seipel favored such schemes. Angleichung could not disturb the delicate diplomacy of the Reich. Even Masaryk and Mussolini were prepared to accept it as inevitable; thus the French opposition was isolated.[25] Wilhelm Kahl, DNVP Reichstag delegate and legal expert, explained:

At this time, every stormy agitation is undesirable and doomed to failure. The immense international difficulties arrayed against our demands cannot be put out of the way by untimely measures. In many instances, such measures would complicate the situation. . . . This does not mean that we should sit with our hands in our pockets and do nothing in the meantime. Here is the place for legal unification. Here is the place for calm progress, for a completed and usable preparation for the union of two states, a preparation no authority can prevent.[26]

Angleichung thus provided a meaningful outlet for the frustrations caused by German inability to act in the realm of foreign policy. It was unquestionably considered as a piece of national unification, "a legal marriage" as one DNVP Reichstag delegate put it. Julius Roller, a Viennese jurist, maintained that legal Angleichung was misnamed; it really was a return to a common law that had once applied to all Germans. But the major advantage of Angleichung was that it promised to achieve more than mere propaganda. Angleichung was unquestionably useful and could provide concrete evidence of ac-

[24] Richtlinien, p. 98; Gliederung des Unterausschusses 1 für Verfassungs- und Verwaltungsrecht, ARk, R43I/109, p. 216; Arbeitsgemeinschaft, *Die Gründung des Reichausschusses für soziale Fragen* (Vienna, 1928), p. 34.

[25] Stresemann, Seipel, Marx conversations, November 1927, NPA Fasz. 464, Ad. 21.25/2597/13/1927; Moellwald (Rome) to Vienna, October 8, 23, 1927, NPA Fasz. 80, Zl. 63, 70 Pol.; Record of protest by Count Chambrun (French ambassador to Vienna), NPA Fasz. 111, 25670 pr. 13 XI 1927.

[26] Wilhelm Kahl, "Einheitliches Recht für Deutschland und Österreich" (ed.) Richthofen, *Jahrbuch für auswärtige Politik: 1929* (Berlin, 1930), pp. 173–74.

complishment. Branca's replacement as Arbeitsgemeinschaft leader, Erich Emminger, wrote that Angleichung concerned "things that apparently have nothing to do with the union but place it half the way there in practice."[27] Erich Koch-Weser expressed similar views to a meeting of the German Jurists Organization held in Salzburg as a sign of unity with the Austrians. The Reichsminister exclaimed: "I hope that the jurists will have so prepared the relationships between us that this union can be created without making a constitution, that it can be instituted by a simple declaration."[28] And, perhaps more important, Angleichung could serve as a real surrogate for the yet uncompleted Anschluss. The *Deutsche Juristen Zeitung* claimed that legal and economic Angleichung would create a situation where "only two politically separated states remain. In internal affairs, these states would have already built a unity that could not be destroyed."[29]

Of all the areas possible, legal Angleichung was by far the most important. The demands for similar laws were rooted in the nineteenth century. They began when Austrian lawyers joined the German Jurists Organization in 1861. By 1911 this group was demanding a common law for both countries. World War I stimulated this movement, and as Germans and Austrians discussed the possibilities of economic union, they began to realize that a unitary economic system necessitated a unified legal code. Most of the proposals concerned various aspects of business law, but Franz Klein, Austrian minister of justice, desired a common civil and criminal law as well.[30]

In 1923 the first concrete steps were taken in this direction. A treaty was signed that gave each state a privileged position with regard to the execution of judgments in the other. In the same year another treaty regulated legal aid for Austrian or German citizens living in the other state. In February 1927 two agreements were signed regulating inheritance and guardianship for Germans living in Austria or vice versa.[31]

Yet these were very small agreements when compared with the most important project of all, Angleichung of the criminal code. By 1927 the work had progressed so far that both governments were

<hr/>

[27] Emminger to Pünder, March 28, 1927, ARk 4619/K1064/K273155.

[28] *Der Anschluss*, September 15, 1928. For an address by Ramek to the same meeting, see *Österreich-Deutschland* 5 (October 1928): 10.

[29] *Deutsche Juristen Zeitung* 33 (1927): 1595.

[30] Franz Klein, *Reden, Vorträge, Aufsätze, Briefe* (Vienna, 1927), II: 967–82; Kahl, "Einheitliches Recht für Deutschland und Österreich," pp. 168–71; Egon Schiffer, "Angleichung: Recht" (eds.) Kleinwaechter and Paller, *Die Anschlussfrage in ihrer, Kulturellen, wirtschaftlichen und politischen Bedeutung* (Vienna, 1930), pp. 463–64; Julius Osner, "Vereinigung im Rechtsdenken," *Juristische Wochenschrift* 49 (1920): 11–13.

[31] League of Nations, *Treaty Series*, XXVII, 88; LXXIII, 205–8.

able to present the outlines of a completed reform to their legislatures. In June, Oskar Hergt, German minister of justice, laid the new criminal code before the Reichstag. He called attention to the fact that the Austrian government was considering a similar proposal: "Walls were erected in the peace treaties that separate us from our German brothers on the other side of the border. But we are of the same blood and of one culture; nothing can hinder us from completing every possible agreement between the two countries."[32] Franz Dinghofer, then Austrian minister of justice, discussed the reform in a very similar vein with the Nationalrat. Dinghofer maintained: "I don't have to use many words in defining the purpose of legal Angleichung. It is not only a clear expression of cultural unity, of a parallel customary and legal outlook between us and the Reich, it is not only a memorial of national unity . . . , it has great practical worth."[33]

Yet such effusiveness was not entirely justified. Although the Austrian and German proposals read word for word in 413 paragraphs, there were still substantial differences between the two documents. The most important concerned the death penalty. Austria had none; Germany refused to relinquish capital punishment. The Anschluss forces feared that the criminal law reform would fail on these few technicalities. Otto Landsberg, a socialist Reichstag deputy, suggested that Germany abandon the death penalty, but he received little support. Yet the general opinion was that this Angleichung would be a success even without agreement upon the death penalty. This was the view of Johannes Schober, president of the Austrian police and an ex-chancellor. It was seconded by Otto Loening, a Prussian legal official, who stated: "I see the equal criminal law as such an important step of rapprochement and unification for both states that I can accept the different opinions on the death penalty."[34]

Still, even if this were true, there were other technicalities involved. To compose these differences, a Criminal Law Conference was created. The Conference included representatives of both the

[32] *Verhandlungen des Reichstags*, CCCXCIII, 10942. See also Martius memo, November 9, 1927, AA 2346/4576/E173011–E173013; Foreign Office memo, November 1927, ibid., E173013; *Die Reichspost*, October 9, 1925; *Berliner Tageblatt*, September 29, 1925, a.m.; Hans Bell, *Deutsche und österreichische Strafrechtsreform* (Berlin, 1930), pp. 1–48; Egon Schiffer, *Anschlussfrage und Rechtsangleichung* (Berlin, 1927) can be found in ARk R43I/109; Wilhelm Bell, "Ansprache des Reichsjustizministers," *Juristische Wochenschrift* 55 (1926): 2044; Ball, *Post-War German-Austrian Relations*, pp. 77–82.

[33] *Stenographische Protokolle über die Sitzungen des Nationalrats*, III Gesetzgebungs Periode, I: 288.

[34] Otto Loening, "Die Todesstrafe im deutsch-österreichischen Strafgesetzbuch," *Österreich-Deutschland* 5 (January 1928): 3. See also Johann Schober, "Internationales Polizeirecht," *Deutsche Juristen Zeitung* 32 (1927): 197; *Der Anschluss*, October 15, 1927.

Reichstag and the Nationalrat. It undertook its work with great eagerness. After all, it had bipartisan support from Stresemann, Marx, and Seipel. And the Conference was loaded in favor of prominent Anschluss supporters. Included were two former justice ministers, Wilhelm Bell and Emminger, as well as Koch-Weser who would soon hold that office. On the Austrian side, Dinghofer was joined by two ex-chancellors, Rudolf Ramek of the Christian Socialists and Karl Renner of the Social Democrats as well as Ernst Schönbauer, Landbund party leader. Von Kahl was the head of the German group; he had already clearly expressed his views on the Anschluss. Thus, even if the subject of Anschluss was not discussed, the impression of nationalistic purpose remained. The *Deutsche Juristen Zeitung* claimed: "If the writers of the Versailles treaty take notice and hear the words that were not spoken, they can only reinforce their impression that the union marches on."[35] Despite all this good will, no agreement was reached. An examination of the Conference's reports shows an apparent widening of differences rather than their resolution. For example, the Austrian and German groups disagreed on eight out of the ten points being considered in the problem of ransom. As for the death penalty, a German report of 1929 concludes: "The Criminal Law Conference has not yet definitively handled the question."[36]

There were two main reasons for the failure of criminal law reform, one concerning internal politics, the other foreign policy. Perhaps the most important was the complicated nature of the task at hand. Even without the complications inherent in Angleichung, the German Reichstag was never able to agree to a criminal law reform. It took Hitler to accomplish this in a way no one thought of or desired in the 1920s. Criminal law touched the most basic questions on the nature of the good society. Certainly the ideological divisions present in politics would also intrude into the area of legal reforms.

Even if the German socialists such as Löbe and Landsberg could forget these conflicts because the result of national unification seemed so important, their Austrian counterparts could not. The new law code was unveiled in Vienna only two months after the July riots. The Social Democrats feared that this revised code was too strong and might be used as an instrument of political repression. When the proposals were debated in the Nationalrat, Social Democrat Arnold Eisler argued that it was scarcely a work of "enlightened humanity"

[35] *Deutsche Juristen Zeitung* 32 (1927): 1595. See also ibid. 33 (1928): 269–70.

[36] *Verhandlungen des Reichstags*, CDXIV, Anlage 3609, p. 4.

and ought to be opposed on those grounds alone. Eisler coupled this argument with the contention that the Seipel regime did not really desire Angleichung. He claimed that the Austrian reforms were constructed in deference to Seipel's Catholic views and thus never challenged official church dogma. Eisler stated that this was clearly shown in the Austrian objection to allowing legal abortions, as was the case in the Reich. "You cannot call that legal Angleichung," he claimed.[37] However strong or weak these arguments were, Eisler might have opposed Angleichung on grounds of sheer political obstinacy. He told Emminger that the Austrian socialists were not pressing for criminal law reform, since they had "already no wish to support the Seipel government."[38]

The other reason concerns foreign policy. The lack of foreign opposition to Angleichung was based upon the premise that such measures would not be turned into spectacular propaganda events. As long as Angleichung attempts were chronicled in the legal journals of small circulation or buried deeply on the second and third pages of the newspapers, the French and the Czech foreign ministries could be relied upon to maintain a relative calm. Therefore the German government, especially, felt it necessary to remain uninvolved. Felix Frank, Austrian minister to Berlin, worried that the efforts for Angleichung could be hindered by too much publicity. He believed that statements connecting Anschluss with Angleichung unnecessarily complicated the realization of both goals. He pleaded with two successive justice ministers, Bell and Hergt, not to discuss the matter during their trips to Vienna. This view was seconded by the German Foreign Office in urging Hergt not to attend the Nationalrat session in which the Austrian version of the criminal code was to be introduced.[39]

The most arresting example of Foreign Office reluctance occurred over the issue of granting citizenship to Austrians living in the Reich. The Anschluss organizations hoped that this could be achieved through the granting of dual citizenship to Austrians who lived in the Reich

---

[37] *Stenographische Protokolle,* III Gesetzgebungs Periode, I: 296. For a similar German view, see Adolf Bachrach, "Bemerkungen eines Deutsch-österreichers zur Ehrereform," *Juristische Wochenschrift* 51 (1922): 360–61. Another writer deprecated an attempt to achieve "an unworthy criminal law with the help of the Fatherland ideals": see Richard Schmidt, "Gesetzmässige und regelfreie Strafrechtspflege," *Deutsche Juristen Zeitung* 30 (1925): 1291. For participation of German socialists in work of Arbeitsgemeinschaft legal committee, see ARk R43I/109.

[38] Berlin to Vienna, October 30, 1927, NPA Fasz. 11, Zl. 219 Pol.

[39] Frank to Vienna, January 4, 1926, NPA Fasz. 11, Zl. 2 Pol.; same to same, September 23, 1927, NPA Fasz. 111, 24462 pr. 27 IX 1927; Köpke to Geneva, September 17, 1927, AA 2346/4576/E173095.

and vice versa. Even Seipel was prepared to accept this solution of dual citizenship. In reply to a socialist-inspired question in 1927, Seipel stated: "I declare in the name of the government . . . that the negotiations with Germany will be swiftly brought forward under the principle of reciprocity."[40] The demands emanating from the DDP faction in 1923 and ex-Justice Minister Koch-Weser could not bring forth action. Stresemann and his predecessor both rejected this scheme. Stresemann stated that giving Austrian citizens the vote in German elections would be considered by foreigners as the first step toward Anschluss and thus unnecessarily complicate German foreign policy. As Stresemann recognized, the granting of dual citizenship also raised great legal problems. Article 278 of the Versailles treaty bound Germany to recognize the new states of Europe and all those who claimed citizenship therein. Therefore, the Austrians living in the Reich were legally bound by the same laws as other aliens. Germany could not make special concessions to the Austrians without offering the same benefits to the other nationals of succession states, even to non-Germans. There seemed no way out of this dilemma. Julius Meinl, an Austrian lawyer, argued that Germans should invoke a völkish law, a jurisprudence higher than mere treaties and constitutions. But such proposals were unconvincing. As Hans Gmelin, a Giessen professor, summed up the German position: "First, there can be no doubt that we Reich Germans would joyfully greet an Austro-German dual citizenship that would serve as the foundation for the German state. But the lively sympathy with which we view dual citizenship cannot wash away the difficulties."[41]

Some Anschluss supporters viewed the failure of Angleichung as a result of the central government's inaction. Others still placed their hopes upon private experts. "It is, above all, a practical problem," they stated. "Therefore the task should be undertaken by practical men."[42] Yet this latter view was incorrect. The accomplishments of Angleichung were almost always the result of governmental coopera- tion. This was the case when Austrian postal regulations were made

[40] *Stenographische Protokolle*, II Gesetzgebungs Periode, III: 117. For the Anschluss organizations, see Mischler letter to Rosenberg, 1921, AA 4491/K920/ K228199–K229200; *Deutsche Einheit*, December 30, 1926, February 28, March 31, 1927; C. Falk, "Doppelte Staatsangehörigkeit für Deutschösterreichischer und Reichsdeutscher," *Österreich-Deutschland* 6 (January 1929): 1–2; Richart Mischler, "Österreichisch-Deutsches Fremdenrecht," ibid. 5 (May 1928): 10.

[41] *Deutsche Einheit*, February 29, 1928. See also Köpke memo, June 7, 1923, AA 4491/K920/K228201–K228202; Stresemann to Interior Ministry, April 30, 1929, AA 4492/K920/K229542–K229543; *Verhandlungen des Reichstags*, CDXXX, Anlage 156.

[42] Ernst Wolf, "Deutsch-österreichische Rechtsannäherung," *Juristische Woch- enschrift* 55 (1926): 2143.

uniform with the German, when visa dues were abolished between the two states. This was the case when the two governments agreed to an Angleichung of railway ordinances in April 1928, signed by Hans Schürff, Austrian trade and transportation minister, and Wilhelm Koch, his German counterpart. Schürff and Koch were proud of their accomplishment. They considered their action as part of the work for Austro-German union. The Austrian Minister told a committee of the Nationalrat that his agreement was "an important work for the Anschluss, that it does an incomparable service for the Anschluss movement."[43]

Private organizations were far less effective than governmental organizations. Although business and employee groups demanded Angleichung in the areas affecting their lives, Angleichung of economic and social law did not proceed with any rapidity. In education the same phenomenon was apparent. A 1926 Austrian school reform remodeled the Austrian Burgschule upon the German Mittelschule, but this was only a small achievement. The problem was complicated by the fact that social welfare and education were the competence of the state, not the federal government. States were reluctant to change their laws and regulations for the sake of foreign policy. Thus the Foreign Office found it easier to give small subventions to Austrian universities than to lower the tuition of Austrian medical students at Prussian universities. But, even if the state governments had cooperated, there was no assurance that the problems were at an end. Private groups would still have to give up their cherished rights. Thus, if German and Austrian academics could cooperate, students of these two lands could not. An attempt to unite the student organizations of both states failed because the Austrians refused to give up their restriction upon Jewish membership. The only apparent way of unifying the student organizations would have been to allow the Austrians to join in two groups—one for socialists and liberals, the other for nationalists. The Prussian government, dominated by the Weimar coalition, could be expected to have none of this.[44]

---

[43] *Stenographische Protokolle,* III Gesetzgebungs Periode, Beilagen, II, Beilage 153, p. 3. See also ibid., I: 1240; *Österreich-Deutschland* 5 (March 1928): 10 (May 1928): 5; *Der Anschluss,* May 15, 1928; *Deutsche Einheit,* February 29, 1928; *Münchner Neueste Nachrichten,* January 12, 1927; *Neue Freie Presse,* August 29, 1925, a.m.; Shiffer, "Angleichung: Recht," pp. 469–76. For visa dues see chapter XIII.

[44] For social legislation see Reichwirtschaftsrat to Stresemann, April 13, 1929, AA 4492/K920/K229534–K229535; Foreign Office memo, May 15, 1929, ibid., K229536; Julius Roller, *Rechtsangleichung: Die nächsten Aufgaben* (Vienna, 1930), pp. 11–12; Adolf Günther, "Grundsätzliches zur sozialpolitischen Angleichung," Arbeitsgemeinschaft, *Gründung,* pp. 10–26; Edmund Palla, "Angleichung: Sozialpolitik und Arbeitschaft" (eds.) Kleinwaechter and Paller, *Die*

Wilhelm Heile thought that many of these problems could be overcome through the creation of a special commission which would mobilize governmental and private interests for Austria. The German cabinet had considered such action as early as 1923, but rejected this course because it would have raised allied opposition and because the Austrians themselves were unenthusiastic.[45] Certainly these forces could be easily mobilized if the Anschluss had actually been completed. But the Anschluss was prohibited, and this fact alone meant that the German central government could not provide the necessary leadership. In Central Europe the state has always been expected to assume the major burden for directing public life. To expect differently after 1918 would have been to ask for a major miracle. Angleichung was in essence private foreign policy. It was supported by the German and Austrian governments but not controlled by them. If these allied prohibitions were withdrawn, an immediate Angleichung of institutions would have been achieved. Only this act would have been called an Anschluss. Thus ultimately the work for Angleichung was subject to the same frustrations as that of propaganda. It was this frustration which united the entire Anschluss movement, which created that common experience that transcended ideological and class differences.

Anschlussfrage, pp. 507–20. For educational Angleichung see Wettstein letter to von Plaesen, August 1, 1928, AA 4492/K920/K229306; *Österreich-Deutschland* 3 (January 1926): 2; (February 1926): 21; 6 (January 1929): 14–15; *Der Anschluss,* January 15, 1928, January 26, March 28, 1929; Viktor Fadrus, "Angleichung: Unterrichtswesen und Volksbildung" (eds.) Kleinwaechter and Paller, *Die Anschlussfrage,* pp. 486–506; Franz Eggersdorfer, *Das reichsdeutsche und österreichische Bildungswesen im Vergleich zu einander* (Munich, 1927), pp. 5–11. For the problem of student organizations, see Foreign Office memo, November 1927, AA 2346/4576/E173043; Frank to Vienna, February 22, 1929, NPA Fasz. 11, Al. 788 Res.

[45] Foreign Office memo, February 27, 1923, AA 4491/K920/K228178; Foreign Office to Heile, March 2, 1923, ibid., K228182.

CHAPTER **VII** THE GERMAN ECONOMY

AND AUSTRIA

Austria's need was not for criminal law reform but for economic aid. The Austrians hoped that German businessmen, agriculturalists, and the Reich government would provide the necessary assistance. At the height of the depression, Germany and Austria would initiate a customs union project that promised some activity in this direction, but, for most of the Weimar era, there was little aid forthcoming. This chapter will concentrate on the period 1923 to 1929, when such hopes were to be frustrated, especially those based upon the assumption that emotional commitments to the unification could be translated into specific economic concessions. German businessmen and farmers did favor the Anschluss; their organizations were constantly cooperating with the Austrians. Yet there were no businessmen and farmers who agreed to make sacrifices out of their own pockets for the sake of the Austrians. To ask for anything different is to demand passion from that area of life least capable of sustaining it. In the arena where the profit motive reigns supreme, it is unreasonable to think that private interests would renounce material gain in favor of national purpose.

Nor would heroic gestures be forthcoming from the Reich Foreign Office until 1931. Economic union and even some kinds of economic assistance were forbidden by the peace treaties. Germany could not unilaterally grant special trade concessions to Austria even if it had wanted to. There were other reasons that made aid to Austria difficult. German energies were mobilized in many directions; the Foreign Office could never focus with single-minded concentration on the small state to the south. Nor could German diplomats renounce all advantages that could be gained in other sectors of public policy for the pursuit of a goal not immediately achievable. This was shown particularly in the trade-treaty negotiations with Austria. Without unswerving government support, German business and agricultural interests could hardly be cajoled into making major concessions to Vienna. Such support was not forthcoming. In fact, these interests were reinforced by the German Foreign Office's economic experts who often considered themselves representatives of the business community rather than slavish followers of Stresemann's policy for economic conciliation with Vienna.

Considering such circumstances, it is surprising that anything at all was done. The large and continuing agitation for customs union and economic aid to Austria is impressive evidence that Germany did have concern before 1931, even if this concern was seldom translated into action. In reality, this agitation itself would be the most important result of German economic policy toward Vienna. It showed that the Germans really did care for the plight of Vienna. And it provided a psychological safety valve for the Reich Germans themselves by transforming unachievable demands for action into satisfying slogans and by changing ordinary intercourse between Austrian and German businessmen into acts of national heroism.

There were two reasons for German concern in this period. First, Germany did not desire any limitation placed upon its future in Eastern Europe. Stresemann realized as early as 1925 that lack of German assistance might force Austria into the arms of the entente and permanently thwart the possibility of Anschluss. At the very least the Foreign Office saw economic aid as an insurance against any radical change in Austrian policy to a pro-Italian or pro-Czech course.[1]

Second, German policy had to respond to public opinion within the Reich. Large and influential sectors of this opinion were committed to helping Austria. Democratic politicians were especially anxious that a customs union be created, and the Anschluss organizations had set up committes to work for a union. Beginning in 1927 the Reischsverband der Industrie and the German Industrie- und Handelstag held common meetings with their Austrian counterparts in order to prepare for economic unification. The interest of the industrial groups was paralleled in the agrarian organizations of both states. For example, the March 1928 convention of the Lower Austrian Agricultural Chamber was turned into a pro-Anschluss demonstration. In attendance were representatives from the Prussian Agricultural Chamber, the Bavarian Peasants' Union, and the Reich Agricultural Chamber.[2]

---

[1] Stresemann to Vienna, January 24, 1925, AA 1483/3086/D613982; Foreign Office memo, November 1927, AA 2346/4576/E172921, E172984–E172985, E173002.

[2] Foreign Office report, n. 1, E172985; *Der Anschluss*, May 15, 1927; *Deutsche Einheit*, March 31, 1927; *Deutschösterreichische Tageszeitung*, March 28, 1929; *Verhandlungsschrift der gemeinsammen Tagung des Deutschen Industrie- und Handelstages und des Oesterreichischen Kammertages in Wien, 1928* (Vienna, 1929), p. 3. This last item was privately printed and labeled as *streng vertraulich!* A copy can be found in NPA, Fasz. 111, 21251.

What were the motives for such agitation? The customs union issue represented a happy juxtaposition of national and economic goals. Stresemann, propagandists for Anschluss, and economic leaders all believed that a customs union was only the first step toward the ultimate goal of political unification. There were good historical precedents for this view. Richard Riedl, ex-Austrian minister to Berlin, stated: "Decisively called into being through the foundation of the German Zollverein in the preceding century, the final goal of economic unification prepares the way for a political union. . . . And so we open our work not only for important economic aims but also for the highest of political goals."[3]

But the adherence of the business leadership was not to be expected on the basis of national loyalties alone. German businessmen would not have supported such a union unless they reaped specific economic advantages. Surprisingly, these advantages were not readily apparent to the business community. The addition of seven million Austrian consumers did not seem interesting. On the other hand, Bavarian industrialists feared Austrian competition, and many Reich economic leaders believed that Austria could only add new burdens to the German economy. The most active Anschluss supporters naturally worried that these opinions would undermine all their efforts for customs union. One of them pleaded with German businessmen to cease judging the economic union by material standards, "because these are so problematical and because they can stand in opposition to the ideal goal—the unification of the political and cultural community."[4]

Yet these fears were groundless. During the war German businessmen had learned about economic possibilities inherent in the domination of Southeastern Europe. They had formed ranks under the slogan *Mitteleuropa*, under the banner of Friedrich Naumann. Naumann died in 1919, but his lineal intellectual descendants, such as Gustav Stolper and Wilhelm Heile, carried on this propaganda, and German business listened. Thus many businessmen expected to derive immense profit from the customs union by utilizing Austria's geographic position in and traditional ties to Southeastern Europe. On this point geopoliticians such as Karl Haushofer, "young conservative" writers like Hans Zehrer, democrats such as Paul Löbe and Wilhelm Heile, businessmen such as Karl Keck and Max Schlenker—leaders of the

---

[3] *Verhandlungsschrift*, p. 76. See Österreichisch-Deutsche Arbeitsgemeinschaft, *Zum wirtschaftlichen Anschluss* (Vienna, 1926), pp. 19–22.

[4] Otto Zweidinek-Südenhorst, "Der deutsch-österreichische Zollverein," *Volk und Reich* 2 (1926): 282. See also *Der österreichische Volkswirt* 18 (1926): 577, and n. 27.

Ruhr heavy industry—all agreed.[5] Well aware that the German steel industry needed new outlets for its wares, Schlenker summed up these advantages:

Austria is the central point of a community of related production and marketing, a community that includes the succession states and the other Balkan lands. Austria has a central geographic position; it is the meeting place of five great European thoroughfares; the Danube is an important waterway that binds it with the East. All these reasons support the conclusion that Austria holds the key to these lands. . . .[6]

The Austrian economic area is the natural bridge to and the natural mediator with the lands of Eastern and Southeastern Europe that lie before it. In this region are the Austrian economy's future tasks that can only be resolved in union with the German economy. The special place of Austria in this region for centuries foredooms any attempt by the small states of the area to combine without it. . . . The German experts along with the experience of the trained Austrian mediation, could serve the whole trade of the East and Southeast. The relationship of the united [Germanic] economic area to the surrounding states could be regulated in the interests of both states [Germany and Austria].[7]

If the Germans had been left to themselves, some form of economic union would have been created. But there were a great many obstacles in the way, almost all of which were the result of foreign pressures. To establish some point of reference it seems simplest to classify these obstacles in three categories: (1) those resulting from Germany's delicate foreign policy position vis-à-vis the allies; (2) those coming from the restrictions of the peace treaties and subsequent Austrian engagements; (3) those caused by the unwillingness of German interest groups to make sacrifices for their co-nationals.

The first of the categories was the most important. Everything hinged upon the views of the French and Czechs. And the French and Czechs were opposed to any agreements between Austria and Germany. Thus the Reich government was often powerless to act, appearing insensitive to Austria's needs, unable to make even the most limited responses to Vienna. This was the case in the early summer of 1922 when the Wirth government refused entreaties to

---

[5] Illustrative of the democratic literature are Wilhelm Heile's article in the *Berliner Tageblatt*, August 15, 1925, a.m. and Gustav Stolper, "Die Vision Mitteleuropas," *Die Hilfe* 35 (1929): 402. For the same view from extreme nationalist sources see Karl Haushofer, "Mitteleuropa und der Anschluss" (eds.) Kleinwaechter and Paller, *Die Anschlussfrage in ihrer Kulturellen, politischen und wirtschaftlichen Bedeutung* (Vienna, 1930), pp. 150–53; Hans Zehrer, "Die Ideen der Aussenpolitik," *Die Tat* 21 (1929): 109.

[6] Max Schlenker, "Österreichs Schlüsselstellung im mitteleuropäischen Raum," *Volk und Reich* 4 (1928): 108.

[7] *Verhandlungsschrift*, pp. 51–52.

save the Austrian currency. In defense of Wirth, it must be admitted that he was hardly confronted with viable schemes. Richard Riedl, Austrian minister to Berlin, asked Foreign Minister Rathenau to begin discussions that would ultimately lead to an economic and political union. The Grossdeutsch Party leader and vice-chancellor in Seipel's new cabinet, Felix Frank, posed the same question to the German minister in Vienna, Maximilian Pfeiffer, and the answer in both instances was negative. Germany could not afford such an adventurous foreign policy at that time.[8]

In August Seipel himself arrived in Berlin with much less sweeping, if more specific, requests for economic aid. But even these were refused. The German government was unprepared to give more than sympathy. As Chancellor Wirth stated: "We ourselves are children of sorrow. . . . In an agitated atmosphere that is filled with other questions (Franco-German relations, Rathenau's murder, the threatened Bavarian secession), we cannot bring in anything new."[9] Thus Wirth encouraged Austria to take its case to the League; this was a journey that would end with new obligations imposed upon Vienna, new obstacles on the road to Anschluss.

In 1925 the Germans were still hamstrung by diplomatic entanglements. England's refusal to evacuate its zone of occupation at the beginning of the year was only a prelude to a series of tortuous negotiations that would lead to Locarno. As we will see in chapter VIII, Stresemann viewed the Anschluss question as an embarrassment to these negotiations. At this time nothing could possibly have come from an attempt by acting Austrian Foreign Minister Alfred Grünberger to initiate plans for an economic union. While the German Minister in Vienna may have believed that the decisive hour had struck for Austria, none of his superiors in the Foreign Office were interested in acting upon Grünberger's request.[10]

Grünberger's statement carried added weight, coming on the heels of those already made by two Grossdeutsch Party leaders. Franz Dinghofer and the ubiquitous Frank had come to Berlin during January. Both leaders had then assailed the German government and public with the now familiar theme: Austria was on the verge of collapse and could only be saved by an immediate customs union with the Reich. But again the German government and press could only give sympathy and verbal assurances. They offered vague hopes

[8] Rathenau's memo on conversation with Riedl, June 20, 1922, AA 1483/ 3086/D613861–D613862; Pfeiffer to Berlin, April 15, 1925, AA 2344/4576/ E171521.

[9] Gottlieb Ladner, *Seipel als Überwinder der Staatskrise vom Sommer 1922* (Vienna, 1964), p. 94.

[10] Pfeiffer to Berlin, April 15, 1925, AA 2344/4576/E171533.

but no specific plans for action. Therefore, in the Reichstag sitting of February 20, Stresemann affirmed his loyalty to Austria and stipulated his desire for the destruction of the economic frontiers separating the two states. But, as for granting any immediate aid, Austria would have to be satisfied with promises alone. "Our goal," he stated, "is to make our relations with Austria as close as possible in every conceivable manner."[11]

Even after Locarno, Stresemann did not act precipitously. As we have seen, Anschluss was not the first priority of German foreign policy. Only the conviction of an imminent Austrian collapse could have moved Stresemann to immediate and direct action, and, paradoxically, this threat seemed to recede after Locarno. The League's financial reconstruction had been only partially successful. Many Austrians, such as Riedl, were convinced that the economy could not last another day, but others had adjusted to the reduced possibilities of the new state. A prime example of this second case was the Austrian chancellor, Rudolf Ramek. After all, what choice did he have? In private discussion during a state visit to Berlin in March 1926, both Ramek and Stresemann agreed that the Anschluss question would have to lie dormant because of the strong allied opposition.[12] Since the allies could not be convinced that an Anschluss was the only solution for Austria, Ramek might just as well have praised the economic achievements of his state. If this act did not aid the campaign for the Austro-German union he supported, still it would allay the fears of foreign creditors. It might even silence the argument that Austria would be a dead weight for the German economy. For these reasons Ramek could overvalue Austria's achievements while undervaluing its internal weaknesses and its temporary setbacks in 1924. He joyously compared the Austrian economic recovery with that of Germany:

Who has prepared this medicine that has wrought such a dramatic change in our state's international prestige? Is it not the Germanic people who with hammer and chisel, with pen and plough, in the workshops and laboratories, behind the counters and in the fields, show the history of our resurrection from abject misery? Every branch of the German people writes its own chapter of this history. The rhythm is different, but the language is the same, and so is the belief in a better and free Germanic future.[13]

---

[11] *Verhandlungen des Reichstags*, CCCLXXIV, 809. See Pfeiffer to Berlin, January 23, 1925, AA 4491/K920/K228283–K228289; Stresemann to Vienna, January 24, 1925, ibid., K228251–K228252.
[12] See chapter V.
[13] Speech can be found in NPA Fasz. 464, 11774.

Such statements were hardly constructed to make Stresemann rush to the side of a dying Austria. But Ramek's predictions were wrong. The remainder of 1926 would not only continue the decline in the Austrian economy but see the fall of his own government. Yet in his own way, the new Chancellor Seipel would reiterate the solvency of Austria. During 1926 and 1927 Stresemann received unfavorable reports from Richard Riedl on the state of the Austrian economy. Riedl was no longer Austrian minister to Berlin, but he was still influential in the Reich and his estimation was seconded by the Austrian Minister to Geneva. Both warned that a desperate Austria, thwarted in joining Germany, might be impelled to become part of a Danubian federation which excluded the Reich. In a November 1927 meeting with Seipel, Stresemann asked whether the Austrian economy actually was in danger. "If, in reality, it is unconditionally necessary for Austria to form a tariff union with Germany, if Austria might otherwise be forced into some other engagement as an alternative scheme (to the Anschluss), it appears essential to undertake a serious discussion of the question."[14] Seipel answered the inquiry with typical indirection, but he did assure the German Foreign Minister that a Danubian federation could not be accomplished. Richard Schüller, the economic expert in the Austrian Foreign Office, more directly allayed Stresemann's fears. Schüller explained: "We cannot wait for any long period, but the present situation is not one of crisis; it is more of a chronic and unresolved nature."[15]

Therefore the first set of obstacles, external allied pressures, had been effective. They had forced Stresemann to act circumspectly. But these were not the only hindrances that Stresemann faced. He was not subject to diplomatic pressures alone. Before the customs union was achieved, he had to solve the problem of legal obstacles as well. Both Germanic states were bound to respect an Austrian independence deemed "inalienable" by Article 80 of the Treaty of Versailles and Article 88 of the Treaty of St. Germain.[16] In addition, Austria had been forced to give new guarantees as a price for the League's financial reconstruction. Signed on October 4, 1922 by Austria, Great Britain, France, Czechoslovakia, and Italy—the Geneva Protocols forged a new link in the legal armor against Anschluss. The vital section of this document occurs in Protocol I:

[14] Stresemann in conversation with Seipel, November 14, 1927, NPA Fasz. 464, 25299, p. 23.

[15] At the meeting above, AA 2346/4576/E173200.

[16] Carnegie Endowment for International Peace, *The Treaties of Peace* (New York, 1924), I: 59, 297.

The Government of the Federal Republic of Austria . . . undertakes, in accordance with the terms of Article 88 of the Treaty of Saint Germain, not to alienate its independence; it will abstain from any negotiations or from any economic or financial engagement calculated directly or indirectly to compromise [this independence]. . . . She [Austria] shall not violate her economic independence by granting to any state a special regime or exclusive advantages calculated to threaten this independence.[17]

These are a truly imposing set of obligations. But were these obligations really such obstacles? Both the German Foreign Office experts and the Anschluss organizations were surprisingly optimistic about the possibility of constructing a viable legal attack upon these documents. Both groups were willing to contend that an Austro-German customs union would not endanger Austria's independence, that these obligations did not apply in the case of customs unions. They called attention to other tariff unions that had not destroyed the sovereignty of the weaker partner—those between Danzig and Poland, the Saar and France, Lichtenstein and Switzerland.

Yet the strongest legal case does not necessarily win in diplomatic contests. A few Anschluss supporters might have been anxious for an immediate test. Ex-Minister Riedl besieged the German government with his scheme for carrying the case to the International Court of Justice. But the Foreign Office knew that such action was illusory. Many Germans and Austrians in the Anschluss movement recognized this fact. Even Arbeitsgemeinschaft head Emmiger thought a customs union was impossible under the circumstances that then applied. Stresemann could count on French and Czech opposition to a customs union, since these nations viewed it as the first step toward a political amalgamation. And he also was aware of the enormous power of retaliation that the allies possessed. As the 1927 report stated:

It is doubtful that the signatory powers of the Treaty of St. Germain and the Geneva Protocols would consider an Austro-German customs union as compatible with the independence of Austria. . . . Considering the overwhelming opposition to the Anschluss, it is doubtful that the necessary approval by the League Council would be forthcoming. Certainly this approval would not come without attachment of impossible conditions. In addition to these objections, every preferential agreement with Austria would be viewed with distrust. It would not only conflict with the peace treaties, but it would also be considered an attack against the most-favored-nation clause.[18]

[17] League of Nations, *Treaty Series*, II: 388–89.
[18] Foreign Office memo, November 1927, AA 2346/4576/E172997. See Emmiger to Pünder, March 28, 1928, ARk 4619/K1064/K273155. Emmiger's and the Foreign Office's view was correct; political considerations did play a major role in the defeat of a customs union project brought to the International Court in 1931.

The debate on the most-favored-nation clause partially echoed the earlier discussion about the peace treaty provisions. Again Anschluss organizations and government experts were agreed that this clause did not legally prohibit unilaterial German concessions to Austria. They argued that the most-favored-nation clause did not apply to customs unions. For that matter, both groups contended that the clause did not apply to any trade agreements between neighboring countries closely related by tradition and economic development. This last principle had been accepted as valid for engagements among Scandinavian countries, between Spain and Portugal, among the Baltic states.[19]

But there was no substantial agreement between the Anschluss organizations and the Foreign Office on implementing the most-favored-nation clause. The Anschluss movement was interested in removing the restrictions associated with this clause as the first step toward a customs union. But the Foreign Office thought such plans too adventurous. Meeting with the leaders of the Austrian Anschluss movement in 1928, Karl Ritter, economic expert in the Foreign Office, opposed any open disavowal of the most-favored-nation clause as "on the one hand, superfluous; on the other hand, dangerous."[20] On numerous other occasions Ritter had pointed out that German trade policy was based upon the most-favored-nation clause. He argued that any hint of its abandonment would jeopardize the Reich's economy. Furthermore, Ritter emphasized the impossibility of Austria circumventing the clause without the unanimous consent of the League Council, highly improbable as long as France maintained a permanent seat. These arguments were almost impossible to answer. The leaders of the Anschluss movement could only rely upon world opinion to force the French government into abandoning its opposition. Riedl argued that the French might relent upon the application of the clause if they could be made to recognize the German customs union as the first of a series of bilateral agreements leading to a European economic integration. The German Foreign Office never could take such a suggestion seriously. But even the most cursory Foreign Office investigation of this scheme was ended by the decisions of the World Economic Conference of 1927. Instead of rejecting the most-favored-

---

[19] Memo n. 18; *Neue Freie Presse*, June 1, 1926, a.m.; Otto von Scala, " 'Die Deutsch Klausel' -Ein Weg zum wirtschaftlichen Anschluss," *Österreich-Deutschland* 5 (1928): 23; Herbert Kniesche, *Der österreichisch-deutsche Wirtschaftszusammenschluss* (Stuttgart, 1930), p. 65.

[20] Ritter memo of conversation with leaders of Austrian Arbeitsgemeinschaft in Vienna, June 22, 1928, AA 2813/6075/E450365. See an earlier statement of November 2, 1925, in Ritter Nachlass 5421/K1124/K290453.

nation clause, the conference concluded that European economic unification could best be served through its universal application.[21]

Riedl's plans could not succeed, since they were conceived more to overcome despair over Austria's plight rather than to deal with political realities. But this hardly made his motives unique. With the failure of traditional diplomacy, many interested Germans began to seek for other solutions that would give at least the appearance of concern for Austria. In 1927 and 1928 a way out of the legal and diplomatic dilemmas seemed to have been discovered. The Foreign Office, business leaders, the Anschluss organizations had found new methods that would apparently bypass the restrictions of the peace treaties and protocols. They sought for means of achieving the substance of economic Anschluss through cooperation between the Foreign Office and various economic interest groups. As the 1927 Foreign Office memorandum stated:

Neither foreign governments nor trade hindrances stand in the way of economic rapprochement between Germany and Austria through autonomous Angleichung measures in the economic area. There could be an Angleichung of tariff formulas, of tariff laws, of production and trade statistics. There could be an adjustment of tariffs themselves, of postal and railroad rates, of taxes and monopolies, of currency standards. The same applies to cooperation between and cartelization of specific branches in industry and trade of both lands. Although the difficulties should not be underrated, the solution of these problems is, in part, the prerequisite and, in part, the consequence of economic union. The achievement of this goal can be prepared by Austrian and German economic leaders and organizations that are already in regular contact with each other.[22]

Such an attack might well have overcome the diplomatic and legal obstacles that stood in the way of an eventual customs union. But new solutions also create new obstacles—in this case the private economic interests themselves. Theoretically there should have been no problem. The major economic interest groups were on record as supporting a customs union, and there was no question that any contradictions between private and national goals could have been overcome in the eventuality of Anschluss or tariff union. If either of these projects came into being, the thought of immediate monetary gain would have been drowned in a flood of nationalist sentiment. But the schemes of the 1920s demanded an effective mobilization

[21] *Verhandlungsschrift der gemeinsamen Tagung*, pp. 71–76; Riedl memorial in Ritter Nachlass 5421/K1124/K290393–98; *Survey of International Affairs, 1929* (London, 1930), pp. 103–4.

[22] Foreign Office memo, November 1927, AA 2346/4576/E172997–E172998.

of private interests before the creation of a customs union. They required businessmen and farmers to renounce profit without giving in return the emotional and economic compensations that a national economic unification would bring.

These hopes were bound to be frustrated. For example much emphasis was placed upon an economic Angleichung achieved substantially through private efforts. As stated in chapter VII, Angleichung attempts were impeded by enormous technical difficulties, even when undertaken under the aegis of government agencies. Therefore the German Industrie- und Handelstag did little more than satisfy its honor when it formed, in conjunction with the Austrian Kammertag, committees to study the Angleichung of tariff and taxation legislation.[23]

Angleichung was not the only difficult scheme that the Foreign Office advocated. All of these proposals would have to overcome serious hindrances; none of them could have been entirely successful. Yet some solutions seemed more appropriate, more resolvable through cooperation between government and private economic interests. For example, such activity fitted well within the established pattern for negotiating trade treaties. Moreover, if the Austrians were to be granted major concessions, the Foreign Office had no choice but to involve these interest groups. Thus the re-negotiations of the 1921 Austro-German trade treaty were begun as a cooperative venture. Although supplemental agreements had been made in 1924 and 1926, the Foreign Office did not believe a general revision was possible without the aid of German business. The 1927 report stated: "The course of the future negotiations between Austria and Germany depends on how many sacrifices our industrialists will make for political reasons to Austria's production and export needs."[24] And at least one industrial group was willing. The German and Austrian cotton yarn industries made a secret convention which nullified the German advantage in the 1924 supplemental agreement.[25]

But the desire for outright German concessions was more easily verbalized than put into practice. At a common session of the German Handelstag and the Austrian Kammertag, Max Schlenker stated that business organizations should work to secure concessions for Austria in the coming trade treaty. He was immediately attacked by an Austrian critic who complained that business interest groups were not suitable vehicles for this task. Schlenker could hardly justify a proposal that he had apparently made only for rhetorical effect. He

[23] *Verhandlungschrift*, pp. 9–26.
[24] Foreign Office memo, November 1927, AA 2346/4576/E172997–E172998.
[25] VA Beilag zu P. 3 Ministerratsprotokoll, Nr. 399, October 9, 1925.

simply retreated and wistfully admitted that such a plan was illusory. "I had only wished for it," he explained.[26]

After all, business organizations were designed to protect special interests. If these interests conflicted with national policy, then the latter would have to suffer. Thus while the cotton yarn industry may have made concessions to the Austrians, the linen yarn industry used the same method to extract advantages. In 1924 a secret convention between a Berlin group and the principal Austrian firm extracted import quotas from the Austrians in exchange for tariff reductions. Other German firms were not as effective in protecting their special interests. Thus the 1924 supplemental agreement brought complaints from industrial organizations representing the umbrella stock and hat industries. The state government at Munich offered a long list of Bavarian industries that were damaged by the treaties; it started off with shoe and papermaking and ended with toys, pencils, and dentist chairs.[27]

Even more important, the influential Reichsverband der Industrie protested against the high Austrian tariffs. As early as 1924 the Reichsverband attempted to postpone any major trade negotiations with Austria. It urged the German government to concentrate on the potentially more profitable negotiations with France and Italy. The German Foreign Office, especially in the person of Karl Ritter, was receptive to the pressure of heavy industry and totally accepted the Reichsverband position.[28] Even when the talks were resumed, the reluctance of German business to make sacrifices would hamstring the Reich delegation. The delegation had a difficult time at best, since the Austrians demanded ten times more concessions from Germany than they were willing to give in return. Yet the necessity for achieving some obvious advantage for Reich industry and agriculture almost wrecked the negotiations and eventually produced, in April 1930, a treaty unsatisfactory to the Austrians.

But the most arduous work did not even concern industrial goods.

[26] *Verhandlungsschrift*, p. 61.

[27] Verband Deutschen Hanfindustrieller to Finance Ministry, 1924, FM IIz V Generalia 49ª, Bd. 3, 13057; Intressengemeinschaft des Deutschen Schirmgewerbes to Finance Ministry, 1924, ibid., Bd. 3, 13468; Finance Ministry memo, 1926, ibid., 13536; Government of Bavaria to Ritter, January 3, 1926, Ritter Nachlass, 5420/K1122/K290086; Reichsverband der Deutschen Industrie to Ritter, ibid., 5420/K1123/K290140–K290141; Wildner and Grunau memo of conversation with von Simson representing Foreign Trade Commission of Reichsverband der Deutschen Industrie, October 17, 1924, AA 1483/3086/D613960.

[28] Ibid., D613959; Reichsverband der Deutschen Industrie to Finance Ministry, Oct. 22, 1924, FM IIz V Generalia 49ª, Bd. 3, 11577. Ritter in conversation with Marx, Stresemann, and Seipel, March 27, 1926, AA 23485/4576/E172484.

The Austrians had been unable to gain concessions from German agriculture in 1924 and had only limited success in 1926. The Viennese government became so frustrated that it was willing to give up far-reaching advantages to German industry in exchange for these concessions. In November 1928 the Austrian negotiators threatened to end the talks unless their countrymen would be allowed to export animals and lumber on favorable terms. The German delegation was only able to make a limited response to these demands. There was strong opposition from the Reich Ministry of Agriculture and its client groups. The lumber industry was able to maintain discriminatory tariffs against the products of Austrian sawmills. The German agrarian organizations opposed with somewhat less success even the most minimal concessions to Austrian animal breeders and raisers.[29]

In the north some of this antagonism was probably due to a latent anti-Austrianism in the Junker-dominated Prussian agricultural organizations, but the primary objections were always economic. Ideological propensities made very little difference. Farmers in Brandenburg and Bavaria had the same economic interests. Both listened politely and refused to make commitments even to such impeccably nationalistic agrarian politicians as Karl Hartleb, Seipel's vice-chancellor in 1927 and 1928. Hartleb pleaded with northeastern German agrarian leaders; he appealed to their patriotism. "We wish," he told them, "to produce a treaty of great scope as the first step toward a customs union."[30]

Fortunately for the Austrian government, Hartleb's missions did not represent the primary thrust of its effort. Demands could be made directly to the German Foreign Office, which felt the need to pacify Austria. The Foreign Office, in turn, was able to convince the Ministry of Agriculture to increase pig imports and to make substantial tariff reductions in 1925.[31] But the Austrians desired more; they wanted outright removal or reduction of the many restrictions upon the importation of animals into Germany. They asked for the liberalization of quarantine measures and the widening of a free-trade zone along the border.

In the importation of animals, the Reich government was only one

[29] Reichslandbund to Marx, July 22, 1924, ARk 4618/K1064/K272654–K272656; Ministry of Agriculture to Finance Ministry, 1926, FM 11z V Generalia 49ᵃ, Bd. 5, 13958; Ministry of Agriculture to Finance Ministry, January 31, 1927, ibid., 28349; Fehr (Munich) to Ritter, November 7, 1925, Ritter Nachlass 5420/K1122/K290005–K290009.

[30] *Neue Freie Presse*, January 29, 1928, a.m.

[31] Lerchenfeld to Berlin, November 20, 1926, FM IIz V Generalia 49ᵃ, Bd. 5, 3006.

of the powers involved. The various state governments, especially Bavaria, would be the principal signatories of any such agreement. Bavaria would be the leader, and, in this case, the Bavarian government was inclined to inaction, since all of the state's farm organizations were opposed to the Austrian requests. Only strong outside pressures could change this situation, and such pressures were not always beneficial for the Austrians. Representing the Foreign Office, Karl Ritter objected to widening the free-trade zones along the border, since this action might have been construed as a violation of the most-favored-nation clause and have needlessly complicated all German trade negotiations. The Foreign Office did favor the lightening of the animal quarantine; thus, there was at least some chance of success in this area.

However the weight of the Reich government was not sufficient by itself to influence the Bavarians. The Foreign Office would have to act in concert with other groups—in this case, the Austrians. The leading Christian Socialist politicians had a special claim on their fellow Catholics in the ruling Bavarian People's Party. They exerted their influence to the fullest in a series of meetings between 1926 and 1929. Yet even with all these forces at work, the Bavarians granted only minimal concessions, such as an agreement in 1926 that decreased the amount of time Austrian animals spent in quarantine from thirty to twenty-one days. Little more could be done. The Bavarian People's Party felt that further agreements would jeopardize its peasant following. Bavarian peasants were restless at the prospect of granting any further concessions to the Austrians. The People's Party feared its rivals would use this issue as a lever to loosen its stranglehold on the rural vote.[32]

In agriculture and industry, the results had been the same. The Foreign Office had been unable to extract major concessions for Austria. As the trade talks dragged on, the Anschluss organizations began to realize the difficulties of overcoming the conflicts between national goals and the profit motive. They demanded drastic solutions. They pleaded that the negotiations be taken out of the hands of civil servants and put into those of the politicians. They reasoned that no German politician would dare forsake national advantage for economic gain. And there was a grain of truth in this deformed logic. Strese-

<hr>

[32] Ministry of Agriculture to Finance Ministry, May 4, 1926, ibid., 13958; Foreign Ministry to Finance Ministry, December 14, 1926, ibid., 4346; Windel to Berlin, January 31, 1927, ibid., 3665; Ritter memo of conversation with Frank, January 26, 1926, Ritter Nachlass 5420/K1122/K289980; Ritter to Frank, December 13, 1926, ibid., 5421/K1124/K290369–K290373; Windel to Berlin, June 12, 13, 1929, ibid., K290624–K290632; Heinl to Berlin, May 4, 1926, ARk R43I/108, 37–46; Frank to Vienna, March 15, 1929, NPA Fasz. 11, Zl. 99 Pol.

mann, the politician, had always viewed the trade talks within the framework of his nationalistic commitment and the wider aims of German foreign policy. When the trade treaty negotiations went sour, he suggested that a customs union might be considered. Stresemann did not mean to put this scheme into practice immediately. The Reichsminister was too wary a diplomat for that. But he was accustomed to thinking of long-term advantage; he was willing to make a beginning and reap the rewards years later. Therefore he suggested to Seipel in 1927: "Hindrances always occur when trade discussions are conducted with reference to only empirical measurement. In order to overcome these, political factors must be included in the discussion. This is true not only because the talks today have proven that it is more than a technical question but also because Austria as well as Germany could progress from this newly-won political basis to other matters."[33]

Yet Stresemann was not the Foreign Office. The very same conflict between national aspirations and economic gain was present in the corridors of the Wilhelmstrasse. On the one side was Stresemann, on the other Ritter. Ritter was forced by the very nature of his position to be more interested in short-term economic gains. He desired to protect German businessmen from the shocks of allied retaliation that could be expected if Germany gave unilateral concessions to Austria. As we have seen, Ritter was an extremely spirited defender of the most-favored-nation clause. Even more important, Ritter worked directly to protect German business against Austrian competition. And acting under Ritter's directions, the German negotiators on the scene went further. In the midst of the most delicate discussions, one reported: "The German economy's interest lies in carrying out these discussions whenever possible on an economic basis, never to let them be switched to a political track. If this last eventuality should occur, it is to be feared that specific German economic interests must then take second place to German politics."[34]

Given these commitments, Ritter naturally was disturbed about Stresemann's offer for political talks. But he did not have to fear. Business interests in the Foreign Office were, for once, seconded by

[33] Stresemann in conversation with Seipel, November 14, 1927, AA 2346/4576/E173202. Julius Curtius, Stresemann's DVP colleague as economics minister was planning for customs union as early as 1927; see his *Bemühungen um Österreich* (Heidelberg, 1947), p. 10 and *Sechs Jahre Minister der deutschen Republik* (Heidelberg, 1948), pp. 188 ff. See discussion in F. G. Stambrook, "The German-Austrian Customs Union Project of 1931: A Study of German Methods and Motives," *Journal of Central European Affairs* 21 (1961): 15–20; and Edward Bennett, *Germany and the Diplomacy of the Financial Crisis, 1931* (Cambridge, 1962), pp. 40–43.

[34] Windel to Berlin, October 8, 1928, Ritter Nachlass 5421/K1124/K290161.

the policies of a Seipel government that also recognized the seeds of Anschluss in these political talks. Ironically, Seipel desired the maximum concessions possible from German business, but he wanted these embedded in a simple trade treaty that would expand Austrian markets. Seipel made his position even clearer in January 1928, as he responded to an incident stemming from a conversation between Count Lerchenfeld, German minister to Vienna, and the Austrian Minister for Trade and Transportation. In this meeting, Lerchenfeld maintained that the trade treaty negotiations were hopelessly mired and advocated that planning be initiated for a customs union. Seipel was immediately informed about this statement. He feared that Lerchenfeld might be signaling a German abandonment of the trade treaty discussions. Thus the Austrian Chancellor angrily telegraphed Berlin for confirmation. The Chancellor was appeased when the German government replied that the impetuous Lerchenfeld had acted without authority.[35]

Yet the leaders of the Anschluss movement remained unaware of Ritter's attitude. They had no means of estimating the strength of business interests in the Foreign Office. They were simply dismayed that government did so little and were unable to understand the great discrepancy between word and deed on the customs union issue. The National Socialists sought to use this discrepancy to embarrass the Social Democratic-led Müller government. Wilhelm Frick introduced an interpellation in the Reichstag on July 4, 1928 advocating that the trade treaty negotiations "should be conducted to further the goal of a tariff and economic union."[36] The Foreign Office predictably had asked the government to ignore Frick. Müller refused; he stated that the issue was too popular to be silenced forever. He pointed to the many unanswered parliamentary questions as proof of this statement.[37] Furthermore, the Social Democrats would be secure against any excessive blame, since their pro-Anschluss stand was well known. Müller could also be confident that business interests would squash the customs union issue before it flared up into a major political debate. The National Socialists could not even count on the full force of the opposition. The DNVP represented too many businessmen and farmers to desire any major concessions from the German economic community.

Thus special privilege once again balked legitimate national goals. But neither the Anschluss organizations nor even the socialist poli-

---

[35] Schubert memos, January 21, 1928, AA 2346/4576/E173274–E173278.
[36] *Verhandlungen des Reichstags*, CDXXX, Anlage 156.
[37] Frank to Vienna, July 6, 1928, NPA Fasz. 11, Zl. 121 Pol.; see Foreign Office material in Ritter Nachlass 5421/K1124/K290731–K290732.

ticians unleashed their fury against these special interests. After all, what choice did they have? Politicians, Foreign Office economists, propagandists—they all hoped German business interests would pull their irons out of the fire. The German government had failed to obtain the necessary assistance for Vienna. Only private business was left. If German entrepreneurs could not provide the necessary leadership and capital, the flagging Austrian economy might force the Vienna government into the arms of the French and Czechs, or even the Italians.

Such a solution had ancillary advantages. Hans Schürff, the perennial Austrian trade minister, thought that this participation would lessen the shock accompanying the eventual economic union. It would provide means for training Austrians in Reich business methods and, therefore, prepare them for meeting the challenge of German business when the national state was finally created.[38] But such reasons were really gratuitous. The industrialists and bankers, the propagandists for Anschluss, the economic experts in the Wilhelmstrasse hoped that these private interests would provide the badly needed accomplishments, the visible signs that Germans did care for Austria and would act in Austria's behalf. It did not matter that German business had opposed trade concessions or that it turned to Austria solely for profit. Even before the fact. the Anschluss supporters were prepared to transform every association of German and Austrian business into an act of national heroism.

To satisfy this need for ostensible action, Stresemann's ministry was constantly urging that Austrian firms be joined to Reich cartels. The Foreign Office warmly greeted the founding of such cartels in the paper and electrical industries. The terms of this agreement not only assured to Austria its home markets but also those of Southeastern Europe for nitrogen and other heavy chemicals.[39]

The Reich government approved of another form of association, the creation of consortiums to develop Austrian water power. Stresemann hoped that the Bavarian government would also use its influence to promote these agreements. As always, the Bavarians were willing to express sympathy but were reluctant to move. Thus the strongest impetus for these consortiums would have to come from the individual Austrian state governments and the major German electrical firms. The fruit of their efforts could be seen in a series of agreements between Austrian and German firms to develop electrical energy in

[38] *Neue Freie Presse*, June 1, 1926, a.m.; see also Erich Giebert, "Angleichung: Wirtschaft" (eds.) Kleinwaechter and Paller, *Die Anschlussfrage*, p. 522.

[39] *Der Anschluss*, September 15, 1927; Foreign Office memo, November 1927, AA 2346/4576/E172986.

Salzburg, Tyrol, and Voralberg. An important byproduct of these conventions was the stream of nationalistic rhetoric they unleashed. They provided the Anschluss propagandists with yet another opportunity to show that a viable national ethic had survived in the business community. The Governor of Salzburg declared, it seemed "good to know that our work for electric power will not stop at the border of the Reich."[40]

A third form of participation was direct investment in Austrian industry. By 1928 German business and banking had invested 300 million marks in seven banks, ten electrical firms, fourteen mining and metallurgical firms, eight in the chemical industry, and eleven in miscellaneous enterprises.[41] And, as both propagandists and industrialists proclaimed, many other opportunities were at hand. Sometimes these investments would lead to a controlling interest in a firm. For the Anschluss movement, these outright acquisitions of Austrian firms were always the major victories. They applauded when Austria's largest glass factory became a branch of a German trust, when the German electrical firms had branches in Austria, when the ubiquitous Krupps were well represented. But the most important acquisition was that of Austria's great steel complex—the Alpin Montangesellschaft—by the United Steelworks Trust of Germany. The pro-Anschluss propagandists breathed a sigh of relief that "the largest firm in the Austrian iron industry is now completely under Reich German influence."[42] As if to reciprocate this approval, Anton Apold, the Austrian firm's director, exclaimed: "The Anschluss is an economic necessity of the first range."[43] Freed from the threat of German competition, Apold led the entire Austrian steel industry into supporting the Anschluss.

But acquisition was a slow process at best and, unfortunately, no other schemes of direct participation were swifter. Differing governmental regulations, problems of currency exchange, even fears about the stability of the Austrian government complicated these transactions. Occasionally Austrian resentment might be a factor as well. Fearing an undue increase in German influence, some Christian Socialist politicians were extremely reluctant to allow German cooperative banks

[40] *Der Anschluss*, September 15, 1929. See also Kniesche, *Zusammenschluss*, pp. 50–51.

[41] *Verhandlungsschrift*, pp. 55–56; Foreign Office memo cited in note 39; Lerchenfeld to Woermann, February 14, 1929, AA 2347/4576/E173834; Woermann memo, February 15, 1929, ibid., E173836.

[42] Kniesche, "Oesterreichischer Wirtschaftsbrief," *Volk und Reich* 3 (1927): 523. See also *Deutschösterreichische Tageszeitung*, April 7, 20, 1927.

[43] *Neue Freie Presse*, June 3, 1927, a.m.

to refund the bankrupt Austrian branch of the German Central Union of Savings Banks.[44] But the most important obstacle was the lack of ready money. The German capital market was hard pressed to finance its own business; it had little to spare for foreign ventures. At the common 1928 Handelstag-Kammertag meeting, a speaker proclaimed: "We Germans cannot at this time lend to you, and I would not be objective if I exaggerated the possibilities of our assistance. We ourselves do not have the money."[45]

The German government was not anxious to alleviate this situation; it showed a great reluctance to intervene in the German money market for the sake of Austrian private firms. In 1928 the Boden Credit Anstalt, Austria's second largest bank, was on the verge of bankruptcy. Its president, Rudolf Sieghardt, appealed for assistance. He held conversations in Berlin with Hjalmar Schacht, Reichsbank president, and Karl Schubert of the Foreign Office, Sieghardt stressed the desirable political consequence of a German funding rather than of a French or Czech. In effect he offered the German government control over the bank's newspapers, including the *Neues Wiener Tageblatt* that had only been lukewarm in its support of Germany and the Anschluss. But when Schacht vetoed the scheme in its infancy, Schubert appeared relieved. The Foreign Office had never been very enthusiastic.[46]

The Foreign Office did show more concern in funding loans offered by the Austrian government. The Reich was frustrated by lack of capital, the restrictions of the peace treaties, and the Reparations Commission, yet it still interceded in behalf of the Austrians. This intercession might take an inexpensive form, such as the discouragement of German banks that raised doubts about collateral behind the old Habsburg loans. It might be more direct, arranging a 6 million mark loan to the Austrian Federal Railway by Mendelssohn and Company, Berlin. In 1925 the Tyrolean state government sought a German loan to avoid becoming dependent upon the French or English money market. At first the Reich government was cautious, but a loan was finally arranged by the Dresdener Bank, guaranteed by the Reich Ministry of Finance. As always there was a rhetorical explosion. The *Neue Freie Presse* described this loan as a "kind of friendship credit which the state of Tyrol could not get from others

[44] Foreign Office memo, November 1927, AA 2346/4576/E173003.
[45] *Verhandlungsschrift*, p. 43.
[46] Schubert memo, February 21, 1929, AA 2346/4576/E173927; Bennett, *Germany and the Diplomacy of the Financial Crisis*, pp. 42–43.

without giving security or agreeing to other oppressive conditions."[47] This rhetoric was actually the most tangible result of work to unite the two economies. The Anschluss movement had dreamed that emotional commitments to German nationalism would act like the chemical placed between two metals in a voltaic cell that could almost magically produce energy from two physically separated bodies. But the magic did not work. The most important fact about the relationship of Germany to Austria remained the separation of these bodies. As long as the Germanic world was politically splintered its institutions would work at cross purposes, its regional and business groups would refuse to exchange their special privileges for a superfluous certification of their national good conduct, particularly one that could not be redeemed for cash.

[47] *Neue Freie Presse*, October 6, 1926, a.m. See also Foreign Office memo, September 22, 1925, AA 2344/4576/E171855–E171856; Radowitz (Innsbruck) to Berlin, October 10, 1925, ibid., E171864; Köpke memo, March 5, 1926, ibid., 2345/4576/E172275.

CHAPTER VIII STRESEMANN'S
FOREIGN POLICY

UP TO THIS POINT, we have concentrated on those elements in German foreign policy that were relatively static. But diplomacy is generated in response to events, and the most carefully constructed policy can fall under the daily pressures faced by any foreign office. There were two major events that had this effect on the Anschluss question in the late 1920s—one concerned the anxieties accruing from the Locarno Accords, the other the maelstrom of opposition raised in response to the Schubert festival of 1928. In both instances the Reich cabinet and, particularly, its Foreign Minister appeared to make statements that contradicted their stated objective of keeping the Anschluss question out of public view and away from the attention of the allied governments. Internal and external pressures as well as Stresemann's own emotional nationalism would often inspire contradictory results. However the contradictions were not necessarily a burden. The Anschluss was not a paramount issue for Stresemann; it could be put off to another day. In any case, he was not given to long-term views; he moved from day to day, from event to event. In fact, it could be argued that the government had really no Anschluss policy. Once reparations were no longer burdensome and the foreign occupation of the Rhineland had ended, the German government was determined to move toward a solution in the east. But there seems to have been no clear formulation of future policy except a rather vague expression that the Polish problem should be settled before the Austrian problem. Yet even this policy could have been changed under the pressure of events. This was precisely what happened after Stresemann's death in 1929.

At first glance, German policy seemed extraordinarily forthright and clear during the negotiations over the security pact. Stresemann told D'Abernon and Mussolini in 1925, as well as Ramek in 1926, that Germany would not initiate an attempt at Austro-German union, that the only German policy on the Anschluss question was to forestall any further obligations of Austrian independence. He stated this in an April 1925 interview with the *Neue Freie Presse* (Vienna). Stresemann contended: "I cannot understand at all what the Anschluss has to do with the security pact. The introduction of this question gives the impression that some want to use this opportunity to force a general concession on all future German policy. I don't need to add that no German government can agree to such a declaration that would strengthen the obligations of the Versailles treaty or would result in a renunciation of the thoughts of Anschluss."[1]

There was naturally opposition to such a policy. Beneš and Polish Foreign Minister Aleksander Skrzyński both actively campaigned for the inclusion of Eastern Europe in the security pact and were only stopped by English and German intransigence. Yet they could not agree on the Anschluss question. Polish eyes were narrowly riveted on their western frontier. This, not Austria, was the single overriding concern in Warsaw. And why not? Even Beneš agreed that the Germans gave priority to the return of their lost Silesian and East Prussian lands over other territorial revisions. There was also another reason for Polish opposition. The Poles were never sympathetic to the Czechoslovak state; they still smarted over the loss of Teschen to Czechoslovakia. The Poles and Czechs remained basically incompatible allies. Beneš went to Warsaw on April 20, 1925, but could do little to change the situation. German diplomats even reported that many Poles thought of trading away Austria for German acceptance of its 1919 frontier with Poland.[2]

The Czechs particularly needed guarantees because of their large German minorities. The most serious attempt to impose new obligations during 1925 was also intertwined with a minority problem—namely South Tyrol. After 1923 Mussolini embarked upon a campaign to Italianize the 250,000 Germans living in this territory that had been ceded to Italy at the close of World War I. Such action would naturally produce an adverse reaction in Vienna and Innsbruck, the capital of Austrian Tyrol. By 1925 this concern for the fate of the South Tyroleans had spread to Germany as well. Mussolini and his diplomats began to fear that Germany might accept *de facto* responsibility

[1] For the *Neue Freie Presse* interview, see Goldmann statement, April 8, 1925, AA 2267/4509/E125926–E125927. See also Stresemann telegram to Rome, May 23, 1925, AA 2344/4576/E171630.

[2] Koch (Prague) to Berlin, April 26, 1925, AA 2267/4509/E126103; Rausche (Warsaw) to Berlin, May 8, 1925, ibid., E126208–E126209; Stresemann memo, April 1925, AA 1483/3086/D614023. For similar Czech-Polish difficulties later on, see Jules Laroche, *La pologne de Piłsudski: souvenirs d'une ambassade* (Paris, 1953), pp. 71–75; Piotr Wandycz, *Czechoslovak-Polish Confederation and the Great Powers* (Bloomington, 1956), pp. 10–12. For a discussion of East Locarno, see Christian Höltje, *Die Weimarer Republik und das Ostlocarno Problem* (Würzburg, 1958), pp. 64 ff.

for the minority rights of the South Tyroleans. Italians did not relish dealing with a Germany whose views carried a great deal more weight in world politics than those of the small Austrian state. Salvatore Contarini, secretary of state in the Italian Foreign Office, told the German Ambassador in Rome: "At this time South Tyrol is an Austrian problem; later it will become a German one."[3]

If the Anschluss were completed, the unified Germanic state would inherit the South Tyrol problem in its entirety. Thus, in the minds of many Italians, any agitation for Anschluss was considered an attack upon the inviolability of the Brenner frontier. *Il Secolo*, the influential Milanese daily, declared that Anschluss was a preliminary step to the reconquest of South Tyrol. Mussolini publicly admitted to the relationship between these two questions in his May 1925 Senate speech. In a dispatch of June 8 to his ambassadors, he clearly stated that the Anschluss would create a new situation on the Brenner frontier to which Italy could not remain indifferent. Konstantin Neurath, the German ambassador in Rome, reported in the same month: "At the present time, anxiety over the loss of South Tyrol dominates the whole Italian public opinion. I have continually stressed in my reports that this is the most sensitive point of German-Italian relations and that every growth of the Anschluss movement must cause great unrest in Italy and has as its consequence an Italian rapprochement with our enemies."[4]

There was a basis for these fears. Not only was the agitation for Anschluss increasing, but anti-Italian demonstrations were springing up in reaction to Mussolini's policies in South Tyrol. The members of the Andreas Hofer Bund in Munich were particularly active and vituperative. A member of the Bavarian cabinet was present at one of the Bund meetings.[5] But the major source of Italian anxieties came from a conversation on May 8 between Stresemann and Count Allesandro Bosdari, the Italian ambassador to Berlin. Bosdari's dispatch to Rome may have been somewhat exaggerated, but it was not radi-

[3] Neurath to Berlin, June 8, 1925, AA 2344/4576/E171676.

[4] Ibid., E171676–E171677. See also *I documenti diplomatici italiani*, serie VII, vol. III: 494–95, 536, 538–39; *Corriere della Sera*, May 21, 1925; *Il Popolo d'Italia*, June 3, 1925; *Agenzie d'Roma* dispatch in AA 4491/K920/K228357. The most recent literature dealing with this problem can be found in Enno di Nolfo, *Mussolini e la politica estera Italiano (1919–1933)* (Padua, 1960), pp. 125–38; Mario Toscano, *Storia diplomatica della questione dell'Alto Adige* (Bari, 1967), pp. 56–96; Alan Cassels, "Mussolini and German Nationalism, 1922–1925," *Journal of Modern History* 35 (1963): 151–54.

[5] Protest of Italian government, June 18, 1925, AA 2344/4576/E171696–E171697; Schubert, Bosdari conversation, June 2, 1925, ibid., E171644–E171655; Schubert memo, ibid., E171662; Haniel to Berlin, June 19, 1925, ibid., E171719–E171720.

cally different from Stresemann's own report. Bosdari did not hide Stresemann's assurance that Germany recognized the difficulties im-implicit in Anschluss—allied opposition and the problem of integrating an enlarged Catholic South with the rest of Germany. But the Italian Ambassador also noted that Stresemann talked of an eventual union with Austria and professed an inability to understand the vehemence of the Italian opposition. Bosdari was wrong to believe that Stresemann was interested in pursuing an immediate Anschluss. He needlessly aroused Mussolini's ire by maintaining this in his report. But the Italian Ambassador did not even mention how Stresemann explicitly associated South Tyrol and the Anschluss. The Reichsminister had argued that an Austro-German union would not increase German irredentism. On the contrary, he contended that it would work to alleviate tensions "because if Germany were Italy's neighbor, we would have an interest in standing well with her."[6]

Was this a trial balloon? Stresemann evidently thought of it as such. Mussolini must have considered the possibility of trading recognition of the Anschluss for a German agreement to treat South Tyrol as an internal Italian problem. He discussed just such a possibility in a circular letter to his ambassadors. But if this was a search for a *quid pro quo*, it was introduced at such an unpropitious time as to cast doubts upon Stresemann's diplomatic ability. In the end, the conversation was embarrassing both to Bosdari and Stresemann. Bosdari did not expect the exasperation that Mussolini would vent. This conversation was the last straw in a very fragile relationship with Stresemann and would eventually lead to the Italian Ambassador's recall. Stresemann, on the other hand, constantly had to set down his work for the security pact and explain his statement to a suspicious Italian government.[7] Upon reflection, Stresemann must have known that the very mention of the Anschluss would disturb the delicate negotiations leading toward the signing of the security pact. He told this to Marx, Löbe, and the Bavarian government. Therefore it is easier to consider Stresemann's comments as an embarrassing eruption of his emotional nationalism. This kind of eruption would occur more than once and be a continuous source of complication for German foreign relations.

Stresemann's mistake was the excuse for precipitating the Italian

[6] Stresemann memo of conversation with Bosdari, May 8, 1925, ibid., E171563. See *I documenti italiani* III: 557–58. For the reaction of Rome see Neurath (Rome) to Berlin, May 14, 1925, AA 2344/4576/E171575–E171576.

[7] Stresemann to Rome, May 15, 1925, ibid., E171577–E171578; same to same, May 23, 1925, ibid., E171626–E171631. Mussolini discussed such a deal in *I documenti italiani* IV: 18.

demands for a Brenner guarantee. It was not the only reason. When the security pact negotiations had started, Mussolini evinced little interest in forcing the issue of a guarantee for the Brenner frontier. It was quite apparent in March that Great Britain was not interested in such an agreement. By that month Mussolini appeared to reject French appeals to include the Austrian and South Tyrol questions in the security pact. On March 14 he had instructed his diplomatic corps that Italy would not press its own special interests during these negotiations. He worried lest "further particular agreements, through the very fact of their existence, should, instead of strengthening, reduce the efficacy of the treaties themselves."[8]

By April the situation had changed. Mussolini began to realize that the security pact might free Germany in the west and allow the Reich greater freedom to pursue an active foreign policy vis-à-vis Austria and South Tyrol. He worried that Hindenburg's election was a signal for a renewed German expansion. In this instance, the fascist leader was not engaged in any schemes for restoring Italian grandeur. Mussolini's actions were essentially conservative—to preserve what Italy already had. Unlike Bosdari, he felt confident that Italy could prevent an immediate attempt at Anschluss. Mussolini was searching for some means of warning Germany about the consequence of taking unilateral action in the future. Perhaps he was considering some means of turning the situation to a profit by arranging a deal at some future date for recognition of South Tyrol. In any case, Italian policy could not have been effective without vigorous public action. Thus Mussolini launched a bitter attack before the Italian Senate on May 21, 1925. Regarding the Anschluss, he declared: "I am sure that the Senate agrees with me that such a flagrant violation of the existing treaties cannot be countenanced."[9] He demanded a guarantee for both the Brenner border and Austrian independence. Mussolini further informed the German and other European governments that Italy could hardly be expected to agree to the inviolability of the Rhine frontier if this would render the guarantees for the Brenner Pass less solid.[10]

In keeping with his aims, Mussolini was careful not to inflame Italo-German relations beyond the point of no return. By the first week in June, the German Foreign Office was receiving reports that Mussolini's speech had been conceived in a fit of momentary anger which was now passing. There was some evidence for this contention. Re-

[8] I documenti italiani III: 485. See also ibid., pp. 431–32, 443, 470, 474.
[9] New York Times, May 22, 1925. See also Il Popolo d'Italia, May 22, 1925.
[10] I documenti italiani IV: 10. Bosdari in conversation with Schubert, June 13, 1925, AA 2267/4509/E126652; Di Nolfo, Mussolini, p. 130.

sponding to a German request, he amended the official text of his Senate speech to exclude the demands for guarantees. He assured Neurath on June 6 that he would make no new proposals without consulting the Germans. Yet on June 8 Mussolini was already instructing his diplomats as to the best means of convincing the English that Italy's borders had to be guaranteed.[11]

Austen Chamberlain, British foreign minister, certainly played a decisive role in instituting the Franco-German rapprochement that was to begin at Locarno. Chamberlain was by no means a proponent of Anschluss. In early April the English ambassador to Berlin, Lord D'Abernon, pointedly asked Schubert if Germany contemplated any active foreign policy vis-à-vis Austria. Schubert answered predictably by assuring the English Ambassador that such a policy would be unfruitful and dangerous. On April 5 D'Abernon made a point of showing Schubert a copy of Chamberlain's letter discussing, among other things, the French need to clarify the fact that additional obligations in the west would not take precedence over existing treaty stipulations in regard to either the eastern frontiers or the inclusion of Austria in the German Reich.[12]

But this was as far as the English were prepared to go. The British Cabinet would decisively reject any eastern or southern guarantee. Chamberlain explained to various Italian and French diplomats the reasons for the British lack of support. English public opinion was not unalterably opposed to the Anschluss; the Dominions would be against such an obligation. Chamberlain accepted Stresemann's assurances that Germany was not contemplating the Anschluss. Unlike the Italians, he accepted Stresemann's contention that there was a strong Protestant and Hohenzollern-loyalist opposition to union with Austria. Perhaps the last statement was an exaggeration and certainly stronger than an interpretation of its source, a statement by Stresemann to D'Abernon, would warrant. Yet Chamberlain's arguments were well grounded in fact. In any case, the British Foreign Minister was not nearly as interested in the nature of these guarantees as in their effect upon Germany's position vis-à-vis Russia. The Locarno Pact was ultimately designed to draw Germany back into the camp of the western powers. Demands concerning Austria could scarcely achieve this result.[13]

Therefore Chamberlain was immune to the Italian arguments.

[11] I documenti italiani IV: 18–19; Prittwitz (Rome) to Berlin, May 22, 1925, AA 2344/4576/E171624; Neurath to Berlin, June 6, 1925, ibid., E171666; Cassels, "Mussolini and German Nationalism," p. 153.

[12] Schubert conversations with D'Abernon, March 31, April 2, April 5, 1925, AA 2267/4509/E125802–E125804, E125861, E125897. I documenti italiani IV: 9.

[13] I documenti italiani III: 476; IV: 18, 23, 26–28, 31, 68–69, 84.

Mussolini carefully explained the line that his diplomats were to take. The Italian leader claimed that creating new guarantees for the Rhine would reduce the treaty stipulations concerning the Brenner Pass to those of second-class obligations. He launched into a long explanation of how the Anschluss question could lead to war. He thought the English were short-sighted in only recognizing the Rhine border as a potential source of European instability.[14] But Chamberlain was unwilling to budge. The only satisfaction he would give the Italians was to restate his position in the House of Commons on June 24. The English Foreign Minister affirmed that no government was considering an Anschluss at the moment. He showed the possible methods of revision, but declared: "The idea that we should set to work within six years of the signature of the Treaty, and after all the labour they involved, rewrite the boundaries of Europe and tear up the settlements there arrived at—to try to create a fresh one—seems to me to be an idea that cannot be conceivable to anyone outside Bedlam."[15]

Mussolini suffered a diplomatic defeat. The English views were to be adopted by France. Despite their rebuff to Italy, Briand and Chamberlain still wanted Mussolini's cooperation. Briand even offered to guarantee the Brenner Pass by a separate French-Italian treaty, claiming he had Chamberlain's support for such an agreement. There is no reason to doubt this, since the British Foreign Minister gave tacit consent to the French engagements with Poland and Czechoslovakia at Locarno. But Mussolini was not interested in special considerations; he hesitated until the last moment before joining the conference to sign the security pact. At Locarno in October, he muttered something about "second-class engagements" but generally remained quiet. Bosdari reported that Mussolini had brought up the Brenner Pass again at Locarno and had been rebuffed by Chamberlain with a gentlemanly, if brusque, wave of the hand.[16]

Here was the time when Stresemann could have been magnanimous in victory. But the German Foreign Minister was not. He distrusted Mussolini; worse, he made fun of the Italian demands. Stresemann saw the Italian government as a threat not only to the Germans in South Tyrol but also to the Reich's newly won freedom of action achieved at Locarno. On December 14 he explicated this view in a long address delivered to a conservative group in Berlin:

---

[14] Ibid., IV: 18–19.

[15] Great Britain, 5 *Parliamentary Debates* (Commons), CLXXXV (1925), 1563.

[16] *I documenti italiani* IV: 13, 26; Schubert to Neurath, October 23, 1925, AA 2272/4509/E130033–E130034; Prittwitz to Berlin, October 2, 1925, ibid., E130177; Stresemann memo of conversation with Bosdari, December 14, 1925, AA 2344/4576/E171882.

I am completely clear, on the other hand, that there are also dangers buried in the Treaty of Locarno. Italy is not at all happy with it. The Italians very often speak of two types of borders in Europe—one of the first class, one of the second. And it is interesting that Italy did make an attempt to bring up the Brenner frontier for discussion. It tried to do so in Paris, London, and Locarno. An attempt has been made through me in Berlin. Since this was first mentioned, I have answered the inquiries in the following manner: I thanked him in principle for the declaration that the Brenner border should be discussed because I gather that no hindrance stands any more in the way of unification with the German Reich. If this were the case, then I could deal with the Brenner border; until then I would assume that it was an Austrian matter. Unfortunately, since the declaration on point 1 had not been given, I had to refuse every declaration on point 2 that was not on the agenda. (*Hilarity and cries of bravo!*)[17]

Stresemann also referred to the possibility of an Italian *Putsch* against North Tyrol. Yet, as late as 1926 Stresemann and Austrian Chancellor Rudolf Ramek discussed the possibility of armed Italian action. Was there any justification for considering this seriously? Mussolini always denied that any attempt was ever planned. Yet the Foreign Office official most directly responsible for Austrian affairs, Gerhard Köpke, would not totally disallow the probability of Mussolini reacting in this manner. However Köpke advised silence on this issue, since he considered a Mussolini-organized Putsch as highly improbable. Stresemann refused. Implicit in this action was the Reichsminister's total distrust of the Italian leadership. Stresemann considered public confrontations with Mussolini both thoughtful and necessary. He was convinced that only publicity would prevent the development of such a Putsch against North Tyrol. In the end, he would try to do just this, not only in the speech of December 14 but also in the Reichstag sitting of February 9, 1926.[18]

There were other reasons why Stresemann felt compelled to intervene in the South Tyrol question. We should not underestimate his emotional commitments to German nationals living under Italian rule. However these commitments were more than reinforced by the needs of internal politics. The Foreign Minister needed support for his agreement at Locarno. By proving that Germany's entrance into the League would be the prelude to serious consideration of the German

[17] *Akten zur deutschen auswärtigen Politik, 1918–1945*, serie B, Bd. I, 1, p. 744.

[18] Stresemann-Bosdari conversation, see n. 16, E171883. Stresemann, Ramek conversations, March 1926, AA 2345/4576/E172464–E172465; Köpke memo of meeting with Frank, January 8, 1926, AA 2344/4576/E171944–E171945; Frank to Vienna, December 9, 1925, NPA Fasz. 11, Zl. 282 Pol.; *I documenti italiani* IV: 158.

minorities, he might gain some needed votes. On November 21, 1925, just before the full-scale debate on Locarno, Stresemann promised the Reichstag that Germany would use its position in the League of Nations to protect the minority in South Tyrol. Yet promises were simply not enough. On December 11 the DNVP delegation introduced an interpellation asking just how Germany proposed to use the League in behalf of German minorities. This was meant to embarrass Stresemann, since the DNVP was in opposition to Germany's entrance into the League in any case. Yet a Foreign Office memorandum advised Stresemann to answer this interpellation anyway. It was his moral duty. Stresemann still hesitated and decided not to answer Mussolini in the Reichstag. He did publicly warn the Italian leader on December 14 that Italy could never bring the proud South Tyrolean peasants to their knees. And, on December 11, Stresemann communicated through diplomatic channels his concern for German children compulsorily educated in Italian. The Foreign Minister proclaimed that no German government could remain idle while this practice continued.[19]

However, the major focus of popular agitation over South Tyrol was in Munich. Bavaria, after all, bordered on the Tyrol; the Bavarians were extremely responsive to the events in the south. There was an organized effort to institute a boycott against the purchase of Italian goods. Leaflets were circulated throughout Munich, particularly at the markets. The Italian Consul complained that a Munich policeman had actually put a handbill into his car. There were attempts to discourage German tourism to Italy. There were even telephone threats against the director and leading soprano of an Italian opera company that was touring Bavaria. The South Tyrol matter was discussed in a committee of the Bavarian Landtag and then in the Landtag itself. The Bavarian agitation culminated with an address to the Landtag by the Bavarian minister-president, Johann Held, on February 5. Held proclaimed: "The Bavarian government is entirely in sympathy with the attempts to make good the injustice done to our German brothers . . . who find themselves in the minority."[20] How else could

---

[19] Oster memo, November 26, 1925, AA 2344/4576/E171921–E171926; *Verhandlungen des Reichstags*, CCCLXXXVIII, 4467–68; CDV, Anlage 1662; CDVI, Anlage 1831; Stresemann-Bosdari conversation, see n. 16. See also Jürgen Spenz, *Die Diplomatische Vorgeschichte des Beitritts Deutschland zum Volkerbund* (Göttingen, 1966), pp. 149–50.

[20] Speech reproduced in AA 2345/4576/E172014. See also Bosdari-Schubert conversation, January 15, 1926, AA 2344/4576/E171958; Neurath to Berlin, January 19, 1926, ibid., E171958; Stresemann to Rome, January 21, 1926, ibid., E171978; Köpke to Rome, January 22, 1926, ibid., E171981; Müller (Bern) to Berlin, February 1, 1926, ibid., E172006; Stresemann memo, no date, ibid.,

this speech be interpreted except as an "official green light" for the boycott movement?

Mussolini considered such actions an insult to the Italian people, and his worst fears seemed realized. He was extremely angry at the boycott attempts. In an interview with Bosdari on February 4, Mussolini so raged against the German menace that his Ambassador interpreted it as "a sign of paranoia."[21] But in an interview with a French journalist, Mussolini took care to give the impression that he was acting out of more than pique. He argued that his actions were those of "a responsible chief of state who sees things as they are and is not afraid to speak out." Mussolini continued: "It was essential to denounce the threat of Pan-Germanism. These people have forgotten nothing, resigned themselves to nothing, and will cling to their dreams of yesterday."[22] Buttressed by Italian public opinion, Mussolini answered Held in an address to the Italian Chamber on February 6. He declared that Held's speech was an insult to the Italian people and contended that South Tyrol was Italian by right of historical development and geographic propinquity.

The boundary of the Brenner Pass is a frontier traced by the infallible hand of God. [Mussolini concluded] A few days ago a Fascist paper reprinted in its columns the following headlines: "Fascist Italy will never haul down her flag on the Brenner." I sent the paper back to the Editor with the following correction: "Fascist Italy will, if necessary, carry the Tricolor further, but lower it never!"[23]

The implication of an attempt upon the north was not lost. Stresemann would publicly proclaim this a threat to both Germany and Austria. The *Vossische Zeitung* diagnosed Mussolini as a political psychopath. The socialist Reichstag deputy, Karl Stampfer, declared: "Mussolini considers himself a Caesar; he is more like a Caligula."[24] The major reaction would come from Stresemann, who addressed a Reichstag sitting on February 9. He took great pains to assure the Italians that his was not an emotional outburst. He read the speech word for word and without his usual flair. He agreed that the South

E171954; Haniel to Berlin, February 11, 13, 18, 26, AA 2345/4576/E172179, E172206, E172236, E172251; Stresemann to Rome, February 6, 1926, AA 1483/3086/D614189–D614192; Günther to Vienna, January 14, February 4, 1926, NPA Fasz. 57, Zl. 1, 2 Pol.

[21] *I documenti italiani* IV: 156.

[22] *New York Times*, February 27, 1926. For similar statements to an Austrian diplomat, see Schüller in conversation with Schubert, March 27, 1926, AA 2345/4576/E172409.

[23] Gaetano Salvemini, *Prelude to World War II* (New York, 1954), p. 101.

[24] *Verhandlungen des Reichstags*, CCCLXXXVIII, 5368.

Tyrol question was a matter of Italian internal politics. Yet he argued that the Reich could not be expected to ignore the situation because of this legal technicality. He stated: "Certainly Germany cannot interfere with the situation in South Tyrol. . . . But this does not change . . . the German cultural concern for a land and people who have been German for centuries and belong to the German cultural community. (*Lively agreement.*)"[25] Stresemann had done what Mussolini feared. He had taken the South Tyrol question out of the hands of the Austrians. Löbe summed up the debate on Stresemann's speech by stating that Germany would protect German minorities "despite concerted attacks and purposeless threats. (*Stormy agreement and hand clapping.*)"[26]

The German and Austrian press also recognized that Stresemann had taken a substantially new position, but the best evidence for this fact comes from the actions of the Austrian government itself. As early as January 6, Felix Frank, the Austrian minister to Berlin, had been assured by the German Foreign Office that his country would not be left to the mercy of the Italians. Even before Stresemann spoke to the Reichstag, Frank was assuring Vienna that the German Foreign Ministry's handling of the situation was all that the Austrians could demand of it.[27] Certainly Austrian Chancellor Ramek must have thought the same. Answering Mussolini in the executive committee of the Nationalrat, Ramek followed the Stresemann line. He even substantiated Mussolini's charges that Germany had taken over the responsibility for South Tyrol when he stated: "As for answering the contentions of the Italian Minister-President that concerned the whole German people without considering to what state they belong, we can calmly leave this to the Foreign Minister of the German Reich."[28]

There was also other evidence to support the Italian contention that the Anschluss question and the problem of South Tyrol had become inextricably related. Stresemann had already associated both in his speech of December 14. On February 23 a mass meeting was held in Munich to support the boycott of Italian goods. At this meeting a certain ex-Captain Milius declared that the Anschluss took precedence over the fate of South Tyrol. Only a unified Germany could bargain effectively with Italy over South Tyrol. A writer in *Die Hilfe* called anyone utopian for considering settlement of the South Tyrol question without an Anschluss. A delegate to the Tyrolean Landtag summed

---

[25] Ibid., 5362.
[26] Ibid., 5381.
[27] Frank to Vienna, December 9, 1925, February 2, 1926, NPA Fasz. 11, Zl. 282 Pol., Zl. 49 Pol.
[28] *Neue Freie Presse*, February 17, 1926, p.m.

up these views in an address to a massive South Tyrol rally organized by the Berlin chapter of the Volksbund. He argued that the South Tyrol problem and the struggle against Mussolini's threats had become a symbol of a wider German unification. It was simply a question of "Who will fight Germany also fights Austria, and who will fight Austria also fights Germany."[29]

These statements went even too far for Stresemann. Despite his public utterances, the German Foreign Minister always attempted to balance his policy. He wanted to warn Mussolini, but his emotional commitments to German nationalism never totally got the better of his belief in the necessity of warding off public discussion of the Anschluss question, as well as his desire to avoid any explosive incident that would jeopardize German foreign policy. Thus the German Foreign Office worked covertly to silence the boycott movement at its source, the Andreas Hofer Bund in Munich. Here the Reich and Bavarian governments were unsuccessful. The Bund leader, ex-Colonel Hörl, organized a mass meeting for the boycott as late as February 23. The Reich's Representative in Munich reported: "Hörl is 'like a bull' who will only be provoked by a direct attempt at instruction."[30] However, the Foreign Office was far more successful with both the Bavarian government and the German press as a whole. The Munich cabinet promised to discourage government officials and the Bavarian press from participating in anti-Italian agitation. It was joined by influential citizens, even by Cardinal Faulhaber of Munich. The North German press also proved amenable to control. While Stresemann was explaining to Mussolini that he could hardly be held responsible for the actions of a free press, the Foreign Office instructed German editors against any intensive handling of the South Tyrol question. The reason given was that it would embarrass the government's attempts to aid the German minority in South Tyrol, since the Italian press interpreted this agitation as a sign of German expansionism aimed at completing the Anschluss by force and then at threatening the Brenner frontier.[31]

Thus the South Tyrol question was allowed to sink slowly out of

---

[29] Österreich-Deutschland 3 (March 1926): 6. See also Milius in Neue Freie Presse, March 1, 1926, p.m.; Karl Ersinn, "Die Not Deutschsüdtirols," Die Hilfe 32 (1926): 516.

[30] Haniel to Berlin, March 3, 1926, AA 2345/4576/E172270. See same to same, February 19, 20, ibid., E172241, E172243. Bavarian Foreign Ministry report, February 28, 1926, ibid., E172271–E172272.

[31] Haniel to Berlin, February 11, 18, 1926, ibid., E172183–E172184, E172233–E172235; Stresemann to Rome, February 6, 1926, ibid., E172022; Köpke to Rome, February 13, 1926, ibid., E172209; Köpke to Vienna, February 11, 1926, ibid., E172116; unsigned press instruction, February 5, 1926, ibid., E172030–E172031.

the public arena. There is some doubt anyway that this issue had enormous appeal outside of Munich. The press reaction in the north had been raised by Mussolini's threats and not by any sustained anxiety over the fate of the Germans in Italy. In any case, the press would soon become almost totally involved in a much more important issue—the struggle over German entrance into the League of Nations. Still this does not mean there was much support for Mussolini. This applied even to the DNVP leadership and press that was sympathetic to the Italian dictator. In a sense, the cruelest blows to Mussolini came from the Right, especially from the Bavarian People's Party, which he had cultivated so assiduously.

It must be admitted that Martin Spahn, the DNVP speaker of February 9, worried that his attack on Mussolini might appear as a defense of democratic policy.[32] After all, Karl Helfferich, a DNVP leader, hoped for an Italo-German alliance once the problems of Anschluss and South Tyrol were solved. Yet only the völkisch radicals, such as Count Reventlow and Hitler, actually defended Mussolini. Their arguments were simple. They turned Stresemann's advocacy of *Realpolitik* against him. Reventlow claimed in the Reichstag that Stresemann was attacking Mussolini for ideological reasons and was sabotaging any possible Italian-German detente. The National Socialist *Völkischer Beobachter* carried a number of articles on this theme by Hermann Esser, Göring, and Rosenberg.[33] Hitler could not wait to discuss the South Tyrol problem in the uncompleted Volume II of *Mein Kampf* and rushed a pamphlet into press in February 1926. After all, the Nazi leader undoubtedly owed money and support to the man he called the "overpowering genius who embodies the national spirit of Italy" and who he now felt was the victim of an international Jewish plot.[34]

Hitler defended Mussolini in page after page of *Mein Kampf* with the peculiar blend of ideological demagoguery and demands for *Realpolitik* that characterized his thought in the 1920s. He attacked Stresemann's foreign policy as an international Jewish and Freemasonic plot against the Germans. He argued that it was conceived to turn Germany away from its true need to revise the Rhine border.

[32] For Spahn, see n. 24, 5371–72. See also *Lokal Anzeiger* (Berlin) quoted in *Bulletin périodique allemagne*, Nr. 333, p. 7. *I documenti italiani* IV: 51.

[33] Reventlow, see n. 24, 5377–99; for National Socialists see *Völkischer Beobachter*, February 10, 11, 13, 27, March 3, 6, 1926. For similar views from Austrian rightist publications see *Deutschösterreichische Tageszeitung*, August 6, 1925.

[34] Adolf Hitler, *Die südtiroler Frage und das deutsche Bundnisproblem* (Munich, 1926), p. 2. For Goebbels this pamphlet destroyed any doubt in Hitler's masterful leadership; see *Des Tagebuch von Joseph Goebbels* (Stuttgart, 1961), pp. 64–65.

He claimed that the democrats were at fault in the first place for negotiating the peace treaty which ceded the South Tyrol to Italy. In any case, these democrats knew that their actions would be unfruitful, since Italy would never renounce its claims to these lands. Hitler concluded: "But they carry on as they do because it is naturally somewhat easier to shoot off their mouths for the recovery of South Tyrol today than it once was to fight for *keeping* it. Everyone does his own part; then we sacrificed our blood, and today this company sharpens its beaks."[35]

Hitler's anti-Austrianism also was a reason for this pro-Italian stand. He urged the Germans not to fight another war for the sake of Austria. He demanded instead for national socialism to "prepare an end to this theatrical hue and cry, and to choose sober reason as the rule of future German foreign policy."[36] As explained in *Mein Kampf*, and even more directly in his unpublished manuscript of 1928, Hitler believed that an Italian alliance was the key to revision of the peace treaties; therefore, Germany would have to sacrifice the South Tyroleans upon the altar of higher national purpose.

This was *Realpolitik* with a vengeance and precisely what Stresemann was not prepared to do. As long as Mussolini embarked upon his Italianization policy in South Tyrol, the German government would be unreceptive to his offer of detente. And the latter was certainly forthcoming. In December 1926 Dino Grandi, under-secretary of state in the Italian Foreign Office, offered a nonaggression pact to Germany. There was no question that Mussolini was interested in improving relations with Germany. In an interview with the *Neue Freie Presse*, the Italian leader even held out the hope of a deal for Anschluss. Mussolini stated: "The Anschluss is an important problem for both Germany and Italy. It will come one day but, as I have already stated, the growth of empire is a slow process."[37] Despite the efforts of Neurath to effectuate a rapprochement with Italy, Stresemann remained unconvinced. He toyed with the idea but rejected it. The Reichsminister distrusted Mussolini, whom he considered both unreliable and overemotional. He did not wish to be drawn into the

[35] Adolf Hitler, *Mein Kampf* (trans.) Ralph Mannheim (New York, 1943), pp. 627–28.

[36] *Hitler's Secret Book* (New York, 1961), p. 192.

[37] *Neue Freie Presse*, January 30, 1927. See Neurath to Stresemann, October 30, November 7, 1926, AA 2345/4576/E172587, E172607; Stresemann to Neurath, November 12, 24, 1926, ibid., E172658–E172659, E172635–E172636; Zech memo, December 6, 1926, ibid., E172672–E172673. Stresemann memo of conversation with Aldrovandi, Italian ambassador to Berlin, December 9, 1926, AA 2582/5271/E326012–E326020; Prittwitz to Berlin, August 25, 1927, ibid., E326054. Mussolini expressed the same idea to Ramek in Rome during 1926, see NPA Fasz. 470, Ad. 23070.

Italian schemes concerning the Mediterranean. He would not pay the price of South Tyrol. By the end of 1927 Neurath was confiding to his Austrian counterpart in Rome that the Foreign Office did not want such a rapprochement. Thus Germany was robbed of support for its schemes for treaty revision. And it was done even with a condescension that would not again characterize relations with Italy until the middle 1940s. In 1928 Schubert explained: "Our Italian policy is very simple. First, we strive to improve our relations with Italy. Second, we are not prepared to protect the special interests of Italy, a thing which Italy has never demanded of us. Third, between us stands South Tyrol. Italy is stupid to let the situation in South Tyrol stand, but that is an Italian affair."[38]

After the explosion of 1926, the Anschluss question remained dormant again until 1928. There were a number of reasons for this. The Seipel government was far less pro-German than that of Ramek. The July 1927 riots in Vienna profoundly disturbed Stresemann. His immediate response was to conclude that German political institutions could not absorb an unstable Austria. Perhaps a customs union was as far as he was prepared to go. He confided to Schubert that: "His opinion was that it would be best if Austria, finally and for all time, remained in this circumstance by which she stays independent and is not annexed to Germany."[39] Schubert must have taken Stresemann seriously, since he had already passed on these views to the French Minister in Vienna.[40]

Yet opinions can change with the times, and the Reichsminister seemed to have different views in August 1928. The Schubert festival in Vienna during July had again raised the Anschluss question. The German and Austrian press considered it an important manifestation for the Anschluss. The French press, from *Le Temps* and *Le Soir* to *Action Française*, saw the demonstration as the beginning of a new German attempt at Anschluss. The French Ambassador warned that the demonstrations in Vienna would have a bad effect upon Franco-German relations.[41] Even the Hungarians were disturbed because of

---

[38] Schubert memo of conversation with Frank, July 6, 1928, AA 2347/4576/E173529. See also Stresemann in conversation with Ramek, March 1926, AA 2345/4576/E172468, and Moellwald to Vienna, October 22, 1927, NPA Fasz. 80, Zl. 69 Pol.

[39] Schubert memo, July 16, 1927, AA 2346/4576/E172848.

[40] Schubert memo of discussion with Peter in Vienna, May 30, 1927, ibid., E172906.

[41] Hoesch (Paris) to Berlin, July 24, 1928, AA 2347/4576/E173575–E173574; Köpke memo, July 30, 1928, ibid., E173578–E173579; Hoesch to Berlin, June 21, 1928, AA 4492/K920/K229210; Foreign Office memo, August 1928, ibid., K229281–K229284; Bülow memo, September 10, 1928, ibid., K229899; *Der Anschluss*, August 15, 1928.

a side excursion of some choral groups led by Löbe to Burgenland, an area Austria had acquired from Hungary after World War I. Schubert wrote Löbe one of those now typical Foreign Office notes with more than a hint of reproach.[42]

There were other danger signals as well. These concerned the negotiations that were taking place for the withdrawal of French troops from the Rhineland. Ex-Chancellor Marx publicly warned against any renunciation of Anschluss in exchange for this evacuation. Ex-Justice Minister Gustav Radbruch again associated these two questions in an address delivered before an influential audience that even included Hindenburg. Radbruch declared: "There is no German that would not be as one with all the Germans in these two demands for union with Austria and liberation of the occupied territories."[43]

Stresemann was aware that the Anschluss problem could not be excluded from the discussions during his forthcoming visit to Paris. He wrote to Schubert: "We must be prepared with what we shall say on our side when such an attack comes."[44] But the German Foreign Minister violated his own instructions. Stresemann was sick and exhausted during his Paris visit at the end of August. This was evident during his conversation with Poincaré on the 27th. Perhaps his weakness made him less clever; in any case, Stresemann was prone to the intrusion of emotional nationalism. When the question came up, Stresemann did start with all the right arguments. He stated that Germany did not contemplate an immediate Anschluss. As long as France was opposed, the Anschluss could never be achieved. In addition, he assured Poincaré that a Catholic Austria might not be suitable for the Reich.

Then the dam burst. Stresemann began to discuss all the agitation for Anschluss. To explain this, he took Poincaré on an interesting excursion through the German soul. Stresemann claimed:

The vast majority in Germany and Austria are for the Anschluss. For this reason, M. Poincaré, you must understand that every meeting of Germans in Vienna will be greeted with joy. We are, in contemporary Germany, more Americanized than any other nation in Europe. We work too much. We have become a people of the haste and inquietude of large cities.

[42] Benzler (Budapest) to Berlin, July 28, 1928, AA 2347/4576/E173576–E173577; Schubert letter to Löbe, August 1, 1928, ibid., E173581–E173582; Löbe to Schubert, August 10, 1928, ibid., E173585–E173586; Benzler to Berlin, August 3, 1928, AA 4492/K920/K229259–K229260; Viennese Embassy report, July 30, 1928, ibid., K229244–K229251.

[43] *The Times* (London), August 13, 1928. For Marx see *Der Anschluss*, September 15, 1928.

[44] Schubert memo of August 6, 1928, quoting letter of Stresemann, dated August 4, AA 2347/4576/E173580.

Our press thrives on sensations. . . . But we recognize in our minds that we have lost a piece of our soul through participation in this modern life. Vienna and Austria appear to us a land where people live differently— a little less modern, quieter and more comfortably. That city conjures up the names of Mozart and Schubert. Then, in Vienna, life was more refined and more gracious. There, even now, theater and literature mean more than a boxing match. When, for this reason, such a great jubilation was expressed for the city itself during the Schubert festival, it was because we seek our lost souls in these people who are of the same blood and have the same feelings as we. This fact has always been so, even after Bismarck created the kleindeutsch government. We have been for centuries in one Reich, and we will feel the same in the future. You must understand this in Paris.[45]

But, of course, this is precisely what could not be understood in Paris. Poincaré was disturbed. The French President was obviously taken aback by this explosion of feeling. He stated that Germany and Austria could have a common cultural identity as long as they remained politically separated. He quickly turned to other affairs and left his considerable doubts for discussion within the French government.

There was obviously some discussion. Briand was already faced with interpellations from all sides. On December 4 the Foreign Minister answered his questioners with the statement that France would never agree to the political suicide of Austria. He told the Chamber: "If, in the national interest, 10 percent of the people wish to safeguard their independence, do you believe that the right of self-determination should prevail? I do not and never shall."[46] The Germans and Austrians were appalled. German Chancellor Hermann Müller and Briand engaged in a public debate. Briand argued that all agitation for Austro-German union would fail, since France would never allow such an action. Müller stated: "There is no Austrian people; there are only Germans in Austria. . . . We are one nation. We bear the same suffering. This has brought us closer together."[47] Julius Deutsch, the Viennese socialist leader, expressed the same view during a German-Austrian football match in Berlin. Referring to Briand's speech, Deutsch declared: "We go with joy to this suicide."[48]

The culmination of this debate occurred during private discussions between Stresemann and Briand at Lugano on December 10. Briand

[45] Stresemann, *Vermächtnis*, III: 360. For a discussion of this meeting, see Jacques De Launay, *Major Controversies of Contemporary History* (London, 1964), pp. 121–24.

[46] *Débats parlementaires, Annales du Chambre des Députés*, CXXXVI, 640.

[47] *Der Anschluss*, January 12, 1929.

[48] *Österreich-Deutschland* 6 (January 1929): 6.

complained of Löbe's participation in the Schubert festival where "Watch on the Rhine" was sung more than once. Stresemann answered that Löbe had not participated in these demonstrations in his capacity as Reichstag president. Stresemann urged Briand to remain calm. He argued that Briand's address could be used by the federalists in Germany, who could argue for the rights of their 10 percent of the population.[49] It was obvious that both foreign ministers were disinclined to let this incident trouble French-German rapprochement. But there could be no question that the French still feared that Germany would turn eastward after the evacuation of the Rhineland and that this fear played some role in slowing down the negotiations for withdrawal of French troops from German soil.

That French anxiety had a real basis cannot be doubted. We have seen in chapter VI that Stresemann was determined to move east as soon as possible. While the question of priorities was not definitely settled, his real disposition seems to have been shown in a letter to the Crown Prince in 1925, where he gave the reacquisition of the lost Polish lands precedence over the Anschluss. His preference for the Protestant North over the Catholic South made him worry about the ultimate disposition of the Austrians in a united Reich. Yet Stresemann also used this proposition as a diplomatic weapon, knowing such statements would please Hohenzollern princes as well as English, French, and Italian statesmen. Stresemann may also have believed that a customs union with Austria was all that could be accomplished until political stability was achieved in Vienna.[50]

Karl Dietrich Erdmann has overstated the case by concluding that Stresemann was always suspicious of an Anschluss, that he never believed a peaceful revision of the Austrian border was possible. Erdmann is correct that Stresemann gave priority to Poland. But precisely what does this mean? Stresemann's Polish policy is as unclear as his Austrian policy. The reclamation of the territories lost in World War I belonged to some distant future. As in the Austrian question, Stresemann alternated between emotional national pronouncements and some sort of appeasement.[51]

[49] Stresemann (Lugano) to Berlin, December 10, 1928, AA 2347/4576/E173625–E173627. See the actual record of the Stresemann-Briand conversations in AA 4492/K920/K229399.

[50] See chapters IV and V.

[51] Karl Dietrich Erdmann, "Das Problem der Ost- oder Westorientierung in der Locarno-Politik Stresemanns," Geschichte in Wissenschaft und Unterricht 6 (1955): 149. For other views see Zygmunt Gasiorowski, "Stresemann and Poland after Locarno," Journal of Central European Affairs 30 (1958): 299–317; Josef Korbel, Poland between East and West (Princeton, 1965), pp. 188 ff. For the most recent and comprehensive overview of the literature, see Hans Gatzke,

Perhaps the answer is that Stresemann believed in Poland first. Perhaps Julius Curtius was right when he considered himself following in Stresemann's footsteps when he initiated the customs union project. We will never know. Stresemann carried these ambiguities with him until his death; they were never dissolved through action. Thus the historian is forced to lament Stresemann's death—not only for its negative effect upon the Weimar Republic but because it enormously complicates the process of understanding his policy. There were ambiguities in his thought and actions that, like the Anschluss question in the 1920s, were unresolvable. Stresemann castigated Löbe for taking part in Anschluss demonstrations and at the very same time needlessly disturbed the Italian government. Sometimes Stresemann thought that unification should never take place; at other times, he demanded that Austria find a place in Germany's future. He had originally supported Anschluss only as a lever against the Versailles system and had not accepted the democratic belief that Anschluss meant the beginning of a new political era, yet his conversation with Poincaré suggested quite the opposite. Toward the end of his life, the Reichsminister was searching for a means to create a true national consensus based upon the republic. The democrats could have been right about the Anschluss from the beginning. Such a union might even have saved the Weimar system.[52]

But the historian does not find a much clearer solution to the Stresemann problem by integrating his actions with the shape of German policy. The Reichsminister's own ambiguities were reinforced by the situation of Germany. Stresemann had to walk a tightrope between two pressures from the Anschluss proponents at home and the opponents abroad. It was an impossible situation for the German diplomats, unable to give either the French or their fellow countrymen the assurances both wanted. It is no wonder that they invented that magical substitute for these assurances, constantly repeated always with the same words whatever the context. As Stresemann stated: "The Anschluss question is not acute."[53] Translated into policy this meant that the Austrian problem did not have to be resolved, that the diplomats had ingeniously found a solution that consolidated the ambiguities within the German position.

"Gustav Stresemann: A Bibliographical Article," *Journal of Modern History* 36 (1964): 1–13.

[52] Stresemann's conversion to the idea of the republic as a vehicle for national integration is discussed in Lothar Doehn, *Politik und Interesse* (Meisenheim a. Glan, 1970).

[53] Stresemann to Neurath, May 14, 1925, AA 2344/4576/E171583.

CHAPTER IX THE AUSTRO-GERMAN CUSTOMS UNION PROJECT

THE DRAMATIC MOVE from Stresemann's policy of restraint to an activist position in 1931 was the result of the changed political situation in the fall of 1929. In 1929 the Austrian government was far more friendly to Germany than at any time since 1922. The German government also had a greater degree of freedom of action than heretofore. An activist policy promised some success and fitted well with the aspirations of Julius Curtius, Stresemann's successor in the Foreign Office. It was in this atmosphere that the customs union scheme was conceived. However, it was unfortunate for Curtius that the diplomatic position of Germany had considerably worsened by the time the policy was put into practice. The failure of the Austro-German customs union scheme was less the result of poor planning than of bad timing. And, once the decision was made, there was no turning back. After having conceived the project in secret, Austria and Germany were forced to abandon it in a series of humiliating public defeats which had disastrous consequences for the governments involved.

In many ways, however, Curtius was pursuing Stresemann's policy to its logical conclusion. Stresemann had to deal with Seipel; Curtius did not. It was the creation of the new Austrian government in 1929 that precipitated the move toward a customs union. Nothing could have been accomplished while Seipel remained as chancellor, but Seipel was forced out of office in April 1929. The short-lived Streeruwitz government was succeeded by the Schober cabinet in September. Streeruwitz had been considerably more pro-German than Seipel, but Schober outdid him. Schober was considered by the press of both states and the Reich Foreign Office to be "a good German."[1] And he did much to substantiate this opinion by concluding a series of conventions that furthered the amalgamation of the social insur-

[1] Lerchenfeld to Berlin, December 25, 1929, AA 1484/3086/D614605. See also chapter XIII.

146

ance, copyright, and patent laws. Schober also brought the very difficult trade treaty talks to a culmination. Furthermore, his constitutional reform of November 1929 could be interpreted as a unilateral Angleichung of the Austrian with the German constitution. The new constitution provided for a president elected by universal suffrage after the pattern of and with powers similar to the German Reichspresident.[2]

These hopes faded for a short time in September 1930, when Schober was replaced by the Seipal-Vaugovin government, but in December Schober was back as foreign minister and vice-chancellor in the Ender government. His pro-German position was fortified by the new political party he headed. The National Economic Block was composed mainly of German nationalists who continuously pressured Schober to undertake a pro-German course of action.

Curtius reacted to the new political constellations in Austria by proposing closer cooperation with Vienna. But even if there had been no change in the Viennese cabinets, the mere continuation of Stresemann's policy would have necessitated thoughts of German intervention. Stresemann stated in 1927 that Germany might have had to offer assistance if a bad economic recession forced Vienna to make further guarantees of its independence in exchange for assistance. By the fall of 1929 the Austrian economy was in another of its periodic crises. The Boden Credit Anstalt, Austria's second largest bank, failed in September. The world economic collapse further heightened Austria's capital starvation and threatened to unhinge the already fragile economic institutions of the Alpine state. Like his predecessors, Schober began to consider reaching agreements with France, Italy, or even the Little Entente in order to alleviate Austria's chronic capital shortage. In early 1930 he apparently showed more interest in securing French loans than in proceeding with the customs union project. The more the Austrians dallied with the French, the more the German Foreign Office would worry. If Curtius was different from Stresemann in this respect, it was only in the tone of the new Foreign Minister, who was far more excitable and less cautious than his predecessor.[3]

Stresemann had also been committed to diplomatic movement in the east once the western questions were settled. So was Curtius. It was left to Curtius to put his plans into operation at a time when there

[2] *Stenographische Protokolle*, III Gesetzgebungs Periode, Bd. III, Beilage, 382; Malbone W. Graham, "The Constitutional Crisis in Austria," *American Political Science Review* 24 (1930): 144.

[3] F. G. Stambrook, "The German-Austrian Customs Union Project of 1931," *Journal of Central European Affairs* 21 (1961): 21–32. See also Friedrich Hertz, *Economic Problem of the Danubian States* (London, 1947), pp. 148, 156; *Neue Freie Presse*, March 5, 1931, p.m.

was a change of climate in which German foreign policy operated. German revisionism had never been so apparently near success as in the fall of 1929 when Stresemann died. Curtius continued his predecessor's work by bringing the Young Plan negotiations to a successful conclusion. Germany was to be freed from the foreign controllers who supervised reparations payments. The last occupation troops were to be withdrawn from the Rhineland in 1930, fully three years ahead of schedule. These concessions seemed to indicate a growing toleration in Great Britain and France for Germany's foreign policy goals. The road to further concessions seemed open.

The problem was in what direction to move. Here Stresemann's legacy was ambiguous. Although Stresemann had always placed the Polish question first and the Anschluss much lower on his list of priorities, tactical considerations might have dictated just the opposite move in 1930. Schubert, Stresemann's secretary of state, argued against an Austro-German customs union in that year. But Schubert had already been replaced by Bernhard von Bülow, who had believed that the logic of Stresemann's revisionism dictated a movement toward Austria. While Stresemann was alive, in the summer of 1929, Bülow, then only a deputy director in Department II of the Foreign Office, prepared the following memorandum:

Normally we would be able to hope that the Rhineland will be evacuated by the spring of next year and that the other problems which keep us and France apart will be settled or postponed. If the British Labour Party is then still in power and, as seems probable, pursues an active foreign policy, then the time will probably have arrived for us to embark on a great activity. The questions of the Corridor, Upper Silesia, and the Anschluss will come to the fore. Coming to grips with Poland would deserve priority. . . . But it could be that the time for raising the Eastern problem may not be ripe and that we must tackle the Anschluss question in one form or another. My opinion is not to work for an Anschluss in the fullest sense of the word but rather of active steps in respect to preferential tariffs and similar things.[4]

Curtius was somewhat less flexible than Bülow and Stresemann; he was committed to a union with Austria as a matter of first priority. This was the result, in part, of his experiences as minister for economics. In 1927 Curtius had instructed officials in this ministry to begin planning for such a union. Planning for the union became an *idée fixe* of his foreign policy. Less than three months after assuming office, Curtius broached the subject to Schober during their discus-

[4] Ibid., p. 20. See similar quote in *Documents on British Foreign Policy,* series II, vol. I, 45–46.

sions in Berlin on February 22–24, 1930. Curtius retained his views as foreign minister, but the emphasis shifted from economic planning to political achievements. He conceived of these technical discussions playing a different role than in 1927. They were designed to keep channels of communication open between Berlin and Vienna until the time was ripe to initiate action. When the discussions were actually initiated they lasted less than two months and produced a draft treaty which resolved none of the hard problems, such as what Austrian industries would have to be protected against German competition. Curtius admitted in February that the allied opposition was too strong to initiate action immediately. What was necessary was to keep Berlin and Vienna talking, "as political constellations were capable of very sudden change. If the overall European situation provided an opening, we must be ready to make use of it."[5]

He was obviously thinking ahead to the end of the French occupation. Certainly this was the signal to begin the technical discussions in earnest. On July 3, three days after the last French troops withdrew from the Rhineland, Ritter wrote to Schüller that they should begin the technical discussion in earnest. During the same month, Briand gave the two Germanic states the opening they needed by advocating a general European economic union. The ensuing discussions brought the whole tariff structure of Europe into disrepute and seemed to lay the groundwork for the mutual reduction of tariff barriers, even in the shape of bilateral customs unions. The time seemed appropriate. The basic decisions had been reached. On January 2, 1931, Ritter slipped into Vienna with the German draft text. Despite all these so-called technical negotiations this treaty was scarcely more than an agreement in principle; the negotiations could move rapidly. On January 6 Schober approved the draft treaty. The Vienna Protocol would soon be signed. All that remained was to make it public before the world.[6]

Unfortunately for the Germans and Austrians the European balance had been altered since 1929. Perhaps the customs union plan might have achieved some success in the winter of 1929–30 when it had been originally proposed. By 1931 the hopes of its realization appeared much more fragile. The depression would not affect all of

[5] Curtius-Schober discussions, February 22–24, 1930, AA 1484/3086/D614747. See also Julius Curtius, *Bemühung um Österreich* (Heidelberg, 1947), pp. 24–25; idem, *Sechs Jahre Minister der Deutschen Republik* (Heidelberg, 1948), pp. 107, 119; Stambrook, "Customs Union," pp. 21–27; Edward Bennett, *Germany and the Diplomacy of the Financial Crisis* (Cambridge, Mass., 1962), p. 44.

[6] Stambrook, "Customs Union," pp. 27–37; Bennett, *Diplomacy*, pp. 41–51; Jürgen Gehl, *Austria, Germany and the Anschluss* (London, 1963), pp. 5–9.

Europe equally; France emerged from the first year of the collapse relatively unscathed. In a scarce capital market the power of money becomes even greater than usual. By the end of 1930 France possessed enormous influence as the only large nation with resources to float large international loans. The French government was not averse to using this power to gain political leverage. A loan to the Italian government was delayed until Paris could be assured the money would not be used for naval expansion. In December 1930, René Massigli, French disarmament expert, told a British diplomat: "France has only to wait a little and Italy will come on its hands and knees and beg France for a loan at any price."[7] And this was a France that was at the core of the opposition to Anschluss, facing a Germany and Austria both seriously weakened by capital starvation.

Yet once plans are set in motion they have a life of their own. They generate emotional commitments that make retreat impossible. Curtius and Bülow had conceived the customs union plan in the relatively favorable situation during the winter of 1929–30. They were unwilling to be dissuaded by the flood of unfavorable comments that greeted their plans a year later. Köpke, still the principal officer responsible for Western Europe, warned of the implacable opposition of France and Czechoslovakia. Gaus, still head of the legal department, doubted the legality of the union. Schubert, now in Rome, and Hoesch, still in Paris, reported on the difficulties accompanying the announcement. Hoesch reminded Curtius that, "without France, let alone against France, none of the problems facing us can be solved." He argued for a policy of "carefulness, patience, and wisdom."[8] Yet Curtius and Bülow ignored these warnings. Curtius even claimed that he had Hoesch's full approval during a meeting in Berlin. Perhaps Hoesch had changed his mind on the train back to Paris. Perhaps Curtius had listened selectively.

This pattern of insensitivity to the international situation would be continuously repeated in the months to follow. Stresemann may have violated his own injunctions to soothe the entente because of the frustrations resulting from his policy of restraint, but Curtius and Bülow seemed to have made a career of needlessly pricking the French. The use of Briand's Pan-European scheme as a justification for the economic union might have appeared an ingenious idea, but it challenged the feasibility of Briand's carefully wrought program and raised doubts about the credibility of anything the Austrians and

[7] *British Documents*, series II, vol. I, 437.

[8] Hoesch memo, March 6, 1931, AA 4507/K936/K240626. See also Köpke memo, February 24, 1931, AA 5426/K1148/K294599–K294603; Bennett, *Diplomacy*, p. 49.

Germans might say. Upon reflection, Briand could only question Schober's motives in his speech before the League Assembly on September 12. The Austrian had then advocated regional economic ententes as "the foundation for the realization of Briand's idea."[9] The French Foreign Minister could understand the explicit fears of the Austrians that nothing concrete would come of his European economic schemes. He might even have thought that the Austrians wanted a regional economic detente to form some sort of Danubian union. But Briand could have no illusions when Schober used this same speech to justify the Austro-German customs union project. Whatever the Austrian motives, the Germans were certainly guilty of duplicity in arguing that the customs union was, in reality, the first step toward Pan-Europe. The German Foreign Office had always viewed Briand's scheme as a guise for the maintenance of the political *status quo* through changing the worst economic features of the Versailles system. Bülow had always considered Briand as a manipulative schemer who could in turn be manipulated. "Dressing up the affair in a Pan-European cloak"[10] was Briand's just reward.

Briand was also stung by the lack of any prior consultation. The governments in Vienna and Berlin had done this purposely in order to give the impression that the project had been hastily conceived to save the foundering Austrian economy. Therefore, they would give no hint of their intentions to the French. When Curtius arrived in Vienna on March 3, the French press had raised the perennial hue and cry. On the same day Briand had sought to calm these fears by assuring the Chamber of Deputies that "if it [the Anschluss question] has not completely disappeared, it is no longer so acute as it was represented to be two years ago."[11] Unfortunately for the French Foreign Minister, Curtius was at that very moment finalizing his plans for the announcement of the customs union project. The original intention of the German and Austrian governments was to announce their project at the organizational meeting of the League's Commission of Enquiry for a European Union. This would have been even more embarrassing for Briand. However, the news leaked out as early as

---

[9] League of Nations, Assembly, *Verbatim Report of Eleventh Ordinary Session, Sixth Plenary Meeting*, p. 5.

[10] Bülow to Prittwitz, January 20, 1931, AA 2384/4620/E199139–E199140. See also Stambrook, "Customs Union," p. 23. For a different view, see Oswald Hauser, "Der Plan einer deutsch-österreichscher Zollunion und die europäischen Föderation," *Historische Zeitschrift* 479 (1955): 45–71. It is interesting to note that even the pre-announcement leaks in the press were using this justification; see *Neue Freie Presse*, March 17, 1931, a.m.

[11] *Survey of International Affairs* (1931): 218. See also "L'accord douanière Austro-Allemand," *Journal des économistes* 99 (April 1931): 8.

March 6. Hoesch's negative reply to Briand's offer of a French loan for German acceptance of the *status quo* assured the French that these rumors were true. The French and their loyal Czech allies began their attack on the customs union even before the Austrian and German cabinets had approved the final plans. On March 18 the French and Czech ambassadors in Vienna introduced a formal protest. It was not until three days later that the announcement finally came. The customs union was launched; the so-called Vienna Protocol was signed under auspices which German Chancellor Heinrich Brüning correctly labeled as "perhaps not especially fortunate."[12]

Curtius had not only misjudged Briand, but he had also underestimated the French power to influence the two undecided states—Italy and Great Britain. At first Mussolini apparently accepted the German and Austrian justifications and viewed the customs union scheme as a hopeful sign for the European economy. His only concern was that the union would not jeopardize Italian economic interests, and he instructed Grandi to enter into direct negotiations with Germany to assure this point. Mussolini further reassured the Austrians that he was willing to view the situation carefully and objectively. However, the Italian government soon found that the customs union would become entangled in its major short-term foreign policy goal. Both Mussolini and Grandi had staked their prestige on resolving their struggle with the French government. This conflict began over the light sentences meted out during 1928 to the murderers of the Italian Consul in Paris. It continued in the Italo-French deadlock during the London Naval Conference of 1930. The arrests of anti-fascists in France during 1929 and the continuous efforts of British mediation were just beginning to take effect. When the French suddenly found fault with the basic agreement over naval parity on March 21, Grandi could only interpret such a move as an attempt to make Italy join the united front against the customs union.[13]

Mussolini, therefore, had to choose between supporting the German action and antagonizing the French or following the French line in the customs union dispute and antagonizing the Germans. This choice really involved two alternative lines of expansion. With France and Great Britain pacified, Italy might hope to expand into the Eastern Mediterranean. With German support, Italy could exert considerable influence over Yugoslavia and the whole Danubian basin. Grandi

---

[12] German Cabinet minutes, March 16, 1931, 3620/K49/K005268.
[13] Schubert (Rome) to Berlin, March 23, 1931, AA 1484/3086/D615062; Bennett, *Diplomacy*, p. 37; Gehl, *Anschluss*, pp. 13–15; Salvemini, *Italian Foreign Policy under Mussolini*, pp. 75–84; *Foreign Relations of the United States, 1931*, I: 540–41, 570, 573.

intimated to Curtius that the Italian approval for the customs union project could be bought if only the Germans could offer *quid pro quo*. The Germans were, as always, reluctant to enter into any combination with Italy. Thus Grandi, against his will, turned to the Franco-British position. He intimated such a change of policy as early as March 21. He told von Schubert, now ambassador to Rome, that "The affair is now considered everywhere as a first step to the Anschluss. You cannot expect Italy to cooperate in such a scheme."[14] By April 29 the Italian government had already informed the British that "as it is conceived, the projected union is not planned in a 'European spirit' in the general interest, but in the restricted interests of Austria and Germany, and more in those of Berlin than of Vienna."[15]

The German and Austrian press saw some hope when the British government at first refused to join in the French protest. The Germans could see that Bülow's prediction of a Labour government's neutrality might have been correct. Perhaps the majority of the Labour Party did agree with the *Daily Herald* in castigating the Anschluss prohibitions as a folly of the peace treaties. But the foreign secretary in the Labour government, Arthur Henderson, was soon forced to take a different position. Henderson was a prisoner of his commitments to European disarmament, which appeared to be jeopardized by the customs union project. If the customs union issue was the cause of the French withdrawal from the naval talks, the failure of the customs union scheme might be necessary to bring about naval disarmament. Italo-French agreement on parity in the Mediterranean was necessary before the limitations on cruisers accepted by the great powers in 1930 could be implemented. This work had to be completed before the crucial conference on land disarmament could begin in 1932.[16]

Even without French pressures, Henderson would have taken the same course of action. Curtius and Brüning had done little more for a year than predispose Henderson to distrust their government. The British Foreign Minister believed that German revisionism, not French intransigence, was the main obstacle to an effective European disarmament. Henderson had already warned Curtius in December that a new, more active German policy would turn Britain toward France. He knew that German activism in foreign policy would so agitate the French that the Paris government might never be willing to compromise on disarmament. The Germans had acted as if to confirm Henderson's worst suspicions. France would never accept complete equality

---

[14] Schubert to Berlin, March 21, 1931, AA 2520/5002/E284373. See also Curtius memo, May 15, 1931, AA 3620/K49/K005533.

[15] *British Documents*, series II, vol. II: 43.

[16] *Survey of International Affairs* (1931): 279–81.

with Germany, yet this was precisely what Curtius and his chancellor, Heinrich Brüning, demanded. In response to Henderson's request for a positive contribution on the disarmament question, Curtius answered on March 18 by demanding complete legal and military equality with France. This response, coupled three days later with the customs union announcement, gave Henderson the impression that the Germans desired a complete revision of their treaty obligations, a position that would destroy all chances of successful limitation on land weapons.[17]

Thrown upon the French, Henderson arrived in Paris on March 23 to find an almost hysterical Briand. The French required some shoring up, and this was precisely what Henderson did. On March 25 the British representatives in Berlin and Vienna received the following cable from Paris written by Sir Robert Vansitart, secretary of state in the Foreign Office:

> German (Austrian) Government should be under no misapprehension as to serious misgivings which have been aroused by their action in many countries and France in particular
>
> Though there may be two opinions as to the exact conformity of the proposed treaty with existing obligations of Austria and, indeed, of Germany, you should make it clear to German (Austrian) Chancellor that state of feeling both in Great Britain and here causes me great concern, and I feel that if nothing is done to calm existing apprehensions the task of those who are anxious that Disarmament Conference should meet under the most favorable conditions will be seriously compromised by any apparent disregard of any treaty obligations by unilateral action.[18]

Vansitart went on to predict dark consequences if Briand's policy of conciliation were undermined by the customs union project. The British official position was to refer the matter to the Council of the League of Nations. Both the Austrian and German governments were further asked to suspend their negotiations at implementing the Vienna Protocol until the question of its legality had been settled. On the same day the Germans were presented with even more disturbing evidence of British intentions. Ernst von Simson, German delegate to the Commission of Enquiry, reported that Henderson was interested in more than the mere legality of the question. Simson expected that the League Council would treat the customs union project under the general provision for settling international disputes.[19]

At this point Germany could have surrendered. All the projections

---

[17] *British Documents*, series II, vol. I: 581–85; Bennett, *Diplomacy*, pp. 85–87; Gehl, *Anschluss*, pp. 15–16.

[18] *British Documents*, series II, vol. II: 12–13.

[19] Simson to Berlin, March 25, 1919, AA 2520/5002/E284409–E284410.

of victory had proven false. Yet it was just as impossible for Brüning to retreat as for Curtius. The Germans simply dug in their heels. They refused to make concessions and, thus, became even further isolated. Their only response was to assert the impregnability of their moral position. Brüning was angered by the British note. Why was the British Prime Minister not equally concerned with the stability of the German government? The election of 100 National Socialist deputies in September 1930 had been a great shock to the German democracy. Brüning had now staked the prestige of his minority government on the customs union issue. He maintained that "Germany had so few rights and if she were going to be checked at every turn the position of his government would become untenable."[20] Brüning particularly feared being branded a disturber of the peace before the League Council. The German Chancellor was not mollified by reports from London that both Henderson and Vansitart did not personally view the customs union as a step toward political amalgamation. Yet he made no attempt to conciliate Henderson. His reply to Henderson was an adamant refusal. "The German government could not admit to an examination of the agreement from a political standpoint as the agreement is of a purely economic character. The negotiations must naturally take their course."[21] All the German Chancellor would offer Henderson was the right to discuss the judicial aspect of the question and an admission that the technical details of the project could not be settled for two or three months.

Fortunately for Henderson, the two allies were not as close as they pretended to be. Curtius had always wanted the customs union for political reasons; Schober needed the economic benefits that would accrue from the Vienna Protocol. In April Schober would try to interest the Italians in a tariff union as well. Ritter could throw up his hands in disgust at such a scheme, which he considered as the purest economic phantasy, but both Ritter and Curtius knew that a third partner would undermine the political objectives of the agreement. In March this same economic priority would apply in Vienna. Schober could not afford to antagonize Great Britain, the center of European finance. It is not surprising, therefore, that his reply to Henderson would state that "the Austrian government has not the intention of making a *fait accompli*."[22]

[20] *British Documents*, series II, vol. II: 15.

[21] Ibid., p. 17. See also Neurath to Berlin, March 23, 1931, AA 3620/K49/K005472; ibid., Bennett, *Diplomacy*, p. 66. For German press reaction, see *Neue Freie Presse*, March 23, 1931, a.m.; *Berliner Tageblatt*, March 23, 1931, p.m.

[22] Ibid., p. 15. See also Ritter to Köpke, April 24, 1931, AA 2520/5002/E284761–E284762; Bennett, *Diplomacy*, pp. 71–74.

Since it takes two partners to negotiate, this statement satisfied the British. Having won his point with the Austrians, Henderson had no intention of further humiliating signers of the Vienna Protocol. He now rejected the French position that the League Council should discuss the political implications of the customs union. Only the legal and financial aspects of the union would be matters for debate. And neither of these would be examined by the League Council. The economic problems of the union would be discussed before the Commission of Enquiry for European Union. The Council would confine itself to requesting an advisory opinion from the International Court of Justice. Yet this compromise did not mean that the British Foreign Minister had softened his position. The official British reply of May 1 to the Austrian and German notes was hardly conciliatory. The British threatened to invoke the most-favored-nation clause if Austria were offered some temporary tariff protection against German competition. It also asked both Germanic powers to consider alternative schemes to the customs union.[23]

All that remained was to play out the scenario already written. The debates at Geneva would perpetuate the French-German deadlock and reinforce Henderson's control over the situation. There were three separate discussions of the customs union in Geneva during the third week in May, but they all led to the same conclusion—the complete isolation of the Germanic powers that Curtius had so cunningly forged. On May 16 the French unveiled their alternative plan before the Commission of Enquiry. André François-Poncet proposed the creation of a European-wide system of cartels that would assign prices and production quotas on a continent-wide scale. He even accepted Schober's proposal for regional economic ententes that would lower tariffs among their members. The French plan also called for "immediate and effective help for Austria . . . to assist her to regain her economic prosperity at a rate sufficient to ensure her separate existence."[24] François-Poncet contended that the Austro-German customs union was hardly the first step toward European economic integration. It would divide the European nations into two groups—German and French—that would engage in continuous political and economic conflicts. The Germanic powers were not impressed with this scheme. Schober forcefully denied the French arguments and claimed that a customs union with Germany was the only

[23] Ibid., p. 38. For Henderson's views on Austrian compliance, see his address to the House of Commons in Great Britain, 5 Parliamentary Debates (Commons) CCV (1931): 720.

[24] League of Nations, Commission of Enquiry for European Union, Minutes of the Third Session of the Commission (CC. 395, M. 158. 1931, VII), p. 22.

solution capable of providing the immediate relief Austria needed. However, no other power came to the support of the two German states. The representatives of Italy, Poland, Czechoslovakia, and Rumania enthusiastically sided with the French. This was an ominous sign for the future.[25]

When the League Council met on May 18, this same isolation was apparent. Although Henderson remained passive while the French carried the debate, he did intervene once to gain from Schober a further renunciation of negotiations until a decision had been reached by the International Court of Justice. Curtius claimed that this was done "in a rough form and tone,"[26] but the German Foreign Minister had some right to be paranoic by this time. The whole meeting was going against him. As the debate dragged into the second day the Italians, Yugoslavs, and Czechs supported the French position. Finally, the discussions completely deteriorated, with Curtius quoting Guizot and Briand, using maxims from Metternich, and both debating the correct interpretation of each other's evidence. At this point Henderson intervened to stop the show. He suggested that the Council request an advisory opinion from the Permanent Court of International Justice on the question: "Would a regime established between Germany and Austria on the basis and within the limits of the principles laid down by the Protocol of March 19th, 1931 . . . be compatible with Article 88 of the Treaty of Saint Germain and with Protocol No. I signed at Geneva on October 4th, 1922?"[27]

Even Henderson's sobriety could not stop this exercise in non-negotiation. The British Foreign Minister had arranged a compromise that satisfied neither side. France was unwilling to abide by the decision of the World Court. Both Briand and Marinković claimed that such an opinion would only be advisory and not binding. They declared that the issue could be returned to the League Council at any time. Curtius was furious. He was convinced that the decision would favor the German case, and any further debate would be tantamount to accusing his nation before the bar of world opinion. "I decline to allow my country to be thus arraigned before any public body as disturbers of the peace."[28] For Curtius the French arguments only strengthened his confidence in the eventual outcome of the decision at the Hague. He wanted reassurance that no further obstacle would be put in the way of completing the customs union. He held this view in the face of the solid opposition of all important European powers.

[25] Ibid., pp. 28–85.
[26] Curtius, Bemühungen, p. 55.
[27] League of Nations, Official Journal XII: 1069.
[28] Ibid., p. 1078.

The German Foreign Minister had become so emotionally committed to the invulnerability of the German position that he made the enormous mistake of attributing his values to the world.[29]

Moral unassailability was all the Germans had left, and this was to be challenged when they lost the decision at the Hague by a vote of eight to seven. Fortunately for the Germans the decision of September 5 was reached in a manner that could scarcely undermine their moral pretentions. The Permanent Court of International Justice had not rendered a monument of international jurisprudence. The failure was certainly not due to a lack of effort. With a thoroughness that would have even pleased the most meticulous Prussian, public hearings were held that lasted two weeks, filling a volume of over 600 pages. Joseph Paul-Boncour, the leading French counsel, dryly commented that this process "guaranteed the judges' minds against all surprise, exhaustively explored, by many detours, all aspects of the problem."[30]

The fault was that the case was too complex to be resolved by traditional jurisprudence. The judges had to determine the validity of two different statements of sovereignty. The Germanic counsel argued for an older view. They contended there could be no abridgment of Austrian independence so long as there were separate capitals in Berlin and Vienna. The Vienna Protocol was constructed to give each partner full equality under the agreement. The French contended that the customs union would have to be judged on the basis of "historical and political realities."[31] This was no ordinary tariff agreement. The desire for political amalgamation in both Germany and Austria would inevitably turn the customs union into a full-scale Anschluss.

The judgments unfortunately had the clarity of neither argument. They lacked both the toughness demanded by the French and the equity demanded by the Germans. The minority opinion refused to consider the French brief. It read: "This Court is not concerned with political considerations nor with political consequences. These lie outside of its competence."[32] Still the minority seemed hardly secure

[29] Bennett, *Diplomacy*, pp. 71–74; Jan Krulis Randa, *Das deutsch-österreichische Zollunionsprojekt von 1931* (Zurich, 1955), pp. 99–122.

[30] Joseph Paul-Boncour, *Entre deux guerres, souvenirs sur la IIIe république. Les lendemains de la victoire 1919–1934* (New York, 1946), p. 176.

[31] Permanent Court of International Justice, *Customs Regime between Germany and Austria (Protocol of March 19, 1931), Pleadings, Oral Statements, and Documents*, series C, No. 53, p. 400. See also Ball, *Post-War German-Austrian Relations* (Stanford University, 1937), pp. 157–85.

[32] Permanent Court of International Justice, *Customs Regime between Germany and Austria, Advisory Opinion of September 5th, 1931*, series A/B, no. 41, p. 75.

in this conclusion. After ignoring political and economic data, the opinion went on to prove that the use of this inadmissible evidence could not have changed its conclusions.

The majority decision was scarcely better. Written by only one judge, Antonio Bustamente, this opinion claimed that the customs union did not violate the peace treaties but only the specific agreements Austria had made in the Geneva Protocol of 1922. However six of the seven judges who signed the opinion appended a codicil that claimed the customs union violated the treaties of Versailles and Saint Germain as well.[33] Only Dionsio Anzilotti, the Italian judge, responded to either of the arguments. In a separate opinion that cast the deciding vote, Anzilotti admitted that Austria would not have violated its independence by concluding a customs union with any other state. "We are concerned with this Customs Union and *this* Customs Union alone . . . . [It] would beyond all dispute assimilate the economic life of the two nations and its effect would therefore be to confirm and strengthen the movement toward incorporation of Austria within a single big German state."[34]

Thus, even in defeat, the Germans could claim a moral victory. The seeming confusion of the judgments, the closeness of the vote, the fact that the majority could not agree upon a single sound line of argument—all these factors were an easy target for Germanic publicists. The Germanic press had a sure set of villains. On one side were the judges from France and her Eastern European allies, buttressed by those from small, inconsequential Central American republics. On the other were judges from the neutral states of Great Britain, the United States, the Netherlands, Belgium, and the Asian countries. The Viennese jurist Stephen Verosta bitterly exclaimed, "The Court makes its debut as a dilettante on the [political] scene."[35] Still it would have been better to win. The Court's decision had come two days after Austria and Germany had renounced the Vienna Protocol in Geneva. The victors could afford to be generous. Even *Le Temps* thought that this decision added little to the French triumph. But for the *Neue Freie Presse* it was that "the last hope has disappeared . . . to save something good from the smoking ruins."[36]

In effect, the customs union scheme was dead even before the League Council meeting in May. The Vienna Protocol could only have

[33] Ibid., pp. 49–52.

[34] Ibid., pp. 68–70.

[35] Stephen Verosta, "Les avis consultatifs de la Cour permanente internationale et le régime douanier entre l'Allemagne et l'Autriche," *Revue de droit international* 9 (April-June 1932): 262.

[36] *Neue Freie Presse*, September 5, 1931, p.m. See also *Bulletin périodique autrichienne*, Nr. 209; *Berliner Tageblatt*, September 5, 7, 1931, p.m.

been pursued to an effective conclusion if Austria and Germany could be immune from foreign pressure. On May 12 all hope of this ended when the Austrian government announced the insolvency of the Rothschild-owned Credit Anstalt, Austria's largest bank. Between 60 and 80 percent of Austrian industry depended on the Credit Anstalt for financing. The government had no choice but to attempt the reconstruction of this bank. Within three days the Austrian National Bank discounted 228,000,000 schillings in Credit Anstalt notes while losing 29,000,000 schillings to foreign creditors who began withdrawing shares from the bank and other Austrian concerns. By the end of May the whole Austrian economy was on the verge of chaos.[37]

How could the Austrian economy be financed? A grant of 100,-000,000 schillings in rediscount credit by the Bank of International Settlements was used up in the first fourteen days of the crisis. On May 15 the League's Control Commission for Austria had authorized the Vienna government to float a 150,000,000 schilling loan, but there had been no takers. As early as May 19 Montagu Norman, governor of the Bank of England, had formed a London committee to study the situation. On May 29 the Bank for International Settlements sent the French expert Charles Rist to study the situation. Yet no loan was forthcoming. The British waited, and an attempt by the Paris Rothschilds to bail out their cousins in Vienna was vetoed by the French government on political grounds. The London committee was broadened by the addition of French, Italian, and American creditors of the insolvent Austrian bank. On June 15 the Head of the Italian Bank Corporation arrived in Vienna. But still no aid was forthcoming. By June 15 the situation had worsened beyond all previous conditions. Seven million schillings were withdrawn from Austrian banks on that day alone. The demand for foreign values increased so rapidly that the National Bank was hardly able to meet inquiries for notes. It was evident that the time for immediate action had come.[38]

It was at this point that French monetary power intervened. There were rumors abroad that the French had precipitated the whole crisis by withdrawing funds from the Credit Anstalt. However, there seems to be little support for such an assertion. Edward Bennett,

[37] *Stenographische Protokolle*, IV Gesetzgebungs Periode, Bd. I, Beilage 126; *Neue Zürcher Zeitung*, May 11, 15, 21, 1931; *Neue Freie Presse*, May 11, 12, 30, 1931; *Vierteljahrshefte zur Konjunkturforschung* 56 (1931): Nr. 4, Part B, p. 6; *The Economist*, 112 (June 6, 1931): 1219, 1245; Howard Ellis, *Exchange Control in Central Europe* (Cambridge, Mass., 1941), pp. 27, 352.

[38] *Foreign Relations, 1931*, I: 23; *Neue Freie Presse*, May 16, June 16, 1931, a.m., June 5, 15, 1931, p.m.; *Berliner Tageblatt*, May 27, 1931, p.m.; *The Economist* 112 (June 6, 1931): 1211; 113 (July 4, 1931): 43; Howard Ellis, "Exchange Control in Austria and Hungary," *Quarterly Journal of Economics* 54 (November 1939): 28.

who has exhaustively studied the financial diplomacy of 1931, believes that the French may have been the source of the leak about the Bank's collapse. Whatever the case, the announcement of the Credit Anstalt's failure could not have been better timed for a French diplomatic offensive, since it came only four days before the Geneva meetings. Even if the French had been ignorant of the Austrian crisis before May 11, they were determined to use the Bank's collapse to extract political concessions from Vienna. Finance Minister Pierre Flandin stated that parliament would never allow any assistance to be given to Austria unless the customs union project were relinquished. On June 16 the Quai d'Orsay informed Vienna that the price for a French loan was for Austria to submit to the League's financial control and to reject unilaterally the customs union.[39]

The Ender government seemed scarcely able to reject these demands. The French government's intention to publish the contents of its note would totally undermine what little confidence was left in Viennese financial circles. The Austrian economy would be plunged into a complete chaos at a time when the government was critically weakened over the internal political consequences of the Credit Anstalt's collapse. The government's stringent pay cuts for civil servants already forced the resignation of Justice Minister Schürff on May 20. The final blow came on the same day as the French ultimatum. Finance Minister Otto Juch resigned rather than accept the government's plan for the assumption of the Credit Anstalt debts. Juch's resignation destroyed Schober's National Economic Bloc and robbed the Ender-Schober cabinet of its majority in the Nationalrat. The Chancellor felt he had no choice but to retire from office.[40]

On the night of June 16, Schober stood alone. He rejected the French ultimatum, but this final act of courage left him defenseless against foreign and internal foes. Some immediate action was necessary to fend off complete collapse of the Austrian economy. The only possible hope was for an immediate massive loan. Fortunately, the British were prepared to act in their traditional role as protector of continental financial stability. Since May 25 Montagu Norman, governor of the Bank of England, had been in constant communication with Vienna and was convinced that the immediate danger to the

[39] *Foreign Relations, 1931*, I: 18. For the argument that the French did not precipitate the crisis, see *Der österreichische Volkswirt* 23 (May 23, 1931): 896–98; Walter Federn, "Der Zusammenbruch der österreichischen Kreditanstalt," *Archiv für Sozialwissenschaft und Sozialpolitik* 67 (1932): 404–21; *The Economist* 113 (July 4, 1931): 43; Bennett, *Diplomacy*, pp. 101–3. For French views, see Hoesch to Berlin, June 11, 1931, AA 2521/5002/E285120–E285121.

[40] *Berliner Tageblatt*, June 20, 1931, a.m. *Neue Freie Presse*, May 16, June 17, 1931, a.m.; Gulick, *Austria from Habsburg to Hitler*, II: 936–37.

European economy would come from that direction. Thus, at the same hour when Ender tendered his resignation, Schober was outlining his country's desperate position to Sir Eric Phipps, British minister to Vienna. The British were astounded at the French ultimatum. Henderson and MacDonald called it blackmail. They feared that the simultaneous announcement of the French ultimatum and the cabinet's downfall would magnify the already growing Austrian panic and have serious repercussions on the entire European financial structure. With the approval and urging of the British government, Norman was prepared to offer aid. He agreed to underwrite the 150,000,000 schilling loan immediately, although he had no authority to take such precipitate action. The news of the decision was telephoned to Vienna at 12 p.m. and was immediately followed by an offer of a 100,000,000 schilling loan from the Bank for International Settlements.[41] Austria had been saved, at least temporarily.

The British intervention only delayed the inevitable. It would keep the same cabinet under a new chancellor, Karl Buresch. It did cause the French to withdraw their condition for the moment and accept 65,000,000 schillings of the rediscount loan. However, the Bank of England was no longer the arbitrator of the world's financial policy. The United States had been seriously weakened, and only France remained able to lend large sums of money. The Bank of England was even forced to turn to the Paris money market for credits. The British loan to Austria could only be extended on a week-to-week basis. On June 13 Henderson informed the French Ambassador to the Court of Saint James that London had done its share for Austria and no further aid could be expected from that quarter. On August 8 Norman informed Schober of the imminent withdrawal of the British loan. The Austrian Foreign Minister was left without any alternative but that of accommodation with France. The French also appeared more conciliatory. By August 10 Schober appealed to the League for aid and the customs union issue was virtually, if unofficially, closed.[42]

Curtius railed at these signs of Austrian duplicity. The Germans had, after all, remained firm against intense pressure. The Credit Anstalt collapse had affected the German economy adversely. The moratorium on war debts and reparations proposed by President

[41] British Documents, series II, vol. II: 74, 85; Foreign Relations, 1931, I: 23–24; Gehl, Anschluss, pp. 30–32; Bennett, Diplomacy, pp. 149–53.

[42] British Documents, series II, vol. II: 224; Official Journal XII: 2121; Der Österreichische Volkswirt 23 (August 15, 1931) 12: 1202; Neue Zürcher Zeitung, July 30, 1931; Neue Freie Presse, June 29, July 31, August 2, 31, p.m.; July 11, 18, a.m.; Ellis, "Exchange Control," p. 28.

Hoover promised such an alleviation of this crisis, but the French demanded concessions before they agreed to Hoover's plan. On June 28 the French government demanded that Germany renounce the customs union and the building of pocket battleships. Henderson and William Castle, United States undersecretary of state, hoped that Germany would voluntarily, in Henderson's words, "allow the customs union to drop as a token of her appreciation of the immense service Mr. Hoover had rendered her."[43] On July 13 the crisis worsened. The great German D-Banks (Darmstädter and Dresdener) failed and could only be restored through massive capital infusions of the German government. Brüning desperately needed money. Only large international loans and the moratorium agreement could save the German economy. Still the Germans remained adamant on concessions. In Paris on July 18 Brüning and Curtius had refused the French suggestions of a political moratorium, including the end of the customs union project, as a price for French loans. The talks were amicable; only later would Curtius claim this refusal as a German moral victory. "They would not bind us in golden chains."[44]

However, much of this German intransigence was for domestic consumption. By August the Austrian diplomat Theodor Hornbostel could report, "the leading people in Berlin were decided under all circumstances from placing any difficulties in the way of the solution of the political and financial questions between Germany and France. Therefore the problem is only to give the customs union an honorable burial."[45] But there was little honor to be gained. The hope that the Germans could renounce the customs union on the heels of a favorable World Court decision proved impossible. Under French pressure Germany and Austria had to agree to a formal renunciation at a meeting of the Commission of Enquiry on September 3, two days before the Court's decision was to be announced. Nor were the Austrians much consolation. Curtius met with Schober on August 31 to set the final details, only to find that Schober was independently and secretly negotiating with the French. Furthermore, Curtius claimed in his memoirs that Brüning desired to make Austria renounce alone, since this would take a great deal of pressure off the German cabinet. Curtius refused, knowing that German silence would only anger the French into demanding further concessions from Vienna. And Austria did get its loan of 250,000,000 schillings and Curtius did renounce

---

[43] *British Documents*, series II, vol. II: 105. See also ibid., p. 180; *Foreign Relations, 1931*, I: 96–97 219–23; *Berliner Tageblatt*, June 20, 1931, a.m.; Bennett, *Diplomacy*, pp. 200–1.

[44] Curtius, *Bemühungen*, p. 65. See also Bennett, *Diplomacy*, pp. 273–74.

[45] Vienna to Berlin, August 17, 1931, AA 2521/5002/E285334–E285335.

the customs union. The German Foreign Minister concluded lamely that the new French plan for European-wide economic union superseded the customs union, since it was the German idea "from the outset, that it should be the starting-point for wider economic agreements in which as many European countries as possible would take part."[46]

Curtius wrote on September 4: "I bear the full responsibility for the breakup of this action."[47] There were many ready to agree with him. Brüning was under attack from the Right-wing press, who were always anxious to criticize his government. National Socialists and German nationalists declared the loss a national disaster, as a sign of the bankruptcy of national policy. The whole Brüning government was endangered. Someone had to take the responsibility. Rather than blame the Chancellor, the moderate *Frankfurter Zeitung* took a line more likely to save Brüning. This paper declared that the loss was the result of the Foreign Minister's miscalculations. Brüning would make the same statement. He pointed out in the cabinet meeting of October 3 that the customs union had never been submitted to the cabinet until a few days before the Vienna Protocol was announced.[48] This was true. Curtius had hardly informed his Chancellor until after the negotiations were well under way. He had never considered the internal political consequences of the union. He had not even consulted the Minister of Trade and Finance. Then, on March 16, as an afterthought, he had promised political gains from his cherished project. "Other circumstances permitting, a united front might be formed on this question reaching from the Social Democrats to the National Socialists."[49] On October 3, Brüning asked for Curtius' resignation. And there would be still another scapegoat. Although his resignation was refused on September 6, Schober was out of office permanently on January 27, 1932.

The defeat of the customs union marked the end of the hopes of revision that were so carefully nurtured by Stresemann. It was not so much that French power was at its zenith in the postwar era as the fact that the world depression had fundamentally changed both internal politics and foreign policy among European countries. The men who had attempted to create a climate of negotiations in the 1920s

[46] *Minutes of the Fourth Session of the Commission* (C. 50 M. 215 1931. III), p. 11. See also Curtius to Berlin, August 31, 1931, AA 3621/K49/K005707–K005712; Curtius, *Bemühungen*, pp. 66–67; Ball, *Post-War German-Austrian Relations*, pp. 152–53.

[47] Curtius to Berlin, September 4, 1931, AA 3621/K49/K005773.

[48] Cabinet minutes of October 3, 1931, AA 1685/3573/D788405–D788407; Ball, *Post-War German-Austrian Relations*, pp. 155–56.

[49] Cabinet minutes of March 16, 1931, AA 1683/3575/D786167.

were also dying. Briand's health began to decline in the summer of 1931, and he would die the next year. Both Seipel and Schober died in August 1932. Brüning would leave office in the same year. His successor, Franz von Papen, was so removed from the pattern of the 1920s that he was indifferent to Austria undertaking any new guarantees of her independence, a violation of one of the standard rules of Stresemann's diplomacy.[50] Stresemann's revisionism had already been laid to rest when Hitler assumed power in the following year.

[50] Gehl, *Anschluss*, p. 43.

ANSCHLUSS VERSUS AUSTRIANISM

CHAPTER X AUSTRIA AND ANSCHLUSS

AUSTRIA IN THE 1920s was truly a unique phenomenon, a state bent on its own self-destruction. The majority of Austrians favored Anschluss and saw it as their only salvation. It is the purpose of this chapter to determine the strength and the limits of this attempt at national suicide. Why did the old Austria leave such an apparently small inheritance to the new? Why did it seem upon retrospect that Austrian civic virtues had been bought at some rummage sale of political ideas—the symbols of imperial order, the loyalties of political Catholicism, a collection of Franz Joseph's virtues? And why, if this were true, could the Austrians not totally reject their heritage?

It is difficult to deny that a majority of Austrians desired the Anschluss. During the 1920s the figure of 90 percent was loosely used. This was based upon plebiscites held in Salzburg and Tyrol where less than 2 and 7 percent, respectively, voted for independence. While there were no opinion polls in the stabler years after 1923, there was other evidence to indicate Austrian support. In 1928 the Austrian Volksbund circulated a petition demanding Anschluss. The Volksbund proclaimed that three out of four Nationalrat delegates signed this document. This author has checked the published lists and has found a somewhat lower number. Still 92 Nationalrat delegates signed this petition which is 9 more than a simple majority of the Nationalrat. And missing were 12 socialists, 2 from the Grossdeutsch Party, and 4 from the Landbund. These groups were unanimous in support of Anschluss. Thus if every delegate had voted his convictions, 108 delegates would have been in favor of the Anschluss.[1]

[1] *Der Anschluss*, December 15, 1928, January 12, 1929. For the Volksbund statement, see NPA Fasz. 402, 20746 pr. 9 II 1931. The best general appraisals of the Anschluss movement in Austria are those by Walter Goldinger and Adam Wandruska in (ed.) Heinrich Benedikt, *Geschichte der Republik Österreich* (Vienna, 1954), pp. 94–103 and passim. See also Ball, *Post-War German-Austrian Relations* (Stanford University, 1937), pp. 8 ff.; Hans Leo Mikoletzky, *Österreichische Zeitgeschichte* (Vienna, 1962), pp. 81 ff.; Ernst Hoor, *Österreich, 1918–1938* (Vienna, 1966), pp. 42 ff.

The minority was composed of the Christian Socialists, yet even then eighteen Christian Socialists signed the Volksbund petition. Some even came from the Viennese wing of the party so dominated by Seipel, long considered cool to this proposition. The signers were distributed over all of Austria; five came from Vienna and the rest from the provinces. Yet Anschluss was so popular that the party as a whole was pressed to take an affirmative stand on this question. In 1918 the Christian Socialist program demanded the reunion of Austria with the German Reich. In 1926 the platform was less specific but still demanded "especially the equality of the German people in the European community of nations and the settlement of relations to the German Reich on the principle of the right of self-determination."[2]

Of course, the Grossdeutsch, Landbund and Social Democratic platforms were far more specific in their demands for an immediate union with the Reich.[3] And there were other indications: for example, the popularity of mass meetings organized by the Volksbund in almost every district (Bezirk) of Vienna, as well as the capitals of all the federal states but one. The meeting at Salzburg was typical. It included two Landtag delegates from the state of Salzburg, as well as one Nationalrat delegate, the Mayor of the city, and a priest at the cathedral. There Karl Renner proclaimed that the right of self-determination was stronger than all treaties and concluded by stating: "We are part of the grossdeutsch Reich and as such want to live."[4] There is also the evidence of foreign diplomats. The American Minister to Vienna noted the steady growth and intensity of the Anschluss movement as early as 1925. Schubert reported on a visit in 1927 how the Anschluss was the major topic of discussion in the diplomatic corps. Furthermore, he stated, "No talk with an Austrian personality can come to a conclusion without an intensive discussion of the Anschluss question."[5]

The Anschluss supporters had no difficulty in providing an intellectual justification. They had only to discover themselves remarkably unexceptional Germans. Then their Austrian traditions would be

[2] Klaus Berchtold, *Österreichische Parteiprogramme, 1868–1966* (Munich, 1967), p. 376.
[3] For the Socialist 1927 program, see ibid., p. 264; for the Landbund program of 1923, ibid., p. 483. For the Grossdeutsch Party, see *Neue Freie Presse*, May 25, 1925, p.m.
[4] *Der Anschluss*, March 28, 1929. For the founding of the Viennese Bezirk groups and other state organizations, see ibid., December 15, 1928, January 1, 12, February 25, March 14, 1929.
[5] Schubert report of Vienna trip, May 30, 1927, AA 2346/4576/E172909. See also USDS, Washburn (Vienna) to Washington, June 10, September 2, 1925, 863.01/35, 863.01/38.

amalgamated with the Reich German, their state reduced to a German province. As the most diligent of the pro-Anschluss propagandists wrote:

1. The Austrians are no special *Volk* but a branch of the Germanic race, no different from the other South German branches. The Austrian is less different from the Bavarian than the Bavarian is from the Prussian or the Saxon. They [the Austrians] speak the same language as the other Germans; they are thus nothing but Germans.
2. The Austrians have a thousand-year history in common with other Germans.
3. The Austrians have the same culture, art and science as the Germans.
4. The Austrians have never stopped considering themselves as part of the German people. Their will to unite with their brothers is no recently conceived notion.[6]

This fourth proposition was the most difficult to substantiate. The dual monarchy had its Prussophiles who advocated their government's dissolution and an Anschluss of German-speaking Austria with the Reich; in addition, they desired the obliteration of Austrian customs and the re-training of Austrians in the Prussian virtues of duty and efficiency. The result of the war seemed to vindicate these Pan-Germans as the only Austrians who did not have to reformulate their national policy. In postwar Vienna, young nationals continued the exaggerated Pan-German rhetoric, absolutely willing to denigrate Austria, dreaming of a future when the "foul air" of Vienna would be purified by the Anschluss.[7]

But the Pan-Germans had been only a small minority of the liberal German parties in the monarchy. The majority liberals had not been able to dispense with either their German nationalism or Habsburg loyalties until St. Germain freed them from the historic contradictions of their existence. The liberals could then believe that Anschluss was Austria's only political solution. Reuniting with the Pan-Germans in the Grossdeutsch Party, they often accepted the former's national myths, sometimes even outdoing these old estab-

---

[6] Friedrich Kleinwaechter, *Selbstbestimmungsrecht für Österreich* (Stuttgart, 1929), p. 23. See also idem, *Der deutschösterreichische Mensch und der Anschluss* (Vienna, 1926), pp. 47–89; the same view was expressed in articles by university teachers Wilhelm Bauer, Robert Lach, and Victor Geramb in (eds.) Kleinwaechter and Paller, *Die Anschlussfrage in Ihrer Kulturellen, wirtschaftlichen und politischen Bedeutung* (Vienna, 1930), pp. 11–19, 245–95.

[7] Joseph Papasch, "Deutsche Kultur und Österreich" (ed.) Herman Ullmann, *Werdendes Grossdeutschland* (Berlin, 1926), p. 12. For similar views, see Victor Geramb, "Ein Brief aus Österreich," *Volk und Reich* 2 (1926): 7. Pan-German Hohenzollern nostalgia was evident in the *Deutschösterreichische Tageszeitung*, August 5, 1927 and passim.

lished practitioners in anti-Habsburg propaganda. A leading Viennese liberal historian, Viktor Bibl, unleashed a hurriedly constructed polemic against the defunct empire, in which he branded the Habsburgs as national traitors who had separated the Austrian Germans from the main body of the nation. Bibl claimed that the Austrian empire had been an anachronism from the day of its founding, the work of a reactionary emperor, Francis I, brought to fruition by a second-rate political hack, Metternich. Designed to break the force of liberal nationalism, the empire was actually doomed to be defeated by these progressive forces in 1859 and 1866, destined for a destruction in 1918 that would bring down a much stronger ally as well.[8]

The socialists underwent a metamorphosis similar to the liberals. The collapse brought relief to the Social Democratic Party from its Sisyphean task of creating national justice and a unified Marxist party within the monarchy. The promise of a viable democratic socialist movement within a future *Grossdeutschland* turned the Austrian Social Democrats rapidly and often callously away from the symbols and ideals of the old regime. As a prime mover in attempts at federalizing the monarchy, Karl Renner had been a strong supporter of a supranational Austrian state. But as the first postwar chancellor, he was more than willing to ignore any remaining associations with and loyalties to the past in return for immediate advantage. He was even willing to junk the new republic's title—"German Austria." If Austria was no longer preserved in name, Renner believed that the allies might have been persuaded to reduce the burdens of government that accrued to the empire's legal successor. Renner's first foreign minister and the Left-wing socialist leader, Otto Bauer, went considerably further. After 1918 Bauer conveniently forgot his widely publicized Austrian commitments and claimed that the socialists had always favored an Austro-German union based on the democratic principles of 1848. Such responses were typical. For most socialists, the whole monarchical experience had become suddenly distasteful, and the Germanic alternatives appeared much more promising. As the party's paramilitary chief, Julius Deutsch, told a German audience, "We do not want to belong to the Habsburg prison again; we want to become part of the German Reich."[9]

[8] Viktor Bibl, *Der Zerfall Österreichs* (Vienna, 1922–24), I: vii, viii, 183 ff.; *Metternich in neuer Beleuchtung* (Vienna, 1928), pp. 5 ff. Bibl's view of Metternich was considered extreme; see Arnold Winkler's review in *Die Reichspost*, July 1, 1928 and Heinrich von Srbik's in *Mitteilungen des österreichischen Instituts für Geschichtsforschung* 42 (1928): 397–409. (Hereinafter this journal will be cited as *MÖIG*.)

[9] *Österreich-Deutschland* 2 (March 1925): 8. Kleinwaechter discusses Renner's attempt to delete Austria in *Von Schönbrunn bis St. Germain* (Graz, 1964),

The speed with which Habsburg allegiances were renounced indicates that the centripetal forces within the monarchy had been weakening for some time. Its intellectual defenders were hard pressed long before 1918. Austrian patriotic historiography had too often merely succeeded in establishing the patterns of a growing central administration without identifying any meaningful relationship between rulers and ruled.[10] Imperial Austria had seemed to many an historic accident held together by a bureaucracy. Such an artificial creation went against the grain of nineteenth-century Germanic wisdom which had discovered the national organism indissolubly uniting each specific *Volk* with its own differentiated land. Only a few scattered authors ever found such organic unity to reside in the dual monarchy which did not even have universally acknowledged geographic limits, let along a single national entity. Austria could alternately be described as the old Habsburg patrimony, or the entire dual monarchy, or merely the Cisleithean provinces. Organic reality seemed to reside in the nationalities, in the historico-political entities, such as the Bohemian or Tyrolean crownlands.[11]

This flaw was also inherited by the republic which could vie in artificiality with the empire. If no longer denounced as multinational, Austria could yet have been indicted as the whimsical creation of allied diplomacy. Its parts did not seem to fit into an organic whole; its capital espoused different values and politics from the rural hinterland; its federal states were often constructed on sounder historical precedents and appeared able to sustain wider loyalties than the central government. Provincial patriotism was so deeply embedded as to be inextricable even by 1961 when 66 percent of a North Tyrolean sample identified Tyrol, not Austria, as their principal national

---

pp. 145–46; Otto Bauer's historiographic *volte-face* can be found in *Die österreichische Revolution* (Vienna, 1923), pp. 49–52; cf. how this differs from even the postwar edition of his classic work on the national question, *Die Nationalitätenfrage und die Sozialdemokratie* (Vienna, 1924), pp. xxviii, 501–2 and passim. The literature on the socialist and liberal attitudes is enormous; this author has only attempted to cite those sources most relevant for his particular purpose.

[10] For imperial historiography, consult Alphons Lhotsky, *Österreichische Historiographie* (Vienna, 1962), pp. 197–212. See particularly, Hermann Bidermann, *Geschichte der österreichischen Gesammt-Staats-Idee* (Innsbruck, 1867–69).

[11] For the problems of historico-political entities versus centralizing forces, see Robert A. Kann, *The Multinational Empire* (New York, 1950), I: 33–38 and Erich Zöllner, "The Germans as an Integrating and Disintegrating Force," *Austrian History Yearbook* III, part 1 (1967): 204–5. Two attempts at explicating an organic unity can be found in Hermann Meynert, *Geschichte Oesterreichs* (Pesth, 1843–46), I: iv–v; and Richard von Kralik, *Österreichische Geschichte* (Vienna, 1913), p. 616. Others are discussed in Heinrich von Srbik, "Österreichs Schicksal im Spiegel des geflügelten Wortes," *MÖIG* 42 (1927): 286–92.

reference group.[12] This defect could only have appeared to substantiate the pro-Anschluss propaganda that denigrated the ability of the republic to secure the allegiance of its citizens. The most influential political journalist in Vienna, Gustav Stolper, argued: "German Austria is not an historically-rooted organism; there is no conception of a German Austrian state. The Tyrolean, Carinthian, Styrian, etc., consider themselves always as Styrians, Carinthians, Tyroleans and then as Germans, never as German Austrians."[13]

Many Austrians did not have to repudiate their past totally. The historian Wilhelm Bauer abandoned his wartime veneration of Austria, but he still thought Anschluss might save the best of Austria and open up a new opportunity for the Viennese as part of a united Germandom.

Our youth that is free from the foolishness of the duality shall have the opportunity to enjoy German history in its entirety. They shall be happy that, beside the hard but essentially sound and efficient North, there stands a South that is weak but colorfully joyous and receptive for everything human. They, both North and South, form the whole of the German way.[14]

Renner himself began to envision Anschluss as a continuation of Austria's tasks rather than an absolute break with the past. In 1927 he declared: "We shall maintain the mission that has been given us in the Southeast . . . when we return to the German Reich with a free heart."[15] He even saw Anschluss as the first step to a United Europe, certainly a political combination which was reminiscent of the multinational empire.

Thus even the strongest Anschluss supporter could retain his nostalgia for the Viennese way of life and for the culture of the Alpine lands. Only the most radical would turn their backs upon these traditions; even Viktor Bibl had an emotional attachment to Austria's cultural heroes and its landscape. A nostalgia for the Austrian past was omnipresent; it even crept into the most technical discussions

---

[12] Doob, *Patriotism and Nationalism* (New Haven, 1964), p. 142.

[13] Gustav Stolper, *Deutsch-Österreich als Sozial- und Wirtschafts-Problem* (Munich, 1921), p. 111. See also Viktor Bibl, *Geschichte Österreichs im XX. Jahrhundert* (Leipzig, 1933), p. 107.

[14] Wilhelm Bauer, *Oesterreich in den reichsdeutschen Geschichtsschulbüchern* (Berlin, 1927), p. 12. See also Bauer's article, "Das Deutschtum und Deutsch-Österreichischer," *Vergangenheit und Gegenwart* 17 (1927): 341–42. Articles by Georg A. Lukas and Wilhelm Erben, both of Graz University, reinforced Bauer, ibid., 14 (1924): 154–57; 17 (1927): 342–54. Alphons Lhotsky suggests that Austrian historians supported Anschluss because they saw their state's sudden territorial implosion not only as a misfortune but as a shameful fact; see "Geschichtsforschung und Geschichtsschreibung in Österreich," *Historische Zeitschrift* 189 (1959): 439.

[15] *Der Anschluss*, December 15, 1927.

on the mechanics of amalgamating with Germany. A major question involved two alternative constitutional plans for the completion of Anschluss. The first intended that Austria be united with the Reich as a single state, eliminating its nine federal governments, basically the old imperial historico-political entities. The second advocated that the federal components be transferred intact into the new Germany, eliminating the central government. Only a few Austrians chose the second alternative. Renner's willingness to abandon Austria in name was a minority view in 1919 and was hardly evident by the mid-1920s. Austrian jurists argued for a compromise solution, but one that demanded an unambiguous life for the central government. The most distinguished Austrian constitutional theorist, Hans Kelsen, proclaimed: "It would be an act of unthankfulness if we became citizens of the German Reich without wishing to remain what we have been for centuries of joy and sorrow—Austrians."[16]

The most interesting attempt to combine love for Austria with German nationalism was undertaken by the historian Heinrich von Srbik. As shown in chapter IV, Srbik attempted to amalgamate all German traditions into a gesamtdeutschmitteleuropäische history. In 1926 he published a Metternich biography designed as a "rehabilitation (Rettung)" on a grand scale.[17] Srbik's Metternich was transformed into a Germanic hero, the model for Bismarck. Srbik continued his attempt to combine Austrian nostalgia with a Germanic future in Deutsche Einheit, published in the 1930s. Again he sought to combine the Germanic mission of the Habsburg with the narrower unification of Bismarck. As early as 1926, Srbik clearly stated: "The first injunction for Germans is grossdeutsch [i.e., the Anschluss], the second is Mitteleuropa. The way is proscribed for us by nature and history; it brings us all through the darkness to the light."[18]

Srbik's attempt to combine the Austrian past with the German future was a difficult task. He was easily misunderstood. Some Austrian scholars considered that he had sold out to the Germans. As for the unreconciled kleindeutsch historians in the Reich, Erich

---

[16] Hans Kelsen, Die staatsrechtliche Durchführung des Anschluss Österreich an das Deutsche Reich (Vienna, 1927), p. 7. See also Ludwig Gerhard, Deutsche und österreichische Organisation der inneren Verwaltung (Munich, 1926), p. 42; Franz Klein, "Deutscher Einheitsstaat oder Deutsch-Österreich," Die Hilfe 34 (May 1, 1928): 201; idem, Reden, Vorträge, Auffsätze, Briefe II: 1006–14; Österreich-Deutschland 4 (October 1927): 4.

[17] Srbik, Metternich, der Staatsmann und Mensch (Munich, 1925), I: xiii.

[18] Srbik, "Metternichs mitteleuropäische Idee," Volk und Reich 2 (1926): 355. See the fuller discussion of Srbik in chapter IV, as well as his article, "Reichsidee und Staatsidee" (ed.) Fritz Büchner, Was ist das Reich? (Oldenburg, 1932), pp. 68–70.

Brandenburg thought Srbik had slighted Bismarckian Germany. He went on, "In this book, which is an intensely personal confession of faith, we clearly see how difficult it is, even yet, for an Austrian to accept as inevitable the great historical occurrences of the nineteenth century."[19] Yet such attacks were unfair. These Austrian and German loyalties were bound into such a package that it was difficult to extricate one from the other. The mix would change with the times, but they would still remain tied together. Thus after 1933 Srbik became a stronger exponent of German expansionism and a weaker advocate of Austrian possibilities.[20] On the whole, Srbik is a good example of the Austrian German caught between his real loyalties to the past and his hopes for a future that might never be realized. Perhaps this Austrianism might have grown stronger in men like Srbik if the new state had proved viable. But it had not. Thus in many ways, the economic question is decisive for the Austrian experience, and this is the subject of the next chapter.

[19] Erich Brandenburg, "Deutsche Einheit," *Historische Vierteljahrschrift* 30 (1936): 769. For discussion of Srbik's Austrian critics, see chapter XII.

[20] Hans Kohn, "AEIOU. Some Reflections on the Meaning and Mission of Austria," *Journal of Modern History* 11 (1939): 521–24; Droz, *L'Europe centrale* (Paris, 1960), pp. 261–62. Adam Wandruska presents a not wholly inadequate case for the opposite interpretation, that Srbik's Austrianism remained stronger than his Germanism; see *MÖIG* 59 (1951): 232–33.

CHAPTER XI ECONOMIC INSECURITY AND PROPAGANDA FOR ANSCHLUSS

MYTH HAS THE ABILITY to revitalize man's relationship to his environment only when it does not repeatedly and dramatically conflict with his estimation of reality. Thus it was difficult to proclaim an intellectual faith in an Austria that only seemed to engender despair of the present and anxiety for the future. In postwar Austria much of this anxiety was associated with an apparent economic decline. The shock associated with political collapse did not subside, but was succeeded by a series of financial and economic crises. Foreign intervention, American relief, and the League of Nations' financial reconstruction brought some semblance of stability. However, radically lowered expenditures by the central government and the recurrent business failures were constant reminders of the economy's fragile structure.

Nor were there any easy solutions for these problems. Major schemes for self-development were frustrated because of insufficient capital; most alternative solutions for expansion of Austria's foreign trade appeared unfeasible. Only the Anschluss, forbidden by treaty, seemed to promise a way out of this impasse. The business community simply held on and awaited the eventual Anschluss. Retailers, wholesalers, small manufacturers, as well as heavy industrialists were committed to this course of action. As the executive organization (Hauptversammlung) of the mining industry declared in 1927: "Only the Anschluss can change the inconsolable situation of Austrian industry."[1]

Many Austrians believed that these economic failures, not nationalist aspirations, were at the root of much of the agitation for the Anschluss. Ignaz Seipel stated more than once that the political interest in Anschluss was secondary to the economic. He told a reporter in Warsaw that "as soon as the economic situation in Austria takes a turn for the better the talk of Anschluss will stop again."[2]

[1] *Deutsche Einheit*, February 28, 1927. For supporting evidence see n. 29.
[2] *Österreich-Deutschland* 4 (May 1927): 8. See also *Kölnische Zeitung*, April 7, 1926, weekly edition.

But economic recovery was difficult and, as Seipel knew, complicated by the little faith that the Austrian middle class had in its own economy. Seipel and his sometime finance minister, Viktor Kienböck, were concerned that their solid political achievements would be undermined by businessmen who would not work for their state. Several authorities are agreed that this pessimism was a primary cause for postwar Austria's feeble power of recuperation. K. W. Rotschild has maintained that Austrian businessmen never realized the potentialities of their markets; he has claimed that they were so convinced of the futility of achieving recovery that they ignored the obvious immediate palliatives. Ferdinand Tremel has also concluded that: "Austria's capability to live was at that time not an economic but a psychological problem. There are few states on earth that are given so many riches in comparison to their population. . . . The cardinal error of the first republic lay not in the lack of economic prerequisites for the reconstruction of the state but in a lack of self-confidence."[3]

It was the self-appointed task of those writers we shall label as pro-Anschluss propagandists to extinguish any spark of self-confidence that remained in the Austrian middle class. Like good Marxists, they had a stake in impoverishment and had made common cause with misery. The perception of common misery was the source of the propagandists' drive. They certainly possessed both the strong commitment and sincerity that the American social psychologist, Leonard Doob, considers a necessary ingredient of the propagandist's mentality.[4] But why should they not have these qualities? After all, the stakes were very high. As a pronouncement of 1928 stated: "The recognition of the instability of the contemporary situation, the worry for the *Volk* and fatherland, the fear in the depth of our souls because our youth lack opportunities, these have moved a number of men . . . to popularize the thoughts of Austro-German economic unification in the broad mass of the populace. . . . We do our duty so that our children will not rightly curse us."[5]

[3] Ferdinand Tremel, "Die wirtschaftliche Situation der ersten Republik Oesterreichs," *Österreich in Geschichte und Literatur* 2 (1958): 156. See also K. W. Rotschild, *Austria's Economic Development between Two Wars* (London, 1947), p. 4; Viktor Kienböck, *Das österreichische Sanierungswerk* (Stuttgart, 1925), p. 137.

[4] Leonard Doob, *Public Opinion and Propaganda* (New York, 1948), pp. 274–78. The definition of propaganda and its basic attributes discussed below are taken from this study.

[5] *Der Anschluss*, April 16, 1928. The relationship between personal insecurity, evidenced by this quotation, and propaganda is discussed by Harold Lasswell, who believes: "Propaganda is talk, and it is no news . . . that people talk when they are unsure. . . . that man is a talking animal who rattles when shaken" (eds.) Alfred Stanton and Steward Perry, *Personality and Political Crisis* (New York, 1954), p. 15.

The propagandists appeared able to achieve their goals. Although unpaid or only partially subsidized, the Anschluss propagandists were as skillful as any of the minions in Goebbels' ministry, as innovative as their contemporaries who were founding modern American advertising. Their message was simple and driven home with remarkable singlemindedness. The propagandists constantly restated their conviction that Austria could never have a viable economy, that the death of their state was a necessary prelude to its economic and moral resurrection as part of a unified German Reich.

The first part of this proposition was the easiest to prove. Many Austrians had already considered their economy doomed from the moment of the republic's inception. For the propagandists, the very fact of separation from the great body of the nation was proof enough. As a German journalist pointed out: "The Austrian state lacks the powerful motor that drives other states. . . . How can we expect them [the Austrians] to have the initiative for reconstruction?"[6] But the propagandists were bound by their education and by their ostensible commitment to natural-law rationality. They had to present a reasonable, educated argument. This was hardly a difficult task and fitted well into the preconceptions of the business community. As the most energetic of them, Friedrich Kleinwaechter, proclaimed without much fear of contradiction:

The German Austrian lands were the directing brains of the entire Austro-Hungarian economic area. As the result of the destruction of the monarchy, this great technical apparatus with its numerous employees is left without a field of activity. Austria's present situation is precisely such as would result if New York State should suddenly be separated from the rest of the United States, cut off from the sea, surrounded by high tariff walls and then required to exist as if nothing had happened.[7]

Detailed analysis of the Austrian economic structure seemed to substantiate this argument. The leading Austrian economists and economic journalists viewed their business structure as a series of overcapitalizations and underinvestments. Austria had too many spindles and too few looms, steel mills but insufficient coal to stoke their blast furnaces or heat private homes. Forced to import foodstuffs and other raw materials to survive, the small republic was unable to export enough to pay for these imports. This continual trade deficit seemed the surest sign of Austria's weakness. The gap between exports and imports was made good by depleting Austrian credit through constant

[6] *Kölnische Zeitung*, June 30, 1926, weekly edition.

[7] Friedrich Kleinwaechter, *Selbstbestimmungsrecht für Österreich* (Stuttgart, 1929), p. 30.

borrowing. The propagandist could reasonably argue that such a solution was hardly a cure, but, in reality, only the last step in the impoverishment of the state and its people.[8]

Yet the propagandists exaggerated the power of their words or, for that matter, of any words. Therefore, counterpropositions assumed tremendous significance and created unjustifiable fears that the Austrian middle class might be convinced that their economy could function adequately. Thus the propagandists felt impelled to make a concerted effort to refute the two League experts who gave the economy a clean bill of health in 1925. Charles Rist and W. T. Layton argued that Austria had made a slow but definite improvement. They told the League that Vienna could find the necessary capital to modernize its industry and agriculture and then could overcome the trade deficit by competing effectively in the world market.[9]

Much to the consternation of the propagandists, the League experts were joined by a handful of Austrians. The most important viper in the midst of the propagandists was Friedrich Hertz—civil servant, who was to become a leading political sociologist in England after 1938. Hertz never attacked the Anschluss directly, but only questioned the possibility of its completion in the near future. Hertz was convinced that Austria would be forced to survive, but that fortunately it could successfully endure. To prove this contention, he addressed himself directly to the heart of the propagandists' argument. He hoped to demolish what was, for him, the fiction of a perpetual trade deficit. He argued that the deficit was partially only a bookkeeping problem, that reliable statistics would show a much more manageable figure. Like Layton and Rist, Hertz hoped that much of the remainder could be overcome by the increased productivity of Austrian industry. He did not believe that this effort would have been as arduous as the propagandists contended, since many industries were ready for a substantial takeoff. Whole sectors of the Austrian

---

[8] Egon Urantisch, "Berufsumschichtung," *Schriften des Vereins für Sozialpolitik* 169 (1925): 185–201; Gustav Stolper, "Die Handelspolitik Deutsch-Österreich," ibid. 171 (1925): 387–406; idem, part 2; *Deutsch-Österreich als Sozial-und Wirtschafts-Problem* (Munich, 1921), pp. 1–103; Siegfried Camuzzi, "Die österreichische Industrie," *Volk und Reich* 2 (1926): 315–19; Herbert Kniesche, *Die grossdeutsche Wirtschaftseinheit* (Leipzig, 1929), pp. 19 ff.; Siegmund Schilder, *Der Streit über die Lebensfähigkeit Österreichs* (Stuttgart, 1926), pp. 47–57; Adolf Günther, *Die wirtschaftliche und soziale Seite der deutsch-österreichischen Anschlussfrage* (Munich, 1926), pp. 32–57; Österreichisch-Deutsche Arbeitsgemeinschaft, *Zum Wirtschaftlichen Anschluss* (Vienna, 1926), p. 8; idem, *Das österreichische Wirtschaftsproblem* (Vienna, 1925), p. 9 ff.

[9] W. T. Layton and Charles Rist, *The Economic Situation of Austria* (M. 162) (Geneva, 1925), p. 43 ff.

economy did not even need new capital investment to increase their production, since they were operating substantially below capacity. What they needed was judicious management.

As exports could be increased, so imports could be reduced. Hertz argued that Austrian agriculture had already become substantially more self-sufficient. More important, he found other economic factors which would reduce the deficit. He envisioned Vienna as a small-scale London that could make enormous profits. Vienna could service the trade of all Danubian Europe through its banking and transshipment operations. Moreover, Austria could also count on a great deal of foreign exchange that would accrue from a properly managed tourist industry. Finally, Austrians held over 430 billion schillings in foreign assets. The dividends from such an enormous investment would have surely wiped out the last of the trade deficit.[10]

Such an extended analysis naturally called forth equally extensive rebuttals. The Anschluss forces claimed that it was Hertz who had misread the statistical evidence. Editor of the influential *Volkswirt*, the most important economic journalist in Vienna, Gustav Stolper alleged that Hertz had ignored the statistics of increasing unemployment, had confused the number of businesses with total productive capacity, had overvalued foreign capital in Austrian hands by 100 percent, and had based his optimistic projections on 1913 data without considering the losses sustained in the succeeding twelve years.[11]

Such arguments were, however, only intellectual shadowboxing. Statistical proofs just convince the already committed. Thus even if Hertz had accumulated all the right data and the propagandists all the wrong, he still never could have changed the opinion of one Anschluss supporter. But Hertz had done much more than accumulate statistics; he had presented a vision of a prosperous Austria, an economic model far more dangerous than any economic fact. He urged his countrymen to consider Switzerland as a prototype for a future Austria thriving on light industry, tourism, and capital accumulation.

The propagandists were determined to destroy Hertz's model before it could provide enough faith to rebuild the economy. They emphasized that Austria had neither the capital nor the ability to

---

[10] Friedrich Hertz, *Zahlungsbalanz und Lebensfähigkeit Österreichs* (Munich, 1925), pp. 13 ff. See also Josef Gruntzel, "Wirtschaftspolitik" (ed.) Eduard Stepan, *Neu Österreich* (Amsterdam, 1923), pp. 379–94; Ludwig Neumann, *Österreichs wirtschaftliche Gegenwart und Zukunft* (Vienna, 1927), pp. 5 ff.

[11] *Der österreichische Volkswirt* 16 (1925): 1297–99; Günther, *Wirtschaftliche und soziale*, pp. 35–57; Schilder, *Der Streit*, p. 21.

produce cheap energy, nor the tourist business to imitate Switzerland. But they did not really have to worry. The most important resistance to the Swiss model was embedded in the psychological and ideological propensities of the Austrians themselves. Hertz may have envisioned a revived Austria competing within the widest framework of international trade between sovereign states, yet he was almost alone in this desire.[12] Such a concept was not only unappealing to German nationalists but to anti-Anschluss forces as well. Here, as before, the propaganda line fitted easily into the generally accepted pattern of belief. The propagandists could argue their case with little fear of contradiction. The business community could not envision successful operation outside of a large protected market. As the propagandists proclaimed, few believed this deficiency could be overcome through international agreement. They considered that a small state not only had an insufficient market but also lacked the muscle necessary to negotiate successful trade treaties.[13]

To citizens who were accustomed to greater space, smallness was more than simply an economic or political catastrophe; it threatened the core of human experience. Many Austrians doubted that a small state could support a satisfactory culture. No one contended that Vienna had not been a great cultural center. But after the war Austria appeared too poor to support its artists, scholars, and scientists who were emigrating to the Reich in increasing numbers. The Austrian government recognized the threat implicit in the problem. In 1926 Chancellor Ramek asked Stresemann to intercede with the Prussian Ministry of Education to stop raiding the Austrian faculties. Ramek also asked that German publishers deposit a copy of each printed book with the Austrian National Library. A memorandum prepared by the Austrian Foreign Office for this occasion stated that inadequate financing of Austrian culture could lead to the de-

---

[12] Friedrich Thalmann accepts Schilder's contention that the major proponents of Austrian viability came from the believers in free international trade; see "Die Wirtschaft in Österreich," (ed.) Benedikt, *Geschichte der Republik Österreich* (Vienna, 1954), p. 510. Confirmation for this view can be found in Layton and Rist, *The Economic Situation*, p. 43; and Hertz, "Wirtschaftliche Probleme des Anschluss," *Der österreichische Volkswirt* 18 (March 13, 1926): 641. However, Layton and Rist often found strong support from those committed to the idea of an independent Austria, from Christian Socialists such as Seipel, and the *Reichspost* editors in their issue of September 4, 1925. See also Ernst Baumgärten, "Die österreichische Presse in ihrer Stellungsnahme zur Anschlussfrage" (dissertation, University of Vienna, 1950), pp. 116–21.

[13] Schilder, *Der Streit*, pp. 10–11; *Der Anschluss*, March 14, 1928; Julius Patzelt, "Österreichs wirtschaftliche Struktur," *Volk und Reich* 2 (1926): 465–66; Herbert Kniesche, *Der österreichische-deutsche Wirtschaftszusammenschluss* (Stuttgart, 1930), pp. 58–60; Eduard Heinl, *Über ein halbes Jahrhundert* (Vienna, 1948), p. 183.

struction of Viennese intellectual preeminence in Southeastern Europe. The report implied serious political consequences if this leadership passed on to Paris.[14]

But even if money had been available, many Austrians would still be unconvinced that their state could support a viable culture. They believed smallness bred decadence. A Catholic historian and propagandist, Karl Hugelmann, unequivocally declared: "A small state like Austria cannot fulfill its cultural tasks."[15] Again the propagandists added little new. Such pessimism was often rooted not in German nationalism but in nostalgia for the old Habsburg empire. Even advocates of Anschluss as committed as Hugelmann or the journalist—Karl Anton, Prince Rohan—paradoxically identified their desire for Anschluss with a return to the Austrian mission. Rohan wrote: "I do not believe that the united strength of the whole world would succeed in making Austria a rich but powerless land. . . . Since the Austrian is a European par excellence, the only politics that can interest him are those with great conceptions. The making of policy in order to assure a peaceful prosperity is scarcely in keeping with the spirit of a people who have borne the world mission of the Habsburgs."[16]

Up to this point, propaganda was able to use the nostalgia for the old empire. But once the discussion stopped revolving around the question of the republic's viability, these two forces would pursue disparate goals. It is true that both the Austrophiles and the Anschluss propagandists were committed to some larger economic area. But they had different models in mind. The propagandists naturally envisioned the enlarged Germanic nation; the Austrophiles were primarily interested in other solutions. Since these models provided the ideological framework for alternative courses of action, the propagandists were determined that only theirs remain intact and defensible.

The propagandists were not overburdened by the task of demolishing these alternative solutions. The opportunities were self-evident for a wider range of activity within the large free-trade area of a united Europe. But all these hopes were in vain. The propagandists could undermine all these dreams by simply showing the difficulty in achieving Pan-Europe. Friedrich Kleinwaechter compared

[14] Peter memo, Deutsche Kultur in Österreich, November 1927, NPA Fasz. 464,11747, and AA 2345/4576/E172498–E172500. See also Günther, *Wirtschaftliche und soziale*, p. 136.

[15] Karl Hugelmann, "Gedanken eines Österreichers über grossdeutsche Kulturpflege," *Volk und Reich* 2 (1926): 37; see also Constantin Dumba, "Das österreichische Problem," *Deutsche Rundschau* 55 (1928): 123; "Das neue Österreich" (ed.) Julius Bunzel, *Schriften des Vereins für Sozialpolitik* 169 (1925): 476.

[16] Karl Anton, Prince Rohan, *Umbruch der Zeit* (Berlin, 1930), p. 147.

the lead time for united Europe with the three centuries necessary for Christianity to emerge as the dominant religion. He wrote with apparent validity: "Austria cannot wait until the ideal of Pan-Europe is achieved. A medicine that does not work in the foreseeable future is, for Austria, no medicine at all. Austria's situation demands immediate aid. Pan-Europe cannot accomplish this end. Thus Austria cannot rely upon Pan-Europe."[17]

Even more important, the propagandists found a method safely to neutralize the Pan-European question by merging it with the demands for Austro-German union. They argued that Anschluss need only be the first step in the process of European economic unification. After the Germanic union would come a Central European economic federation. "The slogan must be from Mitteleuropa to Paneuropa."[18]

If Pan-Europe was rejected as utopian, there were still other alternatives which seemed even more appropriate for Austria. There was the model of a Danubian economic federation covering, at least, the extent of the former monarchy. At first glance, Danubian federation seemed an ideal solution. As its most articulate Austrian advocate claimed, the Austrian economy could well suffer from uniting with a state as heavily industrialized as Germany. Johannes Barolin believed that almost all the Western European industries were too competitive for their Austrian counterparts. He argued that Vienna could only survive in union with a predominantly agricultural area which would provide a protected market for Austrian industrial surpluses. Tied to Austria by historical traditions and geographic propinquity, the Danubian plain was the most natural agricultural region for this amalgamation.[19]

The Anschluss propagandists naturally attacked all of Barolin's assumptions. They claimed that Austria relied less upon Danubian markets than upon those of Western Europe. In the event of a Danubian federation, Western Europe would retaliate against its exclusion from the markets of these countries. Austria would then find its deficit increasing instead of the promised opposite effect. Moreover, the propagandists argued that a Danubian federation would further weaken the economic position of Vienna. The Austrian capital would become only a secondary center of an economic union comprising the poorest region in Europe. The strength of Czech industry would

[17] Kleinwaechter, *Selbstbestimmungsrecht für Österreich*, pp. 51–52. For a definition of Austrophile see chapter XII.

[18] *Neue Freie Presse*, April 3, 1926, a.m. See also Wilhelm Guerge, *Paneuropa und Mitteleuropa* (Berlin, 1929), pp. 5 ff.; Konrad Praxmauer, "Vereinigte Staaten von Europa oder Grossdeutschland," *Die Hilfe* 32 (1926): 512–13.

[19] Johannes Barolin and Kurt Schechner, *Für und wider die Donauföderation* (Vienna, 1926), pp. 23–81.

naturally give Prague the leadership in any such combination. Not only would the Czechs undercut the Austrians in Danubia, but Bohemians would undersell the Austrians in their own internal market and ruin the last protected enclave for native industry.

Such an extended analysis was not really needed to undermine the hopes for Danubian federation. Even Seipel saw deficiencies in this model. Although drawn to Danubian federation because of its superficial correspondence to the old monarchy, he doubted that the succession states would ever abandon the encouragement of new industry behind high tariff walls for the relative insecurity of a free market. Given such doubts among the opposition, the propagandists only had to restate the same arguments to make an acceptable case. As always, Stolper made the most cogent presentation:

The end of tariff restrictions in the affairs of the member states [of a Danubian federation] would only be the first step. They must necessarily set up a common tariff with . . . a common organ to make tariff laws and supervise the administration of the tariffs. In other words, they must renounce a part of their sovereignty to a supra-national organization whose competence must move from the economic to the political spheres and thus create such a close political bond that the newly-won national and political independence would be threatened. Such a combination is only possible between states that are political friends, that are nationally and culturally related, that strive for a close economic agreement as a prelude to even closer political association. But here in Mitteleuropa, the states have just been created; they are jealous of their power and attempt to free themselves from their old economic connections.[20]

Such an analysis seemed to fit the most recent Austrian experience, the distasteful memories of indignities suffered during the dissolution of the Habsburg empire. Many Austrians, including influential Christian Socialists, were unable to forget these painful experiences. Shortly after leaving office as first president of the republic, Michael Hainisch went so far as to claim that even a successful Danubian union would have been unacceptable. Such an attitude seems to contradict the Austrian nostalgia for large economic areas. But most Austrians were no longer interested in multinational forms of government; they wanted security without being forced to rely upon the vagaries of other nations. This could only be accomplished within a Germanic framework. An Anschluss society pamphlet explained:

---

[20] Stolper, *Problem*, pp. 130–31. For other arguments, see Karl Janovsky, *Zollunion Prag-Wien oder Anschluss Wien-Berlin* (Reichenberg, 1927), pp. 1–37; *Neue Freie Presse*, August 29, 1925, a.m.; Michael Hainisch, "Österreich im letzten Jahrzehnt" (ed.) Bernhard Harms, *Volk und Reich der Deutschen* (Berlin, 1929), III: 384.

"Only the Anschluss with Germany means a great assured market not endangered by the instability of a pale legal union achieved through treaties."[21]

The Austro-German union thus promised a fresh start, a method for releasing all the old fears. The Anschluss was always more than a simple economic solution; it was the promised national utopia. Like all good utopias, it was future-oriented and engendered only despair for a present in which it could never be realized. Allied with the perception of common misery, these hopes for Anschluss became a major stumbling block on the road to economic recovery. These hopes thus encouraged the Austrians to remain inactive, to wait for the *deus ex machina* to solve all their problems. This was particularly dangerous in a situation where, as Ludwig Neumann pointed out, "the first prerequisite of success is that every Austrian believe with his whole strength in the possibility of recovery."[22]

The opponents of economic union, Seipel and Hertz, knew that Austrian economic survival depended on mobilizing all energies in the present. But some propagandists feared that these utopian longings would undermine the economy too soon and then play into the hands of the French, who could then introduce new and more stringent controls in order to forestall the Anschluss. The *Neue Freie Presse* attacked statements demanding immediate economic Anschluss as inopportune. Gustav Stolper even went so far as to call upon "the Austrian people to prepare a paradise in the garden of Europe . . . until the day of complete solution in which this land fulfills its only possible European task and becomes part of Germany." But how seriously could any Anschluss propagandist demand the reconstruction of his economy? Stolper wrote these words in an article announcing his departure to Berlin, where he completed his own personal Anschluss. As a parting shot in the same article, Stolper said he was leaving because he was unable to stay in an Austria that "paddles around in the backwater of history."[23] In such a context, he could never have seriously hoped to convince anyone. He may have been intellectually aware of the dangers inherent in constantly denigrating Austria, but he was ideologically and emotionally committed to the utopia of Anschluss.

But who would directly combat the Anschluss? Demolishing utopias wins few friends. Some of the propagandists' opponents,

---

[21] Arbeitsgemeinschaft, *Wirtschaftsproblem*, p. 31.

[22] Neumann, *Österreichs wirtschaftliche Gegenwart*, pp. 37–38. See also Ignaz Seipel, *Österreich wie es wirklich ist* (Vienna, 1953), p. 6.

[23] Gustav Stolper, "Abschied von Österreich," *Der österreichische Volkswirt* 18 (1925): 14.

Hertz especially, even maintained a pro forma allegiance to the union; others, like Seipel, attempted to manipulate German nationalism so as to allow for the continued existence of an independent Austria. So while the propagandists could attack Pan-Europe and Danubian federation as unfeasible, their opponents felt too constrained to challenge the Austro-German union on the same grounds. By refusing to do so, the opponents treated Anschluss as a probable event, perhaps distant but within the realm of possibility. This was the same Anschluss that was forbidden by treaties enforced by allied diplomatic and military power.

Forced by public opinion to reject their best argument, the opponents concentrated on the economic effect of an Austro-German union. Even here they had a substantial case. Hertz and Barolin argued that such a union would overwhelm Austrian business with cheaper German goods. Hertz further stated that Anschluss would deprive Austria of its last few advantages vis-à-vis Germany. Austrian wages and social costs would be raised to the German level and thus Austrian industry would be made even less competitive. These fears were well grounded. Even the advocates of an Austro-German union understood this. As Austrian trade and transportation minister from 1922 to 1929, Hans Schürff knew the disastrous effect an immediate Anschluss would have had on the economy. He thought that the worst effect could be overcome by introducing a transitional stage in which some Austrian manufactures would still have to be protected. But other Anschluss supporters believed this problem could never have been overcome in a short transitional period. Moritz Bonn, the Berlin political scientist, alluded to an Austrian slovenliness which could hardly have withstood North German competition. Karl Trosset, head of the German Trade Chamber for Austria, admitted that economic union would "create a North German storm which would sweep over Austria in the same way as all the bright troops stormed to Alaska as soon as rumors of the gold strike spread."[24] Another Anschluss supporter and business leader, Friedrich Tilgner, declared that in certain circumstances, "the German economy would then appear to play the role of the wolf in the fairy tale that tries to disarm Little Red Riding Hood in order to be able to better eat her up."[25]

The propagandists naturally sought to allay these fears, but they were forced to admit their basis in reality. They had to agree that

[24] Karl Trosset, "Österreichs Wirtschaftsmöglichkeiten," *Deutsche Rundschau*, 53 (1926): 222.

[25] Quoted in Barolin and Schechner, *Für und wider die Donauföderation*, p. 29. See also Moritz Bonn's article in the *Neue Freie Presse*, March 31, 1925, p.m.

some industries would suffer from competition with more efficient German firms. Branches of the textile, machinery, metalware, and porcelain industries would be hard pressed to survive; the chemical industry could never exist in the same market as the big German trusts. Yet the propagandists still maintained that the union would benefit the Austrians in the long run. Austrian luxury goods and raw materials—milk, cattle, wood, and wine—would have easy access to the German market. The Reich's absorption of these commodities would provide the impetus to heal the remainder of the Austrian economy. But no propagandist thought to eliminate German competition. This competition was treated as a positive good, since it would make Austrian business rationalize and learn more effective methods of production. As one Munich expert stated: "A healthy economic rivalry between Austria and Germany would set loose the Austrian strength and energy that has lain dormant."[26]

But however strong this promised reinvigoration, the propagandists really saw Austria as a passive receptacle through which German energies could flow into the Danube valley. The Austrians would contribute their knowledge and experience in Eastern Europe; the Germans would do the rest. Vienna's capital starvation would be ended by association with the German banks. Germany would provide a labor market for the unemployed in Vienna. The Germans would run a unitary transportation system that would considerably reduce the Austrians' shipping costs, and German ports would provide Austria with its needed outlet to the sea. Most important, buttressed by German capital and industrial might, Vienna would be able to expand enormously as a trading center. But along with this prosperity came a hard truth. However much Austrians might confuse their new position with their old supremacy within the Habsburg empire, the Germans correctly proclaimed that Vienna would be an important, but a secondary, center. "Vienna can never return to what it was, to being an old imperial city. But a new era will open a great future to it as the Hamburg of the East."[27]

German energies had become the grace that could achieve Austrian economic salvation. Such passivity had advantages; it placed the resolution of all problems in other hands. But such a solution could only be accomplished by a strong Germany; thus, the demands

---

[26] *Münchner Neueste Nachrichten*, January 8, 1926. Some articles and books not previously cited that repeat this argument are Adolf Günther, *Die wirtschaftlichen Beziehungen zwischen dem deutschen Reich und Österreich.* (Berlin, 1929), pp. 19 ff.; *Der Anschluss*, November 12, 1927.

[27] Wilhelm Heile in *Berliner Tageblatt*, August 15, 1925, a.m. See also Guerge, *Paneuropa und Mitteleuropa*, p. 62.

for economic union fluctuated with the strength of the Reich economy. In 1923, during the height of the inflation, even extreme German nationalists realized that an amalgamation would only mean the sharing of misery. The *Reichspost* could gleefully point to the advantages of separation.[28] But by 1925 the situation had changed. Not only had Locarno initiated hopes for peaceful revision, but Germany's recovery again raised the expectations of the benefits from Anschluss. Agricultural meetings soon resounded with demands for an Austro-German customs union at the very least. The business community showed the same enthusiasm. In 1928 the propagandists founded the Delegation for Austro-German Economic Union (Delegation für den österreichisch-deutschen Wirtschaftzusammenschluss). The delegation comprised the manufacturers' associations for most light industry as well as similar groups from almost all branches of retailing and foreign and internal commerce. The representatives of heavy industry were even more vocal in their demands. They made their weight felt even in the Christian Socialist Party—particularly in the persons of Ernst Streeruwitz, chancellor in 1929, and Emmanuel Weidenhoffer, the leader of Styrian industry. Such concerted agitation would naturally impress foreign visitors. In 1927 Carl Schubert reported to Stresemann on a trip to Vienna. Schubert maintained that Austrian businessmen were losing their fears of German competition and that only a few opponents of Anschluss were left within the business community.[29]

Did the propagandists cause such a groundswell? They obviously could not have been solely responsible. Propagandists can only accelerate processes already set in motion. But this acceleration was an important fact in itself. Movements need words to justify themselves to the world. The propagandists were needed to verbalize barely understood fears and vague hopes. They could rely upon the preconceptions of continual economic decline and upon a nostalgia that denigrated the smallness of the Austrian state and sought after large economic areas. Most important, they were backed by the supercharged emotionalism of Germanic nationalism. It was not a difficult task to demolish the alternatives to Anschluss and to show the advantages of an Austro-German union. But such a union was forbidden. Its proponents could only hope for some change in the political constellation. Until that time, they were left in a state of suspension— unable to cope with the present, unwilling to prepare for the future.

[28] *Die Reichspost*, August 19, 1923. For somewhat more optimistic views of the inflation see *Deutschösterreichische Tageszeitung*, May 27, 1923; *Neue Freie Presse*, May 18, 22, 1923, a.m.

[29] Schubert report, May 31, 1927, AA 2346/4576/E172910. See also *Die Reichspost*, July 8, 1928; *Der Anschluss*, February 15, 1927, April 16, 1928. See chapter VII for further discussion of these organizations.

CHAPTER **XII** THE SEARCH FOR

AN AUSTRIAN IDENTITY

NATIONAL IDEOLOGY and foreign policy were seldom so interrelated as in the search for an Austrian identity. Not only did the Christian Socialists have a stake in finding another solution for Austria besides union with Germany, but foreign powers were also intimately involved. In 1928 Mussolini explained his position to the Austrian Ambassador in Rome. He stated that the Austrians would certainly not wish to be dominated by 36 million Prussians in post-Anschluss Germany. He claimed that the cultural and political differences between Berlin and Vienna were too great for the Austrians to be happy in such a union. In 1927 Poincaré expressed the same sentiments to the Austrian Ambassador in Paris. The French President exclaimed: "I know the Austrian perhaps yet lacks a feeling of nationality, and about this no one is astonished. The Austrians have suffered much. Not enough time has passed since the great misfortune of the war for the Austrians to have found their new role. Despite all that is promised, you will have to wait for some time to become accustomed to being Austrians."[1]

The search for a viable entity goes back to World War I. Instead of repeating the dismal failures of 1859 and 1866, Austria's armies had fought long and hard, expending enough blood to vindicate the empire. The war thus forced many Austrians to alter dramatically their political and national conceptions. They came to view their state as more than a holding operation. Austrians had a purpose, a positive task of their own to reconstruct Mitteleuropa entirely anew, in partnership with the Reich. The Viennese history professor, Wilhelm Bauer, described these changes with a supercharged emotionalism common in wartime.

Austria has changed before our eyes. It has become different from what it was yesterday or the day before yesterday. We look back in wonder.

[1] Grünberger to Vienna, February 3, 1927, NPA Fasz. 59, Zl. 848/2 Pol.; for Mussolini statement, see Moellwald to Vienna, July 7, 1928, NPA Fasz. 81, 84 Pol.

Yesterday what was it to us—a book of memoirs in which our parents and grandparents had written many proud reminiscences, many happy, many melancholy thoughts. . . . Heretofore what had been described as an historical dispute, a political question that necessitated no emotional involvement, has now become a piece of experience for Austria no less than its enemies. Those who have battled on the bloody field, we all, we have in these days experienced Austria.[2]

If Austria existed, scholars owed it a debt. They would have to make up for lost time, for their refusal to consider Austrian nationalism as a realistic possibility; they would have to create a patriotic historiography as the basis for a national reeducation. In 1918 Bauer founded a serious historical journal to pursue this work, to discover the patterns of national growth, to reinterpret Austrian history around the idea of a national community binding its citizens together.[3]

If this sense of destiny was fragile, it did inspire another important if belated discovery, the unearthing of an Austrian national character. National character was peculiarly suited to the Austrian whose conceptions of nation, culture, and traditions were often stronger than those of the state.[4] Thus Austria could not be justified by the best political science. But it could still be saved by constructing what has to be tentatively designated for want of a better name— an "Austrian anthropology." This "anthropology" was Catholic, German, and monarchist, most at home in the Christian Socialist Party, ultimately the work of a small group of Viennese intellectuals—Hugo von Hofmannsthal, Hermann Bahr, Richard von Kralik, Anton Wildgans, Richard Schaukal, Erwin Hanslik, and Richard Müller.

Like the modern anthropologists, these writers attempted to isolate unique cultural traits. Their archetypal Austrians were a composite of elements drawn from their own milieu, the Viennese bourgeoisie and Bohemians, along with an unfamiliar but romanticized Alpine peasantry. This Austrian was venerated as the bearer of a

[2] Wilhelm Bauer, "Oesterreich," *Oesterreich, Zeitschrift für Geschichte* 1 (1918): 1–2. See also Arthur May, *The Passing of the Hapsburg Monarchy* (Philadelphia, 1966), I: 287–89.

[3] Bauer's various articles set the tone for the journal *Oesterreich* which especially emphasized the history of non-German Austria. Its contributors numbered Alphons Dopsch, the famous medievalist, who made a less sanguine contribution in this vein; see his *Österreichs geschichtlichte Sendung* (Vienna, 1917). Another historian working on the same task was Karl Hugelmann in *Historisch-politische Studien* (Vienna, 1915), pp. iv, 171 ff.

[4] It is interesting that the Austrians accepted their exclusion from these political forms more readily than the Germans who emphasized the state as a binding national influence, more important than language. See the attack of Max Weber and Ferdinand Tönnies on Ludo Hartmann who identified nationalism with language and culture in *Verhandlungen des zweiten deutschen Soziologentages*, pp. 50, 187, and passim.

cosmopolitan tradition, the advocate of the old, the universal, of Baroque ideals. This model Austrian was thus the antithesis of the enlightened, progressive man. He was antagonistic to the up-to-date and the functional, essentially human-oriented, unable to commit himself to modern impersonal organizations.[5]

The anthropologists were naturally uncomfortable with the modern state in Prussian or Josephean form. Bureaucracy subordinated culture and morality to politics, created what Hermann Bahr called a paper Austria in place of the authentic. Austria meant more than administrative success. "Austria means to be right," suggested Kralik.[6] The anthropologists viewed Austria as an intellectual fact, a psychological direction, a way of life more relevant than any political program. As Müller proclaimed: "What is called the state in Austria is encumbered with debts, inexact, as empty as a room half-furnished in jest."[7]

Not tied to a particular state, this national character might have found a home in any cosmopolitan political system, even in a German republic which was able to reject the narrow Hohenzollern loyalties. Equally transferable were the anthropologists' patriotic symbols—the

[5] For the roots of anthropological thought see Albert Fuchs, *Geistige Strömungen in Österreich* (Vienna, 1949), pp. 68–76, and Richard von Kralik, "Die Entdeckungsgeschichte des österreichischen Staatsgedankens," *Die Kultur* 18 (1917): 99 ff. Bahr's prewar Austrianism was collected in *Austriaca* (Berlin, 1911); his most important wartime essays can be found in *Schwarzgelb* (Berlin, 1917); see his diaries written in wartime, *1917* and *1918* (Innsbruck, 1918, 1919). Discussions of Bahr's views can be found in Karl Nirschl, *In seinen Menschen ist Österreich* (Linz, 1964), pp. 141–49; and Erich Widder, *Hermann Bahr* (Linz, 1963), pp. 80–83. Hofmannsthal's major wartime essays are to be found in *Gesammelte Werke, Prosa* (Berlin, 1952), III: 189–409. All the voluminous works on Hofmannsthal discuss his Austrianism; of particular relevance are Brian Coghlan, *Hofmannsthal's Festival Drama* (Cambridge, England, 1964), pp. 83–149; Peter Pawlowsky, "Die Idee Österreichs bei Hugo von Hofmannsthal," *Österreich in Geschichte und Literatur* 6 (1962): 177–85; Claudio Magris, *Der habsburgische Mythos in der österreichischen Literatur* (Salzburg, 1966), pp. 214–34. Wildgans's writings can be found in *Sämtliche Werke* (Vienna, 1948–56), VII: 335–62. See also Richard Schaukal, *Zeitgemässen deutschen Betrachtungen* (Munich, 1916); idem, "Oesterreich," *Der Gral* 11 (1917): 37–39. Kralik, in many ways the founder of Austrianism, was an extremely prolific writer; see his *Geschichte der Weltkrieges* (Vienna, 1915 ff.), 1, 2–4 ff.; idem, *Die neue Staatenordnung in organischen Aufbau* (Vienna, 1918), pp. 32–38. Hanslik's and Müller's major works are cited below. The relationship between the major anthropologists is easily documented. Bahr was strongly influenced by Hofmannsthal; see Bahr, *Selbstbildnis* (Berlin, 1923), p. 281. Wildgans and Hofmannsthal reinforced each other's wartime patriotism; *Briefwechsel Hofmannsthal-Wildgans* (Zurich, 1935), p. 49. Bahr knew and read Müller, Schaukal, and Kralik; see *1917*, p. 37; *1918*, pp. 226, 261–62. Kralik edited *Der Gral*, which published Schaukal and Bahr. Bahr dedicated one of his Austrian volumes to Kralik.

[6] Richard von Kralik, *Die Entscheidung im Weltkrieg* (Vienna, 1914), p. 5.

[7] Robert Müller, *Österreich und der Mensch* (Berlin, 1916), p. 43.

Holy Roman Empire, European solidarity, Prince Eugene's victories, and Grillparzer's poetry, even God. These symbols were so vague that they could be counted as common Germanic property after 1918. If they also represented Austrian accomplishments, so much the better; this proved that the Austrian could bring a spiritual dowry to the Germanic marriage even if his country lacked material wealth. Moreover, the anthropologists had unwittingly paved the way for merging the Austrian and German archetypes into a new composite. Müller, Hanslik, and Bahr had argued that a reorganized Mitteleuropa would have stimulated a symbiotic learning process between the various Germanic cultures.[8] But this was as far as they could go. They were committed to a Viennese way of life. They could not envision an existence as part of the Reich.

Thus after 1918, they were without hope. Austrianism became simply another word for despair. The Austrian anthropologists felt robbed of any future. Hofmannsthal and Bahr slipped into their pre-war pessimism. Their wartime expectations were shattered; they were left with only an overwhelming, if pathetic, nostalgia. Bahr may have half-heartedly attempted to transfer the old imperial symbols directly to the republic, but he soon lost belief in the efficacy of this policy. Yet he could not abandon his Austrian loyalties, even at the cost of ignoring reality, even if such an attitude would often lead to jarring contradictions, to rapid alternations in perception and belief. Thus Hofmannsthal could engage in ecstatic prophecy that Austria would survive its catastrophes even while he despaired of the future.[9]

In this environment, the new was almost necessarily viewed with suspicion. The past may have had its problems, but it also had its glories. It offered some security against the postwar chaos. Although more optimistic than the anthropologists, a political and cultural outsider, Joseph Roth, understood the endurance of this nostalgia. In a retrospective essay on Franz Joseph's last years, Roth wrote: "The old sun of the Habsburgs was fading, but it was still a sun."[10] The small republic could certainly not serve as a substitute for even such a reduced image of imperial greatness. On the contrary, this new government's establishment seemed to coincide with the end of

---

[8] Ibid., pp. 19–23; Erwin Hanslik, *Oesterreich, Erde und Geist* (Vienna, 1917), pp. 132 ff.; Bahr, *Schwarzgelb*, pp. 214–16.

[9] Bahr, *1918*, p. 262; idem, *1919* (Leipzig, 1920), p. 306; Bertha Szeps-Sucherkandl, "Gespräch über Österreich," *Hugo von Hofmannsthal* (ed.) Helmut Fiechtner (Vienna, 1949), pp. 337–38.

[10] Joseph Roth, *Werke* (Cologne, 1956), III: 328. This was certainly in the same mood as Roth's major novel about Austrian nostalgia, *Radetzky March* (New York, 1933), pp. 208–11. Robert Schwarz shows how Roth's nostalgia was rooted in Jewish and Eastern European experience, "The Lost World of Joseph Roth," *Phi Kappa Phi Journal* 45 (1965): 51–52.

civilization. Even ten years after the collapse, Hofmannsthal still felt the anguish associated with the death of his world: "Then we had a fatherland, a task and a history, yet now we must continue to live on."[11]

Yet no anthropologist was willing to replace the republic by an Austro-German union. Bahr and Kralik worked actively against the Anschluss. No longer bound by the canons of good taste due military allies, Kralik became a first-class Prussian baiter. He identified the Hohenzollern dynasty with godlessness and materialism; he claimed that Bismarck was the embodiment of the Nietzschean belief in the superman. Hofmannsthal was politically inactive, but even he was prepared to make the grand gesture. He would flee to Switzerland rather than accept an Austro-German union.[12]

Hofmannsthal's answer to the dilemma, both for his person and civilization, was simply resignation. He would learn to live with the chaos and retreat into art. "The misery is great," he wrote in 1919, "but I hear it only as if in a dream. I work on and on."[13] When Hofmannsthal depicted contemporary Austria in his first postwar production, *The Difficult Man (Der Schwierige)*, he was exercising his talent to preserve the memory of a Viennese aristocratic society. But he was also publicizing those Austrian virtues that the anthropologists had so assiduously catalogued. These qualities reposed to a large extent in the difficult man, Hans Karl. Even his rival, the Prussian Neuhoff, could admire them: "substance without pretension, nobility mellowed by infinite grace."[14] Yet despite such obvious nostalgia, this play was not a positive attempt at establishing goals for the future; on the contrary, Hans Karl and his society seemed barely able to survive the modern world. Aware of these fatal imperfections, Hofmannsthal allowed Neuhoff to make the most telling points against the Viennese aristocracy and, implicitly, against the Austrian character itself. "Nobody who circulates in these rooms belongs to the real world in which the intellectual crises of the century are resolved."[15]

---

[11] Helmut Fiechtner, "Die Briefwechsel Hofmannsthal-Redlich," *Wort in der Zeit* 2 (1956): 26.

[12] Richard von Kralik, "Bismarcks Politik als Widerspruch zur deutschen Geschichte," *Schönere Zukunft* 3 (1928): 944; see also idem, *Schönere Zukunft* 4 (1928): 47–50; Rudolf Borchardt, "Hugo von Hofmannsthal" (ed.) Fiechtner, *Hofmannsthal*, p. 354; Bahr's views were expressed in the diaries, but see also *Schichsaljahre Österreich: 1908–1919, das politische Tagebuch Josef Redlichs* (ed.) Fritz Fellner (Graz, 1954), p. 323.

[13] *Briefwechsel Hugo von Hofmannsthal-Carl J. Burckhardt* (Frankfurt, 1956), p. 23.

[14] Hugo von Hofmannsthal, *Selected Plays and Libretti* (New York, 1963), p. 689.

[15] Ibid., p. 729. This interpretation follows that of Emil Staiger, *Meisterwerke deutscher Sprache aus dem neunzehten Jahrhundert* (Zurich, 1957), p. 225. For a discussion of Neuhoff's Prussianism see W. E. Yates's introduction to *Der*

Bahr might gush forth with more sentimentality than Hofmanns-thal but with hardly more hope. In fact, it was Bahr who transformed this resignation into an integral part of the national character. A major character in Bahr's novel, *Austria in Eternity*, could proclaim: "The Austrian is always resigned. . . . We do not revel in great plans; we are thankful to survive."[16] If this statement was made by a self-labeled compromiser, still even the novel's more audacious protagonists could hardly be found sounding a clarion call for action. They hoped that events might force the creation of a national pride, that the "secret will of the nation" would prevail and induce the patriotism apparently lacking in its citizens.[17] Until then there was no solution for the Austrian problem. "Since the death of Charles VI, Austria has become a questionable entity; it cannot go on any longer, but yet it answers back, it endures. The length of time this impossible situation can last appears to be determined by fate."[18]

Even in this weakened state, the anthropologists' mission could only have been entrusted to the Christian Socialist Party, the main political repository of Austrian nostalgia. Catholic, with the strongest commitment to the dead empire, the Christian Socialists loyally retained their old attachments. The semiofficial party organ, the *Reichs-post*, continuously upheld Austrian virtues while attacking the legends of Hohenzollern perfection and the image of Prussian superiority.[19] Many party leaders, including the *Reichspost* editors, were committed to foreign policy alternatives that fitted better with their Habsburg past. They explicitly demanded the construction of some surrogate for the monarchy.

Certainly this was the case with Msgr. Ignaz Seipel, the driving force among the Christian Socialists during the 1920s. Seipel's case is so central to the problem of postwar Austrian patriotism, so representative of the dilemmas within Christian Socialism, that it cannot be ignored. Seipel had been one of the empire's principal intellectual defenders, attacking the nineteenth-century proclivity for building

---

Schwierige (Cambridge, England, 1966), pp. 25–26. Roger Norton has correctly pointed out that *Der Schwierige* was conceived in outline long before World War I, but interestingly Neuhoff was not present in these earlier drafts; see "The Inception of Hofmannsthal's *Der Schwierige*: Early Plans and Their Significance," *PMLA* 89 (1964): 97–103. Hofmannsthal considered this very much a contemporary play; see *Briefwechsel Hugo von Hofmannsthal-Arthur Schnitzler* (Frankfurt, 1964), p. 287.

[16] Hermann Bahr, *Österreich in Ewigkeit* (Hildesheim, 1929), pp. 163–64.

[17] Ibid., p. 104.

[18] Ibid., p. 111.

[19] *Die Reichspost*, June 24, 1925, August 5, 1927, and passim.; Ernst Baumgärten, "Die österreichische Presse in ihrer Stellungnahme zur Anschluss-frage" (dissertation, University of Vienna, 1950), pp. 115–21.

nation-states. He carried his distrust of this political form over into the republic, since its application to the postwar situation would have brought an undesired union with a predominantly Protestant and materialistic Germany. Seipel offered the solution of a cultural, nonpolitical union as an alternative to German national unification. "For us the nation is independent of the property of the state; it is a great community of culture which for us Germans is higher than the state. We do not believe that the state is the only form of life for the nation."[20]

This nostalgia logically forced Seipel to attempt the maintenance of Austria's independence. He wished for a spiritual reconstruction that would give the Austrians confidence in their way of life. He pleaded with foreigners and citizens alike to give Austria a chance, to leave them alone to work out their own destiny. Yet Seipel knew such a situation could not occur. Thus like the anthropologists he often despaired of maintaining the rump state beset by such imposing economic and political problems. Paradoxically even his nostalgia worked against his efforts to obtain security for its citizens. Seipel never felt at ease defending the new Austria, which he believed could ultimately only function as part of some greater state system. Austria needed some surrogate for its imperial task—Pan-Europe, Danubian union, even, at the last resort, a unified Germany. "To cultivate our little garden and to show it for foreigners to make money out of it are no proper tasks for the inhabitants of the Carolingian Ostmark and the conquerors of the Turks."[21]

Since the Christian Socialists controlled the educational machinery of the state, they could transmit their doubts to the next generation. Ministerial decrees did order teachers to consider German and Austrian history equitably but gave no instructions to amalgamate the two streams. Students were to be inculcated with the ideals of *Volk* and fatherland, two generalizations so ill-defined as to fit the most extreme categories of German nationalism or independent Austrianism. This, of course, gave the classroom teacher carte blanche to instruct

[20] Ignaz Seipel, *Österreich wie es wirklich ist* (Vienna, 1953), p. 10. He expressed the same views in France; see *Seipels Reden in Österreich und anderwärts* (ed.) Josef Gessl (Vienna, 1926), p. 323. For Seipel's prewar views see his own *Nation und Staat* (Vienna, 1916), pp. 13 ff.; Kann, *Multinational Empire*, II: 213 ff.; Rolf Wolkan, "Der österreichische Staatsgedanke und seine Wandlungen im Zeitalter Franz Josephs, *MÖIG*, XI Ergänzungsband (1929): 838–39. See chapter XIII for full discussion of Seipel's foreign policy.

[21] Paul Sweet, "Seipel's Views on the *Anschluss*; An Unpublished Exchange of Letters," *Journal of Modern History* 19 (1947): 323. These doubts were often repeated; see Gessl, *Seipels Reden*, p. 322; *Vorwärts* (Berlin), February 6, 1916, edition A.

according to his own prejudice.[22] The three most widely accepted secondary school texts reinforced the impression in official instructions. While advocating Anschluss, these books emphasized the unique characteristics of German and Austrian particularism. Although making an attempt to integrate Austrian history into the main Germanic stream, they too often simply retold the dualistic history, the struggles between Austria and Prussia.[23]

Nor could most of the academic historians, who were committed to an Austrian nostalgia, resolve the contradictions inherent in the textbooks. Otto Redlich, the dean of Viennese historians, was unable to adjust to the new Austria. He could not change the direction of his research and continued to write on the rise of the Habsburg state after the source of inspiration for his work had expired. He could only fall back on the justification that his studies would become useful in the far distant future when an organically constructed substitute for the Habsburg state would be created.[24]

Srbik's academic rival, Raimund Friedrich Kaindl, was far more emphatic. Unlike Srbik, Kaindl had a true Austrian's appreciation of the Hohenzollerns and Prussian-oriented historians. The Graz historian could find no saving grace in the kleindeutsch apologia which he described as "a badly contrived fairy tale."[25] He claimed that Bismarck's unification had not been the fulfillment of the national purpose, but a victory for the narrower Prussian and Protestant ideals.

---

[22] Peter Mosser and Theodor Reitterer, *Die Mittelschulen in Österreich* (Vienna, 1929), pp. 68, 86.

[23] Robert Janeschitz-Kriegl, *Lehrbuch der Geschichte* (Vienna, 1930 ff.), II: 165; Heinrich Montzka, *Woynars Lehrbuch der Geschichte* (Vienna, 1931), II: 231; Andreas Zeehe, *Lehrbuch der Geschichte* (Vienna, 1930), III: 162 ff.; IV: 76–78. In a handbook designed for the teaching profession, Robert Endres demanded more than this vague nostalgia; see his *Handbuch der österreichischen Staats-und Wirtschafts Geschichte* (Leipzig, 1922), pp. 4–5.

[24] See Redlich's 1921 introduction to *Weltmacht des Barock* (Vienna, 1961), p. ix; idem, *Akademie-Festreden* (Vienna, 1958), pp. 49–50; Leo Santifaller, "Oswald Redlich," *MÖIG* 56 (1948): 154–65.

[25] Raimund Friedrich Kaindl, *Oesterreich, Preussen, Deutschland* (Vienna, 1926), p. 11. See also Kaindl's autobiography in Sigfrid Steinberg (ed.) *Die Geschichtswissenschaft der Gegenwart in Selbstdarstellungen* (1925), II: 191–94; Theodor Traber, "Raimund Friedrich Kaindl," *Neues Abendland* 2 (1947): 174–76; Alexander Balse, *Raimund Friedrich Kaindl* (Wiesbaden, 1962), pp. 38–68. Srbik's attack on Kaindl can be found in "Kleindeutsch oder grossdeutsch; ein kritischer Beitrage zu Kaindls Buch: 'Österreich, Preussen, Deutschland,'" *Archiv für Politik und Geschichte* 4 (1926): 251–60; idem, "Unmethodische Geschichtsbetrachtung," *Schönere Zukunft* 3 (1927): 104–6. Kaindl's answer can be found in "Professor von Srbik und mein Buch 'Österreich, Preussen, Deutschland.'" *Schönere Zukunft* 3 (1927): 126–30. Kaindl carried his attack on German historians and advocacy of Mitteleuropa into the German Historical Conference of 1927; *Historische Zeitschrift* 137 (1928): 416.

By abandoning the Austrian Germans to their own devices, Bismarck had laid the foundation for the defeats of 1918.

It was unfortunate for Kaindl's propagandistic intent that his methodology was in disrepute. But even more important, Kaindl was not a strong enough supporter of the Anschluss to suit the academic community. He believed that reconstructing a federal union of the Danubian states took precedence over an Austro-German union. By demanding the complete destruction of mythological and political Prussiandom, he attached so many preconditions to the Anschluss that its completion would have been impossible.

Still this whole generation of historians was never able to go beyond the limited context of the empire in which they had seen themselves as both Germans and Habsburg loyalists. Even Kaindl could not conceive of an Austrian nostalgia disassociated from Germanism. He had spent too much time as an historian of Carpathian Germans to achieve such a task. It would take another generation of historical scholars for nostalgia to take precedence over Germanism in any interpretation. Led by Hugo Hantsch, a priest, several young scholars introduced a new element—Catholicism—which overturned the limited context of the Srbik-Kaindl debates. This Austro-Catholic vision of Germanic culture turned away from the predominantly Protestant Reich to the epitome of Catholic dynasticism, to the Habsburg imperial past. If a nostalgia drawn from monarchical experience made Hantsch doubt the possibilities of a small Austria, still he was more optimistic than either Seipel or the anthropologists. Hantsch considered the postwar Austrian state as the true, if perhaps temporary, repository of nostalgia. He argued that its citizens were Austrians, not Germans. He even approved the allied action which struck "German" from the state's title, leaving "Austria" alone as the official designation.[26]

Hantsch's case was not unique; it proved that Austrian patriotism could exist and that Austrianism did not need to be forever on the defensive. Austria bore a long tradition that appeared to have survived the collapse. By lasting for longer than half a decade, the small Alpine state had proven its Cassandras wrong. The positive features of Austrian mores were again discoverable. A young publicist wrote that compared to the German Reich, "We have the older

[26] Hugo Hantsch, *Österreich, eine Deutung seiner Geschichte und Kultur* (Innsbruck, 1934), p. 16. See also idem, *Die Entwicklung Österreich-Ungarns zur Grossmacht* (Freiburg, 1933), pp. 54–55; Volksdeutscher Arbeitskreis österreichischer Katholiken, *Katholischer Glaube und deutsches Volkstum in Österreich* (Salzburg, 1933), pp. 41 ff.

culture, the one more capable of life."[27] Influential journals supported this position. As, successively, editor and publisher of two Catholic periodicals, Joseph Eberle filled his pages with articles by Kaindl, Kralik, anyone who would attack Hohenzollern myths and support Austrian patriotism. Eberle even supported the small group of serious monarchists. Although not actively engaged in the Habsburg restoration movement, he saw the virtues of allies who always attacked Prussia and rejected the Anschluss as the continuation of Prussia's struggle against the empire.[28]

More important than the retired colonels and generals who led the monarchist movement were a younger and much more radical group of Habsburg loyalists. This intellectual, Catholic and disenchanted youth was informally organized in the "Austrian Action" led by Ernst Karl Winter who would become mayor of Vienna under Schuschnigg. The "Action" was a radical group; its members were very much outsiders to the Viennese bourgeoisie from which they sprang. Winter claimed that his extreme Austrianism had caused his disqualification from university teaching.[29] Yet radicalism does not necessarily mean an ideological divorce from the more traditionally oriented explanations. This was true for the "Action," who lifted most of their ideas bodily from the corpus of "anthropological" thought. What distinguished the "Action" from the older proponents of nostalgia was the vehemence and intransigence with which the young held these views. This extremism was to lead to at least one intellectual innovation. The "Action" abandoned any pretense of allegiance to Germanic culture, an assertion which was beyond the imagination of the anthropologists who were deeply immersed in the German literary world. A leading member of the Action group, Alfred Missong, wrote:

[27] Rudolf Hans Bartsch, "Das österreichische Selbstgefühl," *Das Neue Reich* 6 (1924): 376. Among a host of other works in a similar vein, see Joseph Eberle, "Deutscher Besuch in Wien," *Schönere Zukunft* 3 (1927): 181–82; Karl Diwald, "1529: Oesterreich rettet das Abendland," *Das Neue Reich* 11 (September 14, 1929): 996; Oscar A. H. Schmitz, *Der österreichische Mensch* (Vienna, 1924), pp. 7 ff.; H. Kunz, *Neu-Österreich* (Jena, 1923), pp. 54–55.

[28] *Der Anschluss*, January 15, 1928: Viktor Dankl, "Nochmals: die österreichische Frage," *Das Neue Reich* 7 (1925): 1029–33. For a young monarchist's criticism of his leaders' attempt to maintain the nostalgia intact without revision, see Hans Karl, *Otto von Österreich* (Vienna, 1931), pp. 136–37.

[29] Ernst Karl Winter, "Österreichische Erziehungsprobleme," *Wiener politische Blätter* 4 (1936): 245. See the short biography by Alfred Missong, "E. K. Winter—Mitschöpfer der Zweiten Republik," *Forum* 12 (1965): 245. Winter's rejected dissertation which claimed to find the roots of Austrianism in the Baroque monarchy was published as *Rudolph IV von Österreich* (Vienna, 1934–36), I: ix. See also idem, "Österreich im 19 und 20 Jahrhundert," *Das Neue Reich* 7 (1925): 533 ff.

We cannot talk of an Austrian return to "Mother Germania.". . . . These ideas might suffice for German history texts, but they cannot be considered by Austrians. . . . The idea came out of the old *Ostmark* and completely ignores that the Alpine Austrian of today is culturally and racially different. The Austrian man is racially a synthesis of German and Slav, culturally a synthesis of Roman and Byzantine. . . . We cannot say that Austria has grown out of Germanism alone. Austria cannot return to the Reich since it never belonged to the German Reich of today. The best solution would be the return of the Germans to the Reich, to Austria, to the Emperor.[30]

This unequivocable patriotism was too strong for most Austrians. The Action movement may have been too young and too radical, but even more established sources of Austrian patriotism were only noticed in passing. The response was hardly overwhelming to Anton Wildgans, a famous playwright and poet, sometime postwar manager of the influential Burgtheater. And Wildgans was an ideal exponent of Austrianism, since he was respected by both the generations of Hofmannsthal and of Winter. He had written a patriotic credo as early as 1920 but had delayed its publication, perhaps because of uncertainty about the state's survival. However by 1930 Austria seemed secure, and Wildgans could present his *Rede über Österreich*, first delivered in Stockholm in 1929 and then over Vienna radio on New Year's Day, 1930. Wildgans luxuriated in an Austrian national character that was totally divorced from life in the Reich. Like Hantsch, Hofmannsthal, and Winter, he believed this national character fitted well within an essentially cosmopolitan mission.

The Austrian is a knower of nations, of men, of souls—in one word, a psychologist. And psychology is everything. Psychology is the ability to live with other people and other nations. . . . This knowledge and comprehension is, so to say, the historical nature of the Austrian man. . . . The Austrian man is not a man of action or power, especially in the national movement. This might be considered a lack of progress, a fault from the standpoint of national self-consciousness; it can hardly be considered an error when viewed from the higher plane of humanity. Not without profound cause does the expression "from humanity, to nationality, to bestiality" come from an Austrian, from Grillparzer.[31]

---

[30] Alfred Missong, "Österreichs Politik seit 1866/68," Ernst Karl Winter et al., *Die österreichische Aktion: programatischen Studien* (Vienna, 1927), pp. 111–12. Such radicalism worried the Germans who saw the "Action" as an indication of the failure of communication between Germans and Austrians; see Otto Kunze, "Die oesterreichische Aktion," *Hochland* 25 (1928): 650.

[31] Wildgans, *Sämtliche Werke*, VII: 423. The author's widow has claimed that the radio speech was very popular; see Lily Wildgans, *Der gemeinsame Weg* (Salzburg, 1960), p. 407. However, Wildgans was ignored in many influential circles. The *Neue Freie Presse* did not choose to mention the radio address;

Cosmopolitanism had become the key for any meaningful justification of a distinct Austrian nationalism. In the opinion of the academics as well as the general public, cosmopolitan aspirations seemed irreconcilable with patriotism for any specific political unit. Yet Wildgans and Winter were committed to just this course of action. They believed that Baroque-Catholic-universalism could create the prototype not only for a specific Austrian man but for the supranational European. For these convinced Austrophiles, nationalism and cosmopolitanism did not contain mutually exclusive qualities; both could have found their resolution in an Austria, then small, but in reality the repository of the European future.

Pan-Europeanism had thus merged with the Austrian idiom. After all, the monarchy had been meaningfully called a "little Europe." But the immediate sources of this ideology were the anthropologists. In 1917 Bahr had called himself an "Austro-European."[32] Hofmannsthal wrote in the same year: "Who says Austria says a thousand years of grappling with Europe, a thousand-year mission through Europe, a thousand years of faith in Europe."[33] But neither Hofmannsthal nor Bahr was able to reconcile these values with the small postwar state that seemed the epitome of fragmentation and particularism. Bahr hoped that Austria might merge with other states into some larger agglomerate. Hofmannsthal lost faith even in this idea and transferred his loyalty directly from his prewar Austrian homeland to the concept of a postwar European fatherland. The only political movement he strongly supported was the attempt at continental unity.[34]

It took a Rhenish convert to Austrianism, Oscar A. H. Schmitz, to integrate Pan-Europeanism with Austrianism. Schmitz emphasized Austria's natural role as a mediator between nationalities, Austria's preeminent qualifications to serve as the German-speaking center of Europe. Wildgans and the Action took this argument to its logical conclusion. Winter proclaimed an orientation that was totally "European; the goal is not Mitteleuropa but Europe."[35]

---

given this paper's policies, such action can be taken as less of an attempt at managing the news and more of an indication that the *Presse* saw no threat from Wildgans' direction.

[32] Bahr, *1918*, p. 17.

[33] Hofmannsthal, *Gesammelte Werke, Prosa*, III: 382.

[34] Hofmannsthal, *Prosa*, IV: 412–13, 508–9; idem, *Gesammelte Werke, Aufzeichungen* (Frankfurt, 1959), p. 53; *Briefwechsel Hofmannsthal-Burck-hardt*, p. 227. See Helmut Fiechtner, "Hofmannsthal der Europäer," *Wort in der Zeit* 2 (1956): 33–37.

[35] Ernst Karl Winter, "Vorwort," *Die österreichische Aktion*, p. 5. See also the work of another Action member, the legitimist leader H. K. Freiherr von Zessner-Spitzenberg, "Der österreichische Gedanke und der deutsche Weg," *Schönere Zukunft* 3 (1928): 923; Schmitz, *Der österreichische Mensch*, p. 68.

But the problem remained how to put this nostalgia or this new Austrian nationalism into practice. The Action's program failed not because they remained political outsiders, but because by the time they had reached power the whole framework of society had changed. In the 1920s, the direction of policy fell to the Christian Socialist Party and its leading statesman, Ignaz Seipel. The next chapter attempts to trace the diplomacy of nostalgia as conceived by Seipel and Heinrich Mataja.

The predecessor in Srbik's chair at the University of Vienna held these views even earlier; see August Fournier, *Erinnerungen* (Munich, 1923), p. 10. Among others, Friedrich Schreyvogl attempted to integrate the eventual Anschluss with Pan-Europeanism; the propagandistic intent of these views precluded their serious consideration; see Schreyvogl's *Oesterreich, das deutsche Problem* (Cologne, 1925), p. 61. Contrary to this author's view that Europeanism was the effective component of Austrianism, Magris has isolated two other elements of nostalgia; Viennese hedonism and respect for the imperial bureaucracy. While these did exist, they could hardly be the source for a ground swell of patriotism; see Magris, *Der habsburgische Mythos*, pp. 7–27.

CHAPTER **XIII** THE DIPLOMACY OF

NOSTALGIA

Up to this point, the discussion has concentrated upon the ideological aspects of Austrianism. A larger question still remains unanswered. Could this nostalgia for the old empire or this new Austrian nationalism be put into actual political practice? In internal politics there seemed no genuine Austrian way. The Austrian "Action" did conceive of a new nationalism that would lead to the transformation of the state along Catholic, social reformist, and authoritarian lines. But this was a wild scheme that was hardly suited to a time when democratic governments were the Central European fashion.

The situation was different in foreign affairs. Again the Action presented a utopian proposal, one to make Austria the center of a reorganized Europe. But in the 1920s, such plans expressed the hopes of many sober statesmen as well. More important, the Ministry of Foreign Affairs itself was often dominated by those who were committed into a nostalgia for the old empire, even if they were not thoroughly imbued with the new nationalism of the Action. With the exception of ten months, the period between May 1922 and April 1929 saw the leadership of foreign affairs under the control of men more moved by the symbols of past greatness than by the promises of Germanic nationalism. Contrasting sharply with the preceding Schober government and the succeeding Streeruwitz and Schober cabinets, Seipel's two chancellorships and Heinrich Mataja's foreign ministry tried to find an adequate political form for this nostalgia. Seipel and Mataja sought an enlarged sphere of operations, sought to make Vienna again the center of a vast territory.

How viable was such a policy? To answer this question more is needed than an investigation of ideological propensities. The diplomacy of nostalgia cannot be understood as an isolated phenomenon; it must be considered as part of a larger interplay of events and ideas. The Austrian problem was too much a part of the whole postwar structure to be resolved on any stage narrower than that of a general European settlement. More important, peace treaties aside, Austria could never act unilaterally. Its foreign policy was severely limited by

Vienna's weaknesses; by the external pressures of ententes, both big and little; even by German nationalism within Austria itself.

For these reasons, Seipel and Mataja faced many problems that had little to do with nostalgia. The diplomacy of nostalgia was based upon the search for a wider area in which to operate, but before this policy could be initiated the Austrian economy would have to be put on its feet. And this was no easy task. Often, as in 1922, it became a priority that overrode all others. At that time the economy was in such an imminent state of collapse as to threaten the disruption of political order as well. There was talk of military intervention to forestall this possibility in France, that plans for military occupation were being drawn up by Hungarians and Czechs. Mussolini apparently envisioned a partition of Austria between Italy and Bavaria. The Czech Ambassador to Rome during this period described an interview with Masaryk along the same lines: "Then deep in thought, President Masaryk volunteered the opinion that Austria remained his chief concern. Unless it could unite with Germany, which was excluded, the best solution would be to associate Voralberg and Tyrol with Switzerland and the remainder with Czechoslovakia which might happen as soon as the latter could solve the problem of its Bohemian Germans."[1]

But this alternative was only a last resort. It was unpalatable to the Czechs who did not relish undertaking reconstruction of the Viennese economy. Beneš therefore became Seipel's most able advocate before the League; Czech influence was decisive in organizing the League's financial reconstruction. And international financial reconstruction was just what Seipel had planned. Such a solution did not jeopardize Austrian independence by making the Viennese government a client of some larger power. There was a price paid. The Geneva Protocols did limit Austrian freedom of action in the future. Yet the clever priest knew at whom these protocols were aimed. He realized that the allies would hardly consider any surrogate for the empire as a violation of the Geneva agreements which were only meant to be applied in the case of an Austro-German customs union.

However, the situation in 1922 had been so disastrous that Seipel contemplated giving up the diplomacy of nostalgia forever. If the League's financial reconstruction had not been achieved, he would have been forced to make Austria a mere client of other powers. As we have seen in chapter VII, Seipel's government proffered the plan of an Austro-German customs union. However, this was never really

[1] Vlastimil Kybal, "Czechoslovakia and Italy: My Negotiations with Mussolini," *Journal of Central European Affairs* 14 (1954): 362. Müller (Bern), September 18, 1922, AA 1483/3086/D613865–D613866.

a serious alternative; the Wirth cabinet was both unwilling and unable to act. The more serious proposal was made to the Italian foreign minister, Carlo Schanzer, at Verona during August 1922. Seipel suggested the creation of an Italo-Austrian customs and currency union. Although the Italians were willing, this project was only conceived as a last desperate measure. It would irrevocably tie Austria's fortunes to an Italy that was also undergoing a financial crisis, that was facing a threat of civil war.[2]

The League's reconstruction loan was forthcoming; the Italian government would have to wait. Seipel was acclaimed as the savior of Austria, yet the benefits of such a title were transitory. The League demanded extreme sacrifices from the Austrians as the price of its assistance, and the attempt to share this austerity with the various federal states caused Seipel's fall from power in November 1924. The new chancellor, Rudolf Ramek, was a fellow Christian Socialist, but an avowed supporter of Anschluss. However, Ramek's tenure of office brought about no dramatic shift in foreign relations. The Chancellor was not intimately involved in directing the policy of his government vis-à-vis other countries. Thus his foreign minister, Heinrich Mataja, was far more powerful in office than his immediate predecessors. And Mataja's ideas were very different from those of his chief.

At first glance, Mataja seemed assured of a successful tenure in office. He was socially at home with the Viennese diplomatic establishment and had had foreign experience as well while a member of the Interparliamentary Union. He could not be faulted on grounds of party orthodoxy. He appeared fully able to carry on Seipel's diplomacy. His views were not very different from Seipel's. It was the style of Austrian diplomacy that changed when Mataja assumed office. While Seipel had spread a blanket of calm over Austria's relations with other states, Mataja had a genius for creating an enraged opposition. As Maximilian Pfeiffer, German minister to Vienna, was fond of demonstrating, this was partially due to a lack of political realism. But Mataja's troubles seemed to evolve more from his personality than from his ability to understand the principles of *Realpolitik*. Pfeiffer complained that he was governed by whims; the *Neue Freie Presse* more kindly referred to his "eclectic" tendencies.[3] Although

[2] Gottlieb Ladner, *Seipel als Überwinder der Staatskrise vom Sommer 1922* (Vienna, 1964), pp. 91–93; Pfeiffer (Vienna) to Berlin, April 15, 1925, AA 2344/4576/E171520–E171524; Cabinet Minutes, September 20, 1922, AA 1483/3086/D613868.

[3] *Neue Freie Presse*, see Pfeiffer to Berlin, May 26, 1926, AA 2344/4576/E171623. For Foreign Office appraisal of Mataja, see November 21, 1924, memo, AA 4497/K927/K233572–K233584.

removed by thirty years from the heat of controversy, Walter Goldinger still refers to Mataja's "style possessed by nervousness."[4]

It was this style that forced the discontinuation of the balancing act Seipel had invented, an act which carefully alternated between Austrianism and German nationalism. Seipel could not hide the fact that he was more moved by nostalgia than by plans for an Anschluss. It was obvious to much of the foreign and domestic press, to many diplomats as well. The *Völkischer Beobachter* may have slandered the Austrian leader by calling him a "cancerous sore on Germandom,"[5] yet more moderate sources substantially agreed that he was no firm German nationalist. During a visit by Seipel to the Dutch capital, the German Minister to the Hague reported: "All who meet Seipel here are convinced that he does not possess a deep German commitment."[6]

This impression was in part deliberate, designed for foreign consumption. For the French, Seipel could put on an even better show than he had at the Hague. But for Berlin and Vienna, Seipel would soften his adherence to nostalgia and emphasize his German nationalism. He constantly stated that Austria was a German state, that the Austrians participated in the common German culture. And he seemed sincere enough to convince Josef Wirth and both German ministers to Vienna during his periods as chancellor. Pfeiffer wrote to Berlin in 1925: "I still hold fast to my previous conviction that he is in principle friendly to the Anschluss. Perhaps his close friends are right that he pursues the policy of exhausting all possibilities in order to be able to say that there is no other way out for Austria."[7]

Seipel played this charade also to convince his coalition partners, The Grossdeutsch Party, that he did not oppose an Austro-German union. This was an essential rule of the Austrian political game. But games can only be played by men willing to restrain their emotions. They are not made for men with Mataja's style. The Austrian Foreign Minister was too excitable to restrain his anti-Germanism. He therefore violated the rules of this particular game almost immediately upon assuming office. He seemed determined to weaken the Anschluss

---

[4] Goldinger in (ed.) Benedikt, *Geschichte der Republic Österreich* (Vienna, 1954), p. 139.

[5] *Völkischer Beobachter*, October 7/8, 1926. For other appraisals of Seipel's anti-German feelings, see *Vorwärts*, February 6, 1926; *Österreich-Deutschland* 4 (January 1927): 12–13; 5 (January 1928): 6–7. See also series of press clippings in Vienna to Berlin, December 3, 1926, AA 4491/K920/K228733–K228749, and Rudolf Olden, "Österreichische Köpfe: Ignaz Seipel," *Die Weltbühne* 21 (1925): 162–63.

[6] Lucius (Hague) to Berlin, May 8, 1925, AA 2344/4576/E171559.

[7] Pfeiffer to Berlin, April 15, 1925, AA 2344/4576/E171526–E171527. See also *Der Anschluss*, July 15, 1929; Wirth report on conversation with Seipel, June 13, 1928, AA 2346/4576/E173477.

movement at home at any cost. Thus, in April 1925 he gave an interview to the *Tribuna* (Rome) in which he deprecated the strength of the Austrian Anschluss movement and implied that it was confined mainly to the Grossdeutsch Party. This naturally stirred the Grossdeutsch Party leaders to a frenzy; Dinghofer called Mataja a great enemy of the Anschluss. Mataja sought to appease them by claiming that his remarks had been mistranslated, but this lame excuse satisfied no one. It took a great deal of soothing by other Christian Socialist leaders for the quarrel to be even temporarily settled in May. But then as this crisis blew over, another emerged around the person of the Austrian minister to Paris, Baron Eichoff. Mataja's fragile German nationalism would naturally reinforce the Germanophobes among his subordinates. The Minister to Paris became emboldened and used an interview in *Le Matin* to upbraid publicly the Grossdeutsch Party leaders, Dinghofer and Frank, who had advocated an economic union with Germany.[8]

To appease the opposition, Mataja was forced to shed Eichoff. By the end of June, ex-Foreign Minister Grünberger had succeeded to the Paris post. Yet Mataja lost any good will that accrued from this move by also replacing Richard Riedl in Berlin. It was well known that Riedl was the backbone of Austrian agitation for Anschluss, that he was the leader in demanding a customs union. His dismissal naturally aroused fears in both the German and Austrian Anschluss movements. This seemed another blow directed at sapping the strength of the German nationalists in Vienna, and the uneasiness went unallayed even when Riedl's replacement turned out to be the reliable Anschluss supporter and Grossdeutsch Party leader Felix Frank. Frank would have to use up much of his influence in a vain attempt to end this discontent. He was able to reach some of the key men in the Volksbund, but he still could not stop all public demonstrations. At a farewell gathering on July 6 for the departing Minister, the DNVP Reichstag deputy, Alfred von Kemnitz, declared that Riedl had been removed for espousing pro-German views. Richart Mischler, executive secretary of the Volksbund, then launched into the attack on Mataja that Frank had so desperately tried to avoid.[9]

There were other, more impressive, signs of this change in style. Eichoff excluded German journalists from a press conference that Mataja gave during a June visit to Paris. The Baron stated that he

[8] Pfeiffer to Berlin, April 25, 1925, AA 2344/4576/E171542–E171543; *Der österreichische Volkswirt* 17 (1925): 809.

[9] Frank to Berlin, July 7, 1925, Fasz. 111, 14324 pr. 9 VII 1925; *Berliner Tageblatt*, July 7, 1925; *Neue Freie Presse*, July 7, 1925, p.m.; Clemens Wildner, *Von Wien nach Wien* (Vienna, 1961), pp. 100–5.

had no choice, since many influential French newspapermen would have otherwise boycotted the conference. The Germans could hardly be expected to be comforted with such an excuse. Nor was the German colony in Paris appeased when Mataja issued a separate invitation to journalists from the Reich.[10]

Much more important, Mataja was unwilling to engage in the most perfunctory negotiations with Germany. He even delayed the signing of a harmless accord, eliminating visa dues along the Austro-German border. The Austrian Foreign Ministry had worked hard for this agreement; its economic experts hoped that the German labor market might solve the Austrian unemployment problem. Thus they had designed a treaty eliminating visa dues to facilitate the migration of labor between the two states. This agreement was hailed as a major breakthrough that would cost Austria little and promised possible enormous economic benefits in return. But Mataja postponed the final signing for three months during the late spring and summer. He was filled with excuses. He claimed that Riedl had not explicitly followed instructions from Vienna during the last-minute negotiations, that the Austrian government could not afford the loss of revenue from dues, that the League Control Commission for Austria would not approve this agreement. Finally, he contended that Johannes Schober, then chief of police, was opposed. This last statement was particularly offensive to the German Foreign Office. Schober was known as a persistent advocate of Angleichung. Mataja only used this excuse because Schober was traveling in America and would be hard to reach. Stresemann was maddened by these delays; Mataja was maligned in the corridors of the Wilhelmstrasse; he seemed able to raise the latent anti-Austrianism in even the strongest advocates of Anschluss. Even Pfeiffer closed one of his reports on Mataja's procrastination by proclaiming: "I will not presume to add to this small vignette of Austrian character."[11]

However anti-German Mataja was, he, like all politicians, wanted a good press everywhere. Even as he repudiated German nationalism he worked to reassure the Germans that this was not the case, and, as often happened, his style worked to undermine his strategy. He was so willing to attribute the worst to the Germans that he found it impossible not to alienate the Reich diplomats. Mataja even took

[10] Hoesch (Paris) to Berlin, June 15, 1925, AA 2344/4576/E171680–E171681; Paris to Berlin, June 15, 1925, ibid., E171699–E171705; same to same, AA 4491/K920/K228433–K228434; Mataja to Paris, May, 1925, NPA Fasz. 110, 1382 pr. 10 V 1925.

[11] Pfeiffer to Berlin, May 14, 1925, AA 2344/4576/E171598; same to same, May 14, 19, 1925, AA 2344/4576/E171592, E171595–E171597, E171606–E171608; Riedl (Berlin) to Vienna, March 3, 1925, NPA Fasz. 11, Zl. 274 Pol.

seriously the whimsical suggestion made in 1923 by Friedrich Rosenberg, German foreign minister, who had suggested that Austria might
buy the Anschluss at the price of ten years' starvation. Mataja trum-
peted his unwillingness to pay this fictitious price, although no one
ever demanded it of him.[12]

Mataja's greatest success naturally came while imitating Seipel.
After all, Seipel had managed to maintain the semblance of a friendly
press in the Reich by emphasizing his inability to follow a pro-German
course. Mataja attempted to do the same. He pleaded with Pfeiffer to
recognize the paucity of real alternatives open to Austria. In a style
truly reminiscent of Seipel, he proclaimed to the Center press in
early 1925:

In theory I am a supporter of the Anschluss. In practice I do not believe
that the Anschluss can be completed in the next few years. Therefore I
must construct my policy in these years so that the Austrian state shall
take advantage of the best possible economic and political opportunities.
When I seek the assistance of the allies for at least three years, I cannot
make the impression that I prepare for the Anschluss. For this reason, I am
forced to pursue the policy of an independent Austria, to act in the present
situation in such a manner that the allies will have little interest in refusing
the necessary assistance.[13]

Desperate for any means of reassuring the Germans, other Austrian
diplomats took up this approach. Richard Schüller, economic expert
in the Austrian Ministry of Foreign Affairs, declared to his Reich
colleagues that the necessities of allied control had forced Austria
to pursue its present policies. He stated that Mataja's actions were
dictated solely by tactical considerations, that the Germans had
only to be patient and "the wreck of Austria will one day sail completely unnoticed into the harbor of the German state."[14]

These justifications were more than conjuring tricks to please the
Germans. Their strength lay in the fact that they represented, in some
measure, the state of the Austrian mind. Both Seipel and Mataja
agreed on at least one of the assumptions of such an argument—that
the Austrian state was ultimately doomed. Only their interpretation
of "ultimately" varied. Seipel was never the strong optimist, but he
had confidence in Austria's ability to endure for a time. He told an
audience in Berlin on February 5, 1926: "The German state which
the Austrians have built is not great but it survives and will survive
until one day we perhaps exchange it for another state."[15] But Mataja

[12] Pfeiffer to Berlin, May 14, 1925, see n. 11, E171597.
[13] Paris to Berlin, June 30, 1925, ibid., E171647–E171648.
[14] Pfeiffer to Berlin, May 14, 1925, ibid., E171592.
[15] Vorwärts, February 6, 1926, edition A.

apparently was convinced that the Austrian economy would remain in perpetual crisis, and there was evidence for his contention. It was true that the League's financial reconstruction had brought about a business upswing in 1923. But even the next year saw a decisive change for the worse. First came a plunging stock market in the spring of 1924, then followed a general business decline a year later.[16] These two incidents destroyed the fragile hope that many Austrians had in the League's reconstruction policies. Thus Mataja assumed office at a low point in Austria's economic struggle. Not only had the financial reconstruction failed to stabilize the economy, but it was ending, and Austria needed new credit and new economic support. This money could not be found without the aid of the allied governments. Viewed in this light, there was considerable justification for Mataja's statement to the Center press. For these reasons, any Austrian chancellor would have felt constrained, extraordinarily dependent upon those able to guarantee Austria's international loans. In this situation, every Austrian foreign minister would have had to follow Mataja in what Stresemann contemptuously called "the customary appeasement of the entente."[17]

It is clear that Stresemann quite naturally confused Mataja's dislike for Germany with this aspect of Austrian foreign policy. But the German Foreign Minister was right when he implied that more was involved than merely salvaging the Austrian economy. Instead of supporting German nationalism, Mataja sought to use the fears of Anschluss to draw concessions from other nations. This was the stock in trade of the diplomacy of nostalgia. Seipel had successfully used these fears to generate support for the League's reconstruction. Mataja had, if anything, an even easier task. The negotiations that led to Locarno brought the Austrian question again into prominence. Germany's increasing prestige raised hopes and renewed agitation for the Anschluss. This agitation naturally raised the alarm in France, Italy, and Czechoslovakia. To transform these fears into economic aid for Austria, Mataja only needed to prove a statement that was almost axiomatic in France and Italy. He had only to show that the weakness of the Austrian economy fed the Anschluss movement. Under his leadership, the Austrian Foreign Ministry let few opportunities slip by without making this case. The argument was strongly upheld in a position paper prepared for the eventuality of a French protest against the participation of Austrian socialist leaders in several German

---

[16] For the best discussion of the Austrian business cycle see Friedrich Thalmann, "Die Wirtschaft in Österreich" (ed.) Benedikt, *Geschichte Österreich*, pp. 492–95.

[17] Stresemann to Vienna, May 15, 1925, AA 1483/3086/D614034–D614035.

Anschluss demonstrations. The document stated: "It must be noted that the Anschluss movement is more strongly propelled into the foreground because the economic situation is viewed unfavorably in Austria as well as abroad."[18]

But, this time, it was not the French who were most moved by such statements. The power most receptive to this argument was Italy. Mussolini appeared extremely worried about the effect of a revived and strengthened Germany upon the irredentist movement in South Tyrol. The South Tyrolean problem would certainly have been less pressing if Austria had become dependent on the Italian economy. Furthermore, there were even economic advantages to be reaped from an association with Austria. Austrian business did not directly threaten the Italian businessman; at least this was the undisputed thesis of Richard Schüller. With cooperation appearing so advantageous, various schemes were proposed to facilitate such an economic entente. Some thought was given to the creation of Austro-Italian cartels in several major industries. Chaiarmonte Bordonaro, Italian minister in Vienna, reported that Mataja seemed most interested in the proposal of Bonaldo Stringher, president of the Bank of Italy. Stringher suggested the foundation of a joint Austro-Italian investment bank that would ease the perpetual credit needs of the new republic.[19]

But these moves were only temporary expedients at best. Mataja wanted to do more than simply preserve Vienna's economic structure. He desired to construct a new entity in conformity with his ideological commitments. The problem for the researcher is to ferret out the Foreign Minister's ultimate goals, and this is not easy. For an indiscreet man, Mataja was remarkably silent about his final objectives. Certainly he must have been intrigued by the possibility of constructing a Danubian union as a surrogate for an empire in whose armies he had recently served. At least Mataja implied as much in a June 1925 interview with a correspondent from Le Matin (Paris). But the Austrian Foreign Minister may have made this statement for political reasons; it might not have represented his real belief. He made no secret of his desire to remain on good terms with the French. He could never hurt his standing in Paris by supporting a scheme that was so popular in France as to be approved by the semiofficial Le Temps.[20]

Mataja really seemed to be more interested in another combination that would satisfy the demands of nostalgia, even if the newly

---

[18] Foreign Office memo, 1925, in NPA Fasz. 110, 1220 pr. 13 III 1925.
[19] I documenti diplomatici italiani, serie VII, III: 521–22.
[20] See n. 10.

constructed amalgamation did not fit precisely within the borders of the old empire. After all, nostalgia was really a hope for increased opportunity, a widened area for political action. It did not necessarily have to be tied to one particular project—Danubian union. During a state visit to Rome in April 1925, he suggested that Italy and Austria form a customs union. But he had no intention of stopping with this simple bilateral agreement. He apparently envisioned this union as only the first step toward the construction of a new and powerful economic grouping. He advocated that Italy and Austria invite the succession states to join them. Mataja assured the Italians that this suggestion was made only for reasons of political expedience. He argued that France and England would not apply the restrictive clauses of the peace treaties and Geneva Protocols to such a combination. But, he stated, a simple bilateral agreement between Italy and Austria might run into an invincible opposition. Whatever justification Mataja used, the undeniable consequence of this multilateral combination would be the construction of an economic area even larger and more viable than that of a Danubian union.[21]

As the acknowledged leader of the Little Entente, Czechoslovakia was the key to any such combination. And by 1925, the Czechs had overcome their initial reluctance to aid Vienna. In 1919 Beneš had refused to consider a French suggestion that his government give economic assistance to Austria. He told Philippe Berthelot, secretary general of the Quai d'Orsay, that anti-Austrian feeling in Prague made such action impossible. This animosity never was totally overcome; as late as 1924, some of the Czech press still screamed: "Not a heller for Vienna."[22] But by the beginning of 1921 the Czech government's policy had been reversed. There were a number of justifications for this transformation. There was a growing awareness that Vienna could play a key role in Czech economic exploitation of the Danube. As Beneš told Austrian Chancellor Mayr: "Austria and Czechoslovakia must draw nearer to each other because the economy of Prague cannot be separated from that of Vienna."[23]

Much more important, Beneš and Masaryk feared that the Anschluss might come about if Austria was left to its own devices. This would have been a disaster for the Czechs. A unified Reich would not only have surrounded Czechoslovakia on three sides but exerted enormous pressures upon the Bohemian economy. Beneš believed

[21] See n. 19, also *I documenti italiani* IV: 38; Marek to Vienna, July 10, 1925, NPA Fasz. 63, Zl. 103 Pol.

[22] Translation can be found in NPA Fasz. 822.

[23] Foreign Ministry memo, December 2, 1921, NPA Fasz. 822, 6885 pr. 2 XIII 1921.

that supporting the Austrian economy was the best means of assuring Austrian political independence. Thus in 1921 he began a series of moves designed to achieve these goals. His first step was to negotiate a nonaggression pact, the Treaty of Lana, that was signed by the Schober government on December 16, 1921. The Austrian Foreign Office not only desired the improvement resulting from the stabilization of their formal relationship with Prague, but viewed this agreement as the first step toward far-reaching economic engagements. As the first installment on these expectations, Vienna was given a credit of over 500 million Czech crowns (around $16 million).[24] In the following year, the Czechs continued this policy by enthusiastically supporting the League's financial reconstruction.

Yet however much the Czechs searched for means of assisting Vienna, they could never overcome their pessimism about the utility of such a policy. In 1925 Beneš confided to Italian diplomats in Geneva that he considered the 1922 solutions as only provisional. He stated that some final settlement of Austria's economic difficulties was necessary if the small Alpine state were to survive.[25] And Mataja was now offering a final solution to the Austrian problem. It was certainly in the interest of Beneš to consider a tripartite tariff union scheme. He had encouragement from other powers. While the English were opposed, Beneš could count upon some support from his major ally, France. Even the timing was right. In 1925 Beneš and Masaryk were worried about substantial German revisions on the Czech and Austrian frontiers. They saw Germany's refusal to guarantee its eastern borders as an ominous sign for the future. This fact could only encourage the Czechs to end the Austrian economy's chronic instability while they still had a chance.[26]

Thus in May 1925 Beneš told several Italian diplomats that Czech-Italian cooperation was a necessary precondition for any definitive solution of the Austrian dilemma. He claimed to view favorably an economic agreement between these two states and Austria. He even committed the Czech government to monetary sacrifices in order to

[24] Ibid.; Höffinger (Belgrade to Vienna), November 19, 1921, NPA Fasz. 822, 6546 pr. 20 VI 1921; Ladner, *Seipel als Überwinder*, pp. 22–23. For a full discussion of Czech policy in the 1920s, see Foreign Office memos January 9, 1922, October 24, 1923, NPA Fasz. 855, Z 128/1B, 3038 pr. 25 X 1923. Meeting of Beneš with Seipel, May 1924, with Mataja, December 1924, ibid., 13437 pr. 7 VI 1924, 42030 pr. 9 XII 1924. *Berliner Tageblatt*, May 12, 15, 1925, p.m.; Eduard Beneš, *The Diplomatic Struggle for European Security and the Stabilization of the Peace* (Prague, 1925), p. 10.

[25] *I documenti italiani* IV: 4–5.

[26] Grünberger to Vienna, September 29, November 10, 1925, NPA Fasz. 59, Zl. 6117 ex. 1925, Zl. 6635 ex. 1925.

bring this scheme to completion.[27] By June Mataja, Beneš, and Vittorio Scialoja, representing Italy, had initiated discussions that could have led to the establishment of preferential tariffs among their respective states. Such an agreement had some advantages over a simple customs union. Not all goods had to be included; each government could still assure protection to its most cherished interests. Furthermore, tariffs did not have to be equal. Instead of abolishing customs dues, the three governments could have manipulated them to assure fair competition.

Thus Mataja's scheme seemed able to succeed. The fears of the Czech and Italian governments, the renewed German diplomatic offensive of 1925, the advantages of a preferential tariff system—all these circumstances gave force and direction to the hopes of nostalgia, to the promise of a larger economic area for Austria. Yet despite such a happy juxtaposition of events, the preferential tariff system was stillborn. Its success depended upon a continuous Czech-Italian cooperation. If their complementary interests in Austria pushed them in this direction, their differences were too great to keep them moving along the same lines indefinitely. Mussolini hardly fitted Beneš' model of the solid statesman. In November 1924 Beneš warned Mataja against associating with the Italian Prime Minister, who was in the bad graces of Europe. In 1926 Beneš blamed Mataja for ever including Mussolini in the tariff union scheme. Moreover, Beneš worried that any cooperation would jeopardize Czech policy in other areas. He could not forget that his ally in the Little Entente, Yugoslavia, had been engaged in the most serious diplomatic conflict with the fascist leader.

On the other hand, the Italians were just as suspicious. Bernardo Attolico, vice-secretary general of the League, informed Mussolini that Beneš was too much a confidant of Briand and Chamberlain to ever become a friend of Italy. Attolico repeated conversations with other diplomats who thought that Beneš was considering a pact with Austria alone. While these rumors went too far, the Italians were right not to trust Beneš. The Czech Foreign Minister soon refused to consider the preferential tariff system. He argued that his partners in the Little Entente had refused to surrender their rights under the most-favored-nation clause. This excuse seemed lame. Mataja, Ramek, and Mussolini were all convinced that Beneš had left them in the lurch.[28]

[27] *I documenti italiani* IV: 5.
[28] Ibid., pp. 5–11, 37–38, 94; Marek to Vienna, July 10, October 5, November 7, 1925, January 19, 1926, NPA Fasz. 62, Zl. 149, 169, 183, Pol., Zl. 18 Pol.; Marek to Vienna, November 22, 1924, NPA Fasz. 822, 15797; Beneš, Mataja

Yet even if Beneš had agreed, Mataja still would have had enormous obstacles to overcome. The Foreign Minister's unpopularity did not bode well for a plan that was sure to arouse the opposition of those Austrians committed to the Anschluss. It is doubtful that even as adept a politician as Seipel could have secured its approval by the Nationalrat, and Mataja had none of Seipel's skill. His anti-German posture had only succeeded in forewarning the opposition of his plans. The socialists were especially active in the attack. The *Arbeiter Zeitung* castigated Mataja for undermining Austria's good relations with the Reich, while intriguing to create a tariff union with Czechoslovakia and Italy. Under the leadership of Social Democratic deputy Wilhelm Ellenbogen, the executive committee of the National-rat revoked the cabinet's power of lengthening trade treaties without parliamentary consent. This move assured a full-scale debate on even the first steps toward implementing Mataja's scheme. The pro-Anschluss forces rejoiced. The *Volkswirt* stated that Mataja had planned to achieve a Danubian union under the guise of harmless treaty revisions. But, proclaimed the *Volkswirt*, he had been defeated. "The friends of Anschluss are awake; they have found their organization."[29]

By October 15 the opposition was demanding Mataja's head. In the Nationalrat, Social Democrat Karl Leuthner launched into a full-scale attack. "Mataja is against the Anschluss," he proclaimed. "Not only do we maintain this, but every man in Europe recognizes this fact."[30] Ramek was embarrassed by his Foreign Minister's unpopularity, but no prime minister in his right mind could accept the opposition's demand for the removal of a subordinate. Thus Ramek felt obliged to defend his choice as foreign minister. However, the Prime Minister must have been relieved when Mataja became involved in a financial scandal during the closing days of 1925. In January 1926 Ramek assumed the office of foreign minister in addition to his duties as head of the government. He embarked upon a quiet pro-German course for the following ten months. But this policy was not to last the year. In October 1926 a new Seipel government was formed.

This new Seipel ministry was an ideal instrument for the diplomacy of nostalgia. Seipel was committed to other solutions than

---

conversations, see n. 22; Ramek in conversation with Mussolini, 1926, NPA Fasz. 470, Ad. 23070; Ramek in conversation with Stresemann, March 1926, NPA Fasz. 464, 1174 pr. 6 IV 1926.

[29] *Der österreichische Volkswirt* 17 (1925): 1089. Borchers (Vienna), June 24, 1925, AA 2344/4576/E171731–E171734.

[30] *Stenographische Protokolle*, III Gesetzgebungs Periode, III: 2727. See *Arbeiter Zeitung*, June 25, 1925.

Anschluss; he was the strongest and most able politician in Austria. If the diplomatic situation seemed less fluid than in 1925, appearances can be deceiving. Both Czechoslovakia and Italy were searching for new forms with which to shape development in Central and South-eastern Europe.

Yet old problems held back the creation of these new forms. The South Tyrol problem erupted again in 1928. The Austrian Chancellor could not ignore the increasing agitation of the Grossdeutsch Party and Tyrolean Christian Socialists. On February 17, 1928 he finally launched a full-scale criticism of Mussolini's policy. Seipel invoked a higher morality than even international law for the protection of the South Tyroleans' minority rights. And Mussolini, who recognized no law higher than his state, naturally took affront. As a consequence, Il Duce withdrew the Italian Minister from Vienna and broke off any meaningful talks with the Austrians. Since the Italian government's agreement was essential before new international loans could be granted, this action put Seipel in an embarrassing position. The Austrian Chancellor would have to face financial ruin or submit to Mussolini. Seipel naturally chose the latter course. He issued a public statement conforming to Mussolini's position that South Tyrol was a question of internal Italian politics. In June the Italian Minister returned, but the government in Rome still remained suspicious. While Mussolini claimed to appreciate that Seipel could not control the actions of private citizens, the Italian leader still was infuriated by insults coming from Innsbruck and Vienna. As late as October he warned that it was difficult to agree to an Austrian loan as long as the anti-Italian agitation continued.[31]

This was bad enough, but South Tyrol was not the only obstacle to an Italian-Austrian detente. The main problem was Mussolini's repudiation of the status quo. By 1926 Contarini's influence over Italian foreign policy was declining. Mussolini was no longer interested in arguments against expansion. On the contrary, as part of a planned expansion into Southeastern Europe, Mussolini began to cultivate the Hungarians. In 1927 this rapprochement culminated in a military con-

[31] Foreign Ministry memo, 1927, NPA Fasz. 464, Ad. Z. 25.297/13 ex. 1927; Moellwald to Vienna, February 12, May 7, October 20, 1928, NPA Fasz. 109, Zl. 53, 116 Pol.; Schubert memo on conversation with Frank, July 6, 1928, AA 2347/4576/E173522–E173529; Austrian Foreign Ministry memo presented to Schubert, no date, ibid., E173556–E173572; Neurath to Köpke, July 18, 1928, ibid., E173541–E173546; Papers Relating to the Foreign Relations of the United States, 1928, I: 907–12, 914; Berliner Tageblatt, March 5, 1928, p.m.; Enno DiNolfo, Mussolini e la politica estera Italiano (1919–33) (Padua, 1960), pp. 136–37; Mario Toscano, Storia diplomatica della questione dell' Alto Adige (Bari, 1967), pp. 103–6, 110–12.

vention. In the event of war with Yugoslavia, both parties were resolved to launch an attack upon Belgrade through Austria. The Austrian government was never informed of this action, but there can be no doubt that Seipel would have opposed such a scheme.

Yet this did not mean that Mussolini and Count Bethlen, the Hungarian prime minister, were not interested in dealing with Vienna. In order for their military plans to succeed, they needed a friendly government in the Ballhausplatz. For this reason, they made an agreement with the paramilitary Heimwehr in August 1928. Mussolini agreed to support the Heimwehr with money and weapons worth one million lira. The Heimwehr was to be the agency through which the Austrian government would be secured. Berlin, at least, envisioned the possibility that a new Right-wing government in Vienna would unite with Hungary and Italy in an ideological and diplomatic front, a fear that would become a reality in 1932. The *Arbeiter Zeitung* had worried about a Hungarian-inspired monarchist *Putsch* as early as 1925. In 1928 Seipel and Bethlen engaged in a stormy exchange about Hungarian-trained paramilitary bands operating in the Austrian province of Burgenland. Seipel knew that the Hungarians had more than ideological commitments in this province that they had ceded to Austria in 1919. Hungarian Foreign Minister Louis Walko was besieging Berlin with plans for an alliance between Germany, Italy, and Hungary. As a price for agreeing to Anschluss, Walko desired the return of Burgenland. The repeated Hungarian offers only succeeded in causing Stresemann to lose his patience.[32]

With the Italians written off, nostalgia could best be transformed into action with the cooperation of the Czechs. These hopes were very fragile. In 1925 Beneš had been constrained by the anti-Austrianism of the other Little Entente members. In 1928 the situation had scarcely improved for Vienna. There was still strong sentiment in Rumania and Yugoslavia against assisting Austria. The Rumanian Foreign Minister, Ion Mitilneu, expressed this view.[33] In Yugoslavia some minority parties even went further and were willing to dump the whole Austrian problem into the lap of the Germans. Such a

[32] Foreign Ministry memos, 1926, 1927, NPA Fasz. 464, 1174–13; no number. Moellwald to Vienna, February 12, 1928, NPA Fasz. 109, Zl. 11 Pol.; Stresemann-Ramek conversations, March 1926, AA 2345/4576/E172479; Zech memo, 1927, AA 2346/4576/E172938–E172939; *Arbeiter Zeitung*, January 3, 1925, *Deutsch-österreichische Tageszeitung*, September 2, 1928; *Der Anschluss*, March 15, December 15, 1928; Karl Heinz Ritschel, *Diplomatie um Südtirol* (Stuttgart, 1966), pp. 116–17; A. Macartney, *A History of Hungary* (New York, 1956), pp. 56, 72; Lajos Kerkes, "Vorgeschichte der Annexion Österreichs," *Acta Historica* 7 (1959): 359; idem, "Italien, Ungarn und die österreichische Heimwehrbewegung, 1925–1931," *Österreich in Geschichte und Literatur* 9 (1965): 1–13.

[33] Foreign Ministry memo, June 21, 1927, NPA Fasz. 470, Ad. Z. 23070.

solution, they argued, would cost nothing and might bring economic advantages to Yugoslavia. Svetozar Pribićević, leader of the Independent Democratic Party; Jovan Jovanović, head of the small Serbian Peasants' Party, and Stepan Radić, leader of the influential Croatian Peasants' Party—all thought that Austria could serve as a useful intermediary for achieving beneficial economic ties with the Reich. Jovanović and Pribićević were even willing to discuss the Anschluss publicly as an acceptable political consequence of this economic rapprochement. There were even ideological reasons to support such a policy. As Jovanović proclaimed: "Can we prevent what must inevitably come. No. . . . Nothing can prevent the Anschluss. Least of all can we, who were united on the principle of nationalism, fight against the Anschluss."[34]

But despite these opinions, there had been one basic change in Yugoslavia since 1925. Momilco Nincić had been replaced as foreign minister. Although Nincić was a member of a government that formally maintained a strong opposition to Anschluss, he was not at all convinced that this was the correct posture. Despite rumors in 1926 of an Italo-Yugoslav agreement against the Anschluss, the German and Austrian press caught nuances of Nincić's weakening resistance. The rumors of the Italo-Yugoslav agreement were false, but Nincić's unusually moderate statement to the Yugoslav parliament in 1925 was a matter of record. And the German Foreign Office had much harder evidence. Nincić and his Minister to Berlin both apologized for reasserting this opposition in any form at all. The Yugoslav Foreign Minister appeared restive under Czech leadership in the Little Entente. He made a point of telling the German Minister to Belgrade that Yugoslavia had rejected any special engagements designed to forestall Anschluss by bolstering the Austrian economy. The German Minister reported: "In the course of the conversation, Nincić had spoken of his allies . . . as though he had to take them into consideration against his wishes."[35]

But Vojislav Marinković, Nincić's successor, was cut from a different piece of cloth. Marinković was committed to following the French and Czech leadership on the Austrian question. With the new Yugoslav Foreign Minister's aid, Beneš attempted to transform the

---

[34] *Der Anschluss*, September 15, 1929. See also ibid., June 15, August 15, 1928; Camillo Morcutti, *Grossdeutschland, Gross-Südslawien* (Vienna, 1928), pp. 18 ff.

[35] Olshausen (Belgrade) to Berlin, July 23, 1925, AA 2344/4576/E192779. See also Müller (Bern) to Berlin, February 27, 1926, AA 2345/4576/E172263; Dodge (Belgrade) to Washington, June 26, July 3, 1925, USDS 863.01/36, 863.01/37; *I documenti italiani* IV: 172; *Neue Freie Presse*, July 14, 1925, a.m., February 26, a.m.; *Berliner Tageblatt*, March 5, 1926, a.m.

Little Entente into an instrument for aiding Austria and combating the Anschluss. As usual, he could count on the aid of the French, especially that of Berthelot. Moreover, the economic refashioning of the Danubian states had already become a matter for serious public discussion. A former Hungarian minister, Elemér Hantos, organized a series of Central European conferences and institutes for studying the possibilities of economic unification in the Danube valley. For this reason, his schemes were viewed favorably by the Christian Socialist *Reichspost*.

Yet Hantos was no slavish follower of Beneš. He did include Germany within the geographic limits of his scheme. However, he was still less than a favorite with the Anschluss supporters. From their narrow perspective, Hantos' German colleagues opposed any economic union that was not preceded by the Anschluss. Since Hantos did not agree, the Anschluss propagandists labeled him a French, even a Habsburg, agent.[36] And there was an element of a self-fulfilling prophecy in such statements. German intransigence made the Czechs the principal beneficiaries of Hantos' plans. Thus Beneš' scheme to remold the Little Entente appeared as the most practical measure yet undertaken in that direction.

With all these factors working for him, Beneš could count on achieving some success. He carefully prepared the way at the Little Entente meetings at Temesvar in 1926 and Jachymov in 1927. At the Bucharest Conference of June 1928, Beneš and Marinković enunciated a plan for the economic unification of Central Europe. They especially advocated an agreement between Austria and Czechoslovakia. By 1927 Beneš had already enough confidence to elucidate this plan to the Austrians. He envisioned a general unification between Austria and the Little Entente in the areas of railway and postal service, visa regulations, and tariff formalities. Beneš stated that Czechoslovakia and Austria could even go further. Ferdinand Marek, the Austrian minister to Prague, reported: "Beneš claimed that just we two—Austria and Czechoslovakia—can begin to work for the good end. And he believes that we can today or tomorrow finally achieve, if not a unitary customs union, some kind of tariff union or, at the very least, minimal reciprocal tariffs."[37]

The syntax of this report might have been muddy, but the general

[36] Marek to Vienna, October 28, 1927, NPA Fasz. 64, Zl. 153 Pol.: *Die Reichspost*, June 2, 1928; *Der Anschluss*, June 15, 1928.

[37] Marek to Vienna, March 25, NPA Fasz. 63, Zl. 49, Pol. See also same to same, July 14, October 6, 1927, NPA Fasz. 64, Zl. 94, 136 Pol.; same to same, March 3, 1926; April 28, May 12, 1927; May 31, June 1, 1928, NPA Fasz. 855, 11227 pr. 5 III 1926, 22041 pr. 29 IV 1927, 22286 pr. 13 V 1927; 22712 pr. 2 VI 1928, 22780 5 VI 1928; same to same, July 11, 1928, NPA Fasz. 111, 2345 pr.

direction was clear. For once events seemed to be on the side of the advocates of a foreign policy based on nostalgia. Beneš promised a larger arena for the absorption of Austrian energies. He appeared to have the ideal solution to the dilemma that Seipel had discussed in an inter-office memorandum of 1928. Seipel wrote: "If one wishes to separate Austria politically from the Reich, as it has been separated since 1866, then one must bind it to some kind of greater unity and not let it be isolated."[38]

Moreover this new union would have been in a familiar zone of Europe. Beneš presented a unified economic area that closely corresponded to the extent of the Habsburg empire. It was the first really viable plan for a Danubian union, only thinly disguised by Beneš' refusal to use this term. How could Seipel resist a scheme that so complemented his commitments? Seipel could see that Beneš was promising an entrance point into a market deemed essential for Austria's survival. Even a report addressed to the pro-German Schober government could state: "It is commonly recognized that the success of such an economic rapprochement to the states of the Danubian basin is a matter of life and death."[39]

Yet despite these advantages, Seipel and the Austrian Foreign Ministry did not place much hope in an economic alliance with the Little Entente. The Foreign Ministry was extremely skeptical of Beneš' ability to overcome the obstacles to his plan. It had rejected similar overtures in 1921 for the same reason.[40] The Rumanians were only peripherally involved; there was opposition in both Yugoslavia and Czechoslovakia. More important, Beneš was often uncertain and contradicted himself when discussing economic proposals. After speaking to Beneš in 1925, the Austrian Minister to Bucharest was impressed by the Czech leader's willingness to aid Austria. But the Austrian diplomat also believed that Beneš did not know how to pursue this goal. In 1927 Marek reported the same frustrations. The Minister to Prague wrote: "I can get no clear picture of what he concretely means."[41]

---

13 VII 1928; Robert Machray, *The Little Entente* (London, 1929), pp. 345, 348; John Vondracek, *The Foreign Policy of Czechoslovakia: 1918–1935* (New York, 1937), pp. 282–87.

[38] Seipel memo, August 13, 1928, NPA Fasz. 111, Z. 23805–13.

[39] Höffinger (Belgrade) to Vienna, December 6, 1921, NPA Fasz. 822, 7131 pr. 11 XII 1921.

[40] Ibid., Foreign Ministry memo, NPA Fasz. 822, 6885 pr. 2 XII 1921; Prague to Vienna, November 23, 1921, ibid., 6834 pr. 30 XI 1921.

[41] Marek to Vienna, October 6, 1927, NPA Fasz. 64, Zl. 135 Pol. See also Carlbach (Bucharest) to Vienna, May 10, 1925, NPA Fasz. 822, 13262 pr. 11 V 1925; Foreign Ministry memo, June 27, 1927, NPA Fasz. 470, Ad. 252.9713/1927.

In the Czech Foreign Minister's defense, it must be admitted that he could hardly complete his plans while still lacking the full agreement of his partners in the Little Entente. But there were other reasons for this vagueness. Beneš was unquestionably more interested in political than in economic arrangements; he only turned to the latter as a last resort. Thus his vagueness on economic questions was representative of his true state of mind, and it gave the appearance of insincerity. Seipel seemed to worry that Beneš would only give enough economic concessions to draw Austria irrevocably into the Czech camp. With Austria inextricably tied to the Little Entente, the Czechs and their partners could do as they wished. Austria would have paid the price with restrictions on its freedom of action. It would not gain economic security in return. Seipel communicated the substance of these fears in an interview with Ritter in June 1928. The Austrian Chancellor doubted that Austria could ever join a group of states so unsympathetic to Vienna. In the same month, he told the Nationalrat: "We have refused because the Little Entente is a political alliance and cannot put economic interests in the foreground."[42]

There was another fundamental reason for rejecting a detente with Czechoslovakia. The Czechs were the chief status quo power in Central Europe. The Austrians were unsatisfied with the postwar settlement. Beneš desired a Central European Locarno that would assure the frontiers of Czechoslovakia; Seipel was searching for new and larger areas in which to operate. In one sense, however, these policies were complementary. The diplomacy of nostalgia could not function unless the antagonisms in Central Europe were diminished. As a Foreign Ministry memorandum stated: "We also can hope that a solid Central European system would lessen the eternal danger of conflict and facilitate its emancipation from the great powers."[43] But, as with the economic proposals, the Austrians were not sure what role Beneš envisioned for them. On the one hand, Beneš appeared to have been satisfied with a simple neutralization of Austria. On the other, he seemed to demand that Vienna play an active part in his plans.

Thus Seipel must have suspected that this scheme was simply a device to lure Austria into an anti-German posture. During his meeting with Beneš in Prague on February 12 and 13, 1928, Seipel expressed profound suspicion of a Central European Locarno. Even before Beneš could utter a word, the Austrian Chancellor had exclaimed that such a scheme would be worthless without the great

[42] *Stenographische Protokolle*, III Gesetzgebungs Periode, I: 1360. See also Ritter memo, June 26, 1928, AA 2347/4576/E173499.
[43] Foreign Ministry, 1928, NPA Fasz. 473, 20705 pr. 15 II 1928. See also same, 1927, NPA Fasz. 464, Ad. Z. 25.297/13.

powers. And could Austria agree to accept the partition of South Tyrol forever? Would Germany accept a virtual renunciation of the Anschluss? Beneš was lucky even to get Seipel's agreement to a watered-down version that called for the signing of only bilateral pacts.[44]

There was another reason for Seipel's reluctance to unite with the Czechs. The Austrian Chancellor was engaged in a continuous struggle with the socialists, one that erupted into violence after 1927. To maintain his parliamentary majority, he needed the support of the nationalist parties who were committed to Anschluss. Seipel had to maintain a careful balancing act between his own desires and the need to maintain the governing coalition. This was made more difficult by the suspicions about Seipel that the nationalists held. In these circles any dealings with the Czechs were bound to be considered the equivalent of treason. Even the pro-Anschluss Chancellor Ramek was attacked for meeting with the leading Czech statesmen. It is not surprising that Seipel would have to buttress his status within the coalition by making pro-German statements in response to questions from the Landbund and the Grossdeutsch Party.[45] He could not afford to appear as an opponent of the Anschluss. Thus in 1927 Seipel pleaded with Stresemann and Marx not to publish any clear priorities for German foreign policy. He was convinced that the Anschluss question would come behind that of the Polish Corridor and that this would be extremely embarrassing to his government.[46]

Thus, for all intents and purposes, Seipel rejected a detente with Czechoslovakia. The Anschluss supporters were pleasantly surprised; they had feared the worst. Instead they saw what seemed a rejection of the diplomacy of nostalgia. In his June speech to the Nationalrat, Seipel had firmly renounced joining any combination "directed against a particular Central European state that is dear to us." Even more explicitly he stated: "At no time do we believe that the Central European question can be solved without including Germany in the solution."[47] The liberal *Wiener Neuste Nachrichten, Neues Wiener*

[44] Seipel, Beneš conversations in Prague, February 1928, NPA Fasz. 402, 20878–13.

[45] See Landbund interpellation, NPA Fasz. 822, 11606 pr. 25 III 1925. Seipel's promise to Grossdeutsch Party questioner to become more pro-German in *Der Anschluss*, December 15, 1927. Seipel in conversation with Schubert, AA 2346/4576/E172890.

[46] See Peter's minutes of meeting with Stresemann and Marx, November 1927, NPA Fasz. 464, 2529 pr. 21 XI 1927. The Germans never understood Seipel and thought that he was complaining about the low priority given to the Anschluss, see Pünder's minutes of the meeting, AA 2346/4576/E173192–E173195.

[47] *Stenographische Protokolle*, III Gesetzgebungs Periode, I: 1359.

Tagblatt, the *Neue Freie Presse,* even the Catholic *Grazer Tagespost*—all agreed that Seipel had abandoned his opposition to the Anschluss. Only the *Arbeiter Zeitung* held out. It accused Seipel of being a Habsburg legitimist and urged Austrians to reject his " 'Central European [mitteleuropäische]' phantasies."[48]

And, if only by chance, the socialists were right. Seipel had no intention of abandoning the diplomacy of nostalgia; he was just searching for a new form in which to house this policy. This interpretation of Seipel would agree with those of Klemmens von Klemperer, now writing his definitive biography, and Adam Wandruska, the most perceptive student of the first republic's ideology.[49] Seipel had only abandoned small-scale unions; his mind now turned to larger schemes that would include all the Central European powers. This change was due, in part, to Seipel's frustration in dealing with Italy and Czechoslovakia. But it was also based upon an apparent transformation in European diplomacy. After all, Briand was preparing to propose a European union. Pan-Europe was more than compatible with the diplomacy of nostalgia. Like Wildgans and Winter, Seipel hoped that a new Austrian sense of destiny might grow up in conjunction with the rising forces of European cosmopolitanism. Such was the tone of several statements he made in 1928. To a German friend, Seipel still wrote as though the Anschluss were a possibility. But he stated that such a union was only feasible if the "Austrian Germans have trifled away their historical task for all time." In contrast, he talked of a new mission that "might be placed before them [the Austrians] once more, either as an Austrian, an eastern European, a central European, or a pan-European task."[50]

Seipel's resignation from office in April 1928 was a severe blow to the diplomacy of nostalgia. His immediate successors, Streeruwitz and Schober, were committed to the Anschluss. Things had so far advanced in Austria that the Germans could be accused of dragging their feet. In October 1930 Curtius asked the Austrian Minister to Berlin why the Anschluss effort had been moving so slowly. The Minister, somewhat untruthfully, answered: "We in Austria have missed the right resolution from the Reich."[51] The response was

[48] *Arbeiter Zeitung,* June 30, 1928. See also *Neue Freie Presse,* June 28, 1928, p.m.; *Bulletin périodique autrichienne,* Nr. 191, pp. 7–9; Lerchenfeld to Berlin, July 3, 1928, AA 4492/K920/K229113–K229118.

[49] See von Klemperer in *Austrian History Yearbook* 2 (1966): 315–18; Wandruska in (ed.) Benedikt, *Geschichte Österreich,* p. 325.

[50] Sweet, "Seipel's Views," p. 322. See also *New York Times,* April 15, 1925; *Vorwärts,* February 6, 1926, edition A.

[51] Frank to Vienna, October 27, 1930, NPA Fasz. 11, 21.296. Pol.

forthcoming in the shape of the customs union project which further undercut the diplomacy of nostalgia, even among its proponents.

Seipel was never able to resist the possibilities of such action. He wanted to pursue detailed trade negotiations while foreign minister in November 1930, although the final achievement of a customs union project may have been far from his mind. Out of power in March 1931, Seipel privately supported the project and urged Curtius to take the lead, since weakness might make the Austrians settle for only 10 percent of what they could achieve.[52] Surprisingly, the *Reichspost* also favored the customs union. Although many Austrians were concerned about German economic competition, only the ultra-monarchists attacked the Vienna Protocol. On March 28 over 1,000 members of the Monarchist Party presented a memorandum to the Hungarian, Italian, and British ministers in Vienna claiming that the customs union would forever destroy Austrian independence and bar the restoration of the Habsburgs.[53]

But Christian Socialist support for the customs union was not conditioned by intense nationalistic commitments. They were summer soldiers in the fray. The *Reichspost* was considerably less critical of the French than was the rest of the Austrian press. It even worried that a favorable decision before the World Court would exacerbate the international situation, since British and French opposition made the completion of the customs union impossible. When the Ender cabinet fell in June 1931 over its failure to gain foreign credits, Seipel, the savior of 1922, was asked to form a cabinet. Both the nationalists and Social Democrats feared that this would mean abandonment of a pro-German policy. They feared Seipel could gain the financial support of France in exchange for renunciation of the customs union. Thus Seipel could not form a majority, although the fears of the socialists were exaggerated. Yet whatever the case, the Christian Socialist Right wing began to advocate a pro-French policy. The *Neues Wiener Journal* carried an article defending the legitimacy of the French position and the necessity for Austrian economic independence. The *Reichspost* contended that French policy was designed "to liquidate the serious conflict and put Austria at ease."[54]

[52] Lerchenfeld to Berlin, November 15, 1930, AA 1484/3086/D619908; Reith to Berlin, May 7, 1931, AA 2520/5002/E284629–E284630; Clodius (Vienna) to Berlin, June 20, 1931, AA 2521/5002/E285139.

[53] *New York Times*, April 13, 1931; *Berliner Tageblatt*, March 23, 1931, p.m.; *Neue Zürcher Zeitung*, March 2, 1931.

[54] *Die Reichspost*, September 4, 1931. See also ibid., May 11, June 18, September 5, 1931; *Berliner Tageblatt*, May 8, September 4, 1931, a.m.; *Der österreichische Volkswirt* 23 (August 8, 1931): 1188.

The full circle had turned. Still the victory did not belong to the diplomacy of nostalgia, but rather to a new generation of men who were less committed to the ideals of the old empire and sought to create an independent Austria through other means, internal reconstruction and Italian alliances. Dollfuss' accession to power in 1932 clearly marks the end of an era. In the 1920s most Austrians desired the destruction of their state in some greater amalgamation. In the 1930s there was a serious attempt to build an independent small state, a sort of freedom-hating Switzerland.[55]

[55] The Anschluss movement in the 1930s is best chronicled in Ulrich Eichstädt, *Vom Dollfuss zu Hitler* (Wiesbaden, 1955), and in Jurgen Gehl, *Austria, Germany and the Anschluss.*

BIBLIOGRAPHY

UNPUBLISHED DOCUMENTS

AUSTRIA

Haus-, Hof- und Staatsarchiv (Vienna), Neues Politisches Archiv.

Faszikel		
10	78–81	464
11	110–111	470
57	234	473
59	240	822
62–64	402	855
	454	

In footnotes, the document number follows the Faszikel number. In the case of chronological reports from diplomatic posts (10–81), the number designating the order of receipt is used.

Verwaltungsarchiv (Vienna), Ministerratsprotokolle, 1925.

GERMANY

Foreign Office documents deposited at National Archives (Washington), microcopy T-120:

Serial Number	Roll Number
2411	4655
2520	5002
3086	1483–84
3573–75	1685
4509	2267
4576	2344–47
4665	2411
5271	2582
7478–79	3270
K49	3620–21
K55, K56	3269
K920	4491–92
K922	4495
K936	4507
K1148	5426
K1184	5540
Saint Anthony's	25

Ritter Nachlass
K1122   5420–21
Stresemann Nachlass
7313   3143
7318   3168
Columbia
University   3
These documents are cited as follows:
roll number/serial number/document number.
Koch-Weser Nachlass deposited at Bundesarchiv Koblenz, diary 1925–29.

Finance Ministry documents deposited at Bundesarchiv Koblenz, IIZ, V Genernalia, 49ᵃ

Alte Reichskanzlei documents, deposited at Bundesarchiv Koblenz, Bestand R43I, 107–111.

These documents were examined in the original, but those microfilmed are cited in the normal manner as Serial K1064, rolls 4618, 4619.

UNITED STATES
Department of State, National Archives, Reports from Vienna and Belgrade, 1925.

PUBLISHED DOCUMENTS

Almond, Nina and Ralph Lutz, eds. *The Treaty of St. Germain.* Stanford University, 1935.

Austria. *Rot-Weiss-Rot Buch.* Vienna: Druck der österreichischen Staatsdruckerei, 1945.

————. *Stenographische Protokolle des provisorischen Nationalversammlung für Deutschösterreich.* Vienna: Druck der deutschösterreichische Staatsdruckerei, 1919.

————. *Stenographische Protokolle über die Sitzungen der Konstituierenden Versammlung.* Vienna: Druck der österreichische Staatsdruckerei, 1919, I.

————. *Stenographische Protokolle über die Sitzungen des Nationalrats* with *Beilagen.* Vienna: Druck der österreichische Staatsdruckerei, 1920–31. I, II, and III Gesetzgebungs Periode.

Carnegie Endowment for International Peace. *The Treaties of Peace, 1919–1923.* 2 vols. New York: Carnegie Endowment, 1924.

France. *Débats parlementaires, Annales du Chambre des Députés.* Paris: Imprimerie des Journaux Officiels, 1930. CXXVI.

————. *Débats parlementaires, Annales du Sénat.* Paris: Imprimerie des Journaux Officiels, 1926. CII.

————. Ministère des Affaires Étrangères. *Bulletin périodique de la presse autrichienne.* 1923–31.

————. Ministère des Affaires Étrangères. *Bulletin périodique de la presse allemagne.* 1925–31.

Germany. *Akten zur deutschen auswärtigen Politik, 1918–1945.* Göttingen: Vandenhoeck and Ruprecht, 1966. Serie B, Band I, 1.

———. *Die Regierung der Volksbeauftragten.* Düsseldorf, 1969.

———. *Die Regierung des Prinzen Max von Baden.* Düsseldorf, 1962.

———. *Statistik des deutschen Reichs.* Berlin: Verlag Reimar Hobbing, 1928. Band CMI, Teil I.

———. *Verhandlungen der Verfassungsgebenden Deutschen Nationalversammlung.* Berlin: Verlag der Norddeutsche Buchdruckerei, 1919–20.

———. *Verhandlungen des Reichstags, Stenographische Berichte.* Berlin: Druck und Verlag der Reichsdruckerei, 1925–30. CCCLXXIV–CCCXCIII.

———. *Verhandlungen des Reichstags, Anlagen.* Berlin: Verlag Julius Gittenfeld, 1926–31. CCXIV, CDXXX.

Great Britain. *Documents on British Foreign Policy, 1919–1939.* London: His Majesty's Stationery Office, 1957. Series II, Volumes I, II.

———. *Parliamentary Debates* (5th series) (Commons). London: His Majesty's Stationery Office, 1925–31. CLXXXV (1925). CCV (1931).

Italy. Ministero delgi Affari Esteri. *I documenti diplomatici italiani.* Rome: Liberia dello Stato, 1957–59. Serie VII, Vol. I, II, IV.

League of Nations. Assembly. *Verbatim Report of Eleventh Ordinary Session.* Geneva, 1931.

———. *The Economic Situation of Austria.* Report presented to the Council of the League of Nations by W. T. Layton and Charles Rist. Geneva, 1925. D.568 M.232 1926. II.

———. Commission of Enquiry for European Union. *Minutes of the Third Session of the Commission.* Geneva, 1931. CC.395 M.158. 1931.

———. Commission of Enquiry for European Union. *Minutes of the Fourth Session of the Commission.* Geneva, 1931. C.50 M.215. 1931. III.

———. *Official Journal.* Geneva, 1931. XII.

———. *Treaty Series.* Geneva, 1922–28. XII, XXVII, LI, LXXIII, CLIV.

Mantoux, Paul. *Les délibérations du conseil des quatre.* Paris, 1955.

Permanent Court of International Justice. *Custom Regime between Germany and Austria, Advisory Opinion of September 5th, 1931.* The Hague, 1932. Series A/B no. 41.

———. *Custom Regime between Germany and Austria. Pleadings, Oral Statements, and Documents.* The Hague, 1932. Series C, no. 53.

United States. Department of State. *Papers Relating to the Foreign Relations of the United States, 1918, 1928, 1931.* Washington: United States Government Printing Office, 1930–46.

———. *Papers Relating to the Foreign Relations of the United States: The Paris Peace Conference, 1919.* Washington: United States Government Printing Office, 1942.

NEWSPAPERS

The following newspapers have been reviewed for the entire period, 1923–29:

Arbeiter Zeitung (Vienna)
Berliner Tageblatt
Deutschösterreichische Tageszeitung (Vienna)
Kölnische Zeitung
Münchner Neueste Nachrichten
Neue Freie Presse (Vienna)
New York Times
Die Reichspost (Vienna)
Völkischer Beobachter (Munich)
Vorwärts (Berlin)

After 1925 the foreign press is cited in the Anschluss journals. For 1925 the following papers were used: *Corriere della Sera, Le Figaro, Il Popolo d'Italia, Le Temps.* The *Frankfurter Zeitung, Vossische Zeitung,* and *Rote Fahne* were used for 1926 only. The *Berliner Tageblatt, Neue Freie Presse, Neue Zürcher Zeitung, New York Times,* and *The Times* (London) were used for 1931.

PERIODICALS

The following periodicals were used in their entirety for the period 1923–31.

Der Anschluss
Archiv für Politik und Geschichte
Deutsche Einheit
Deutsche Juristen Zeitung
Der deutsche Volkswirt
Engelhaafs historisch-politische Jahresübsicht
Mitteilungen des österreichsichen Instituts für Geschichtsforschung
Neues Abendland
Das Neue Reich
Österreich-Deutschland
Der österreichische Volkswirt
Schönere Zukunft
Schriften des Vereins für Sozialpolitik
Survey of International Affairs
Vierteljahreshefte zur Kunjunkturforschung
Volk und Reich

The historical journals are cited in chapter IV; the economic journals are in chapter XI. The legal journals can be found in chapter VI.

PUBLISHED WORKS

The following is a bibliography of only the more important secondary literature. The specialized contemporary studies can be found under topics in the chapters listed above. The literature on nationalism can be found in the Introduction. The two major bibliographic sources for these contemporary works are *Bibliographie zum deutsch-österreichischen Anschlussgedanken*, Stuttgart, 1926; and Friedrich Kleinwaechter and Heinz von Paller, *Die Anschlussfrage in ihrer kulturellen, politischen und wirtschaftlichen Bedeutung*. Vienna, 1930.

Ball, M. Margaret. *Post-War German-Austrian Relations*. Stanford University, 1937.

Benedikt, Heinrich (ed.). *Geschichte der Republik Österreich*. Vienna, 1954.

Bennett, Edward. *Germany and the Diplomacy of the Financial Crisis*. Cambridge, Mass., 1962.

Berchtold, Klaus. *Österreichische Parteiprogramme, 1868–1966*. Munich, 1967.

Bracher, Karl Dietrich. *Deutschland zwischen Demokratie und Diktatur*. Bern, 1964.

———. *Die Auflösung der Weimarer Republik*. Stuttgart, 1957.

Braunthal, Julius. *Otto Bauer*. Vienna, 1961.

Cassels, Alan. "Mussolini and German Natonalism, 1922–1925," *Journal of Modern History* 35 (1963): 137–57.

Coghlan, Brian. *Hofmannsthal's Festival Drama*. Cambridge, 1964.

Cord Meyer, Henry. *Mitteleuropa in German Thought and Action*. The Hague, 1955.

Curtius, Julius. *Bemühung um Österreich*. Heidelberg, 1947.

———. *Sechs Jahre Minister der Deutschen Republik*. Heidelberg, 1948.

DeLaunay, Jacques. *Major Controversies of Contemporary History*. London, 1964.

DiNolfo, Enno. *Mussolini e la politica estera Italiano (1919–1933)*. Padua, 1960.

Doehn, Lothar. *Politik und Interesse*. Meisenheim a. Glan, 1970.

Dumin, Frederick. "Background of the Austro-German *Anschluss* Movement, 1918–1919." Dissertation, University of Wisconsin, 1963.

Fuchs, Albert. *Geistige Strömungen in Österreich*. Vienna, 1949.

Gasiorowski, Zygmunt. "Stresemann and Poland after Locarno," *Journal of Central European Affairs* 30 (1958): 299–317.

Gatzke, Hans. "Gustav Stresemann: A Bibliographical Article," *Journal of Modern History* 36 (1964): 1–13.

———. *Stresemann and the Rearmament of Germany*. Baltimore, 1954.

Gehl, Jurgen. *Austria, Germany and the Anschluss*. London, 1963.

Gulich, Charles. *Austria from Habsburg to Hitler*. Berkeley, 1948.

Hammen, Oscar. "German Historians and the Advent of the National Socialist State," *Journal of Modern History* 13 (1941): 163–88.

Hannak, Karl. *Karl Renner und Seine Zeit*. Vienna, 1965.

Hauser, Oswald. "Der Plan einer deutsch-österreichischer Zollunion und die europäischen Föderation," *Historische Zeitschrift* 479 (1955): 45–71.

Herzfeld, Hans. "Staat und Nation in der deutschen Geschichtsschreibung der Weimarer Zeit," *Veritas-Justitia-Libertas, Festschrift zur 200-Jahrfeier der Columbia Universität.* Berlin, 1954, pp. 129–43.

Hertz, Friedrich. *The Economic Problem of the Danubian States.* London, 1947.

Hertzman, Lewis. *DNVP, Right-Wing Opposition in the Weimar Republic.* Lincoln, 1963.

Heuss, Theodor. *Friedrich Naumann.* Stuttgart, 1954.

Höltje, Christian. *Die Weimarer Republik und das ostlocarno Problem.* Würzburg, 1958.

Hoor, Ernst. *Österreich, 1918–1933.* Vienna, 1966.

Keleher, Edward. "Deutschland, Deutsch-österreich und die Anschlussfrage in den letzten Wochen des Ersten Weltkrieges," *Österreich in Geschichte und Literatur* 12 (1968): 132–43.

Kent, George. *A Catalogue of the Files and Microfilms of the German Foreign Ministry Archives.* Stanford, 1962–70.

Kerekes, Lajos. "Italen Ungarn und die österreichische Heimwehrbewegung," *Österreich in Geschichte und Literatur* 9 (1965): 1–13.

————. "Vorgeschichte der Annexion Österreichs," *Acta Historica* 7 (1959): 355–90.

Kleinwaechter, Friedrich. *Von Schönbrunn bis St. Germain.* Graz, 1964.

Kogan, Arthur G. "Genesis of the Anschluss Problem," *Journal of Central European Affairs* 20 (1960): 24–50.

Kohn, Hans, "AEIOU. Some Reflections on the Meaning and Mission of Austria," *Journal of Modern History* 11 (1939): 521–24.

Korbel, Joseph. *Poland between East and West.* Princeton, 1965.

Krill, Hans-Heinz. *Die Ranke Renaissance.* Berlin, 1962.

Ladner, Gottlieb. *Seipel als Überwinder der Staatskrise vom Sommer, 1922.* Vienna, 1964.

Lhotsky, Alfons. "Geschichtsforschung und Geschichtsshreibung in Österreich," *Historische Zeitschrift* 189 (1959): 379–448.

Machray, Robert. *The Little Entente.* London, 1929.

Magris, Claudio. *Der habsburgische Mythos in der österreichischen Literatur.* Salzburg, 1964.

Meyers, Duane. "Berlin versus Vienna: Disagreement about the *Anschluss* in the Winter of 1918–1919," *Central European History* 5 (1972): 130–75.

————. "Germany and the Question of Austrian *Anschluss* 1918–1922." Dissertation, Yale University, 1968.

Mikoletzky, Hans Leo. *Österreichische Zeitgeschichte.* Vienna, 1962.

Mommsen, Wilhelm. *Deutsche Parteiprogramme.* Munich, 1960.

Nelson, Harold. *Land and Power.* London, 1963.

Neumann, Sigmund. *Die Parteien der Weimarer Republik.* Stuttgart, 1963.

Nirschl, Karl. *In Seinen Mensch ist Österreich.* Linz, 1964.

Reimann, Viktor. *Zu Gross für Österreich: Seipel und Bauer im Kampf um die Ersten Republik.* Vienna, 1968.

Renner, Karl. *Österreich von der Ersten zur Zweiten Republik.* Vienna, 1953.

Ringer, Fritz. *The Decline of the German Mandarins.* Cambridge, Mass., 1969.

Ritschel, Karl Heinz. *Diplomatie um Südtirol.* Stuttgart, 1966.

Rohe, Karl. *Das Reichsbanner, Schwarz Rot Gold.* Düsseldorf, 1966.

Rothschild, K. W. *Austria's Economic Development between Two Wars.* London, 1947.

Schallenberg, Horst. *Zum Geschichtsbild der Wilhelmischen Ära und der Weimarer Zeit.* Ratingen bei Düsseldorf, 1964.

Schulz, Gerhard. *Zwischen Demokratie und Diktatur.* Munich, 1954.

Schwend, Karl. *Bayern zwischen Monarchie und Diktatur.* Munich, 1954.

Srbik, Heinrich von. *Geist und Geschichte.* Munich, 1951.

Staiger, Emil. *Meisterwerke deutscher Sprache aus dem neunzehnten Jahrhundert.* Zurich, 1957.

Stambook, F. G. "The German-Austria Customs Union Project of 1931: A Study of German Methods and Motive, *Journal of Central European Affairs* 21 (1961): 25–44.

Stiefbold, Rodney et al. *Wahlen und Parteien in Österreich.* Vienna, 1966.

Stirk, S. D. *The Prussian Spirit.* London, 1941.

Sweet, Paul. "Recent German Literature on Mitteleuropa," *Journal of Central European Affairs* 3 (1943): 1–24.

Thimme, Anneliese. "Gustav Stresemann: Legende und Wirklichkeit," *Historische Zeitschrift* 181 (1956): 292–338.

———. *Gustav Stresemann.* Hanover, 1957.

Toscano, Mario. *Storia diplomatica della questione dell' Alto Adige.* Bari, 1967.

Tremel, Ferdinand. "Die wirschaftlichen Situation der ersten Republik Oesterreichs," *Österreich in Geschichte und Literatur* 2 (1958): 154–59.

Turner, Henry Ashby. *Stresemann and the Politics of the Weimar Republic.* Princeton, 1963.

Wehler, Hans-Ulrich. *Sozialdemokratie und Nationalstaat.* Würzburg, 1962.

INDEX

THE JOHNS HOPKINS UNIVERSITY PRESS

This book was composed in Caledonia text and Palatino display type
by Maryland Linotype Composition Company, Inc. It was printed on
Warren's 60-lb. Sebago stock and bound in Columbia Llamique cloth
by Universal Lithographers, Inc.

Library of Congress Cataloging in Publication Data
Suval, Stanley.
    The Anschluss question in the Weimar era.
    Bibliography: p.
    1. Anschluss movement, 1918–1938.
2. Austria—Politics and government—1918–1938.
3. Germany—Politics and government—1918–1933.
I. Title.
DB48.S85   1974   320.9'43'085   73–17174
ISBN 0–8018–1502–9